Cosmic Holiday

J.C. ROMERO

I would l like to thank the following people for helping make this book possible: Jennifer Zaczek Kepler at Cypress Editing, Amy Mae Romero, Jennifer Pickens, Conrad and Marian Young, Lori Rosenberg and Don Romero.

For Mae.

Matt dealt another hand of our nightly poker game. I saw the cards in front of me, but I didn't pick them up. Matt smirked devilishly, organizing his hand as if he'd already won. In that moment I was hit with an epiphany. Like a lightning bolt, the universe reached down and smacked me right in the face, screaming, "Wake up!"

Resolved, I stood up and said, "That's it. I'm done. I'm out of here."

Part I

Chapter One

I was never afraid of the dark, but I seemed to be now. The smoke from my cigarette burned my eyes as I navigated the shadows. I forged ahead down the long path to my mom's cabin. The rain was light but constant. *I should have stayed in town until morning*, I thought, flicking my cigarette butt on the ground. Remembering I was in the forest, I chased down the butt to make sure it was out. Though it was raining, burning down the forest was the last thing I wanted.

My mom's property was a twenty-mile drive from Apple Hill, California, a tiny, one-traffic-light town in the Sierra Nevada Mountains. Surrounded by farms, apple orchards, and deeply forested woods, Apple Hill used to be a thriving mining town back in the 1800s that later became a lumber town. Today, it's just apples and tourists during the springtime. Apple Hill was beautiful and slow paced—the kind of small mountain town you might see in a movie. You know the one: small town, big drama. My mom had moved there twenty years ago, having converted an old miner's camp into an artist's retreat surrounded by nature. I wished I were here to pursue art, but unfortunately, I was in desperate need of solitude and soul-searching.

You see, my girlfriend of three years abruptly ended our relationship, leaving me brokenhearted. A broken heart of unimaginable magnitude. If my heart were an earthquake, California would have fallen right into the sea. I'd had breakups in the past, but this one left me feeling soulless, empty, and unable to see any glimmer of light at the end of the tunnel. I was devastated, and I needed some time to get myself right again.

My ex, Ashley, and I had agreed to move to San Francisco after her acceptance to SF State. She was happy to be a student, and I was content to continue my life as an optimistic twenty-three-year-old freelance artist. She had moved to San Francisco to begin school, and I had planned on joining her in a month. That day never came. Out of the blue, she'd started to become distant, and I knew something in her had changed. After I pressured her to tell me what was going on, she said she was unsure about how she felt and needed time to herself to "figure it out."

"Figure it out"? We already did! We talked about getting married someday. What is there to figure out? I was convinced it was another guy. She promised it wasn't, but my mind wouldn't let go of this conclusion. My constant barrage of questions and insulting accusations of her fidelity drove her to cut ties and cease all communication with me.

Why did she do this? How could she do this? We were in love! These questions and so many others had been running through my mind over and over for the past few months. I just couldn't figure out what had gone wrong, and she would no longer talk to me. I felt abandoned, betrayed, and desperately alone. After a certain point, my friends and family no longer wanted to listen or talk to me about it anymore. My mom had invited me to stay at her place while she traveled overseas, but I was reluctant to go there alone. She and I did not have the best relationship, and I wasn't keen on hanging out in her home. Her place always made me anxious. But my outburst at poker night forced me to look at my life, and after talking with Matt, he convinced me it was a great opportunity to get away from all the memories and reminders of Ashley at home. I reluctantly accepted my mother's invitation and decided to leave the very next day so I wouldn't change my mind.

I packed a bag and jumped into my yellow VW Bug. I waved goodbye to my best friend and headed north into the unknown. The drive from Orange County to Camino had taken a good eight hours. The hardest part of the journey had been entering Northern California. Eventually, I-5 splits west to San Francisco and east to Sacramento. With delusions of grandeur, I had pulled over and sat thinking of how I could surprise Ashley, fantasizing that she would happily take me back. I really wanted to go west toward San Francisco, but I forced myself to go east.

When I finally arrived, it was late in the night. Making my way through the dark gauntlet of fears and ferns, I was finally awarded by a beacon of light just a few yards away. The small cabin was dark except for the porch light illuminating a note pinned to the door. I could hear it snapping in the wind as I approached. Thinking I'd heard something, I looked over my shoulder and up into the drizzling mist but realized it was just the creaking and swaying of the fifty-foot-tall trees that surrounded the rustic cabin. I snatched the note.

Jason, this is your mom.

"Yeah, no kidding," I muttered.

The door is open and there is nothing in the fridge, so you will need to go to the store. Also, I left a couple of books for you to read that might help you. Make yourself at home, and we will see you in a few weeks. If you are still here, great. If not, good luck.

—Your mom

Well, that sounded like my mom, no-nonsense and straight to the point. I pushed the door open and entered the cabin. I hadn't been here in over ten years. I flipped on the light to see the warm, inviting interior. It was exactly as I remembered, cedar walls, leather furniture, and various works of art and treasures from her travels. The smell of campfire from the wood burning stove permeated the air from years of use. I used the badly needed bathroom and decided to confirm the empty fridge, hoping that something had been left behind. Yep, empty except for a lone beer. "Score!" I snatched up the beer. I found a bag of chips, and with my beer, I plopped down on the couch and turned on the TV. Nothing held my interest because my mind kept reverting to Ashley, wondering what she might be doing and whom she was with. I thought about calling her to let her know I was at my mom's house. *Who knows, maybe she might want to see me*, I thought. I looked over at the phone. *Don't do it!* I struggled, and with no one to distract me, I was my own worst nightmare. *Why am I such a mess? She doesn't want me to call her.* Based on my past phone attempts, I knew it was best if I didn't call. I finished my beer and soon fell asleep.

Chapter Two

I awoke to the sun beaming through the windows, hitting straight across my face like a spotlight. The TV was still on from the night before, and the bag of chips had spilled onto the floor. I stretched like a cat before getting up and cleaning the mess. I made my way to the bathroom for a long-overdue shower. Surprisingly, I had slept through the night, and for the first time in a while, I felt fairly rested. *Heartache is an exhausting business*, I thought. I was proud of myself for not calling Ashley last night when I felt alone and vulnerable. The hot shower washed away more than just dirt. It soothed my tired and aching muscles from the long drive. As I toweled off, a familiar feeling came over me—one I hadn't felt in quite some time. I was hungry, which was unusual. I'd lost a few pounds due to my depressed state of mind. I just couldn't eat. My friend Matt told me that I was on the "broken-heart diet." I debated ignoring my hunger pains, but my stomach growled, as if in answer. I decided my next task would involve grocery shopping.

I stepped outside and walked down the long path to where my road-dirty VW Bug was parked. *Not so scary in the daytime*, I thought as I looked around the property. I realized I'd parked next to a huge pine tree that I had a history with.

I walked over to the tree and placed my hand on the now healed gouges I'd inflicted on the tree many years before. I had decided I was somewhat of a mountain man and was going to teach myself how to throw a hatchet. It was after I'd hurled the hatchet over two dozen times into the majestic tree that I heard my mom scream.

"What the hell are you doing to my tree!"

I hadn't realized that I'd done anything wrong until she'd yelled. She ran over to me and snatched the hatchet out of my hand. Seeing the rage in her eyes and fearing she might hit me over the head with the hatchet, I took a few steps back and nervously looked down. She gave a speech on nature being sacred and explained that I was incredibly disrespectful. She made me apologize to the tree, which I thought was silly at the time.

Standing before the tree all these years later, I was surprised that the scars were still visible. I looked up at the tree, and in my mind, I apologized again.

The property was both beautiful and secluded. Old Man Dave, the nearest neighbor, was about a mile away. He had lived out here for many years. He liked to wander around the forest, shooting crows that gathered around his house. When you drove to town from my mom's cabin, you passed right by his place. Sometimes you could see him talking to himself and yelling at the birds. He never looked at you when you drove by, almost as if he were deaf or didn't care for human connection.

The road to the general store was as I remembered. My little Bug sped along, smoking out of the tailpipe in the brisk morning chill. I patted the dash, thanking the car for doing such a great job of getting me to my destination safe and sound. I passed through the one traffic light and rolled into the empty parking lot of the Camino General Store. The bell rang loudly as I entered and inhaled the smell of pine. It was October, and the store had already been decorated with Christmas wreaths, lights, and ornaments. I'd been here many times as a kid, but since I wasn't a local, the store clerk asked if I needed help finding anything.

"I'm fine." I half smiled.

The only thing I'd been able to stomach since the breakup was Tiger's Milk bars and chocolate milk. A Tiger's Milk bar is basically an energy bar made of creamy peanut butter and chocolate. My dad would buy them for me when I was a kid, and they were still just as tasty and comforting to me as they were back then. I grabbed all they had, along with a few frozen pizzas and some ice cream. I made my big purchase and drove the winding road back to the cabin. I looked for the old man shooting birds, but as I passed his place, I didn't see him around, and I wondered if he still lived there.

By the time I returned to the cabin, the morning sun had faded and was replaced by the gray mist I'd encountered the night before. It was fall, and the weather was on time. I put my sparse groceries away and hurried back to the hum of the still running TV. Ever since I was a little kid, television had brought me comfort. Being raised in a house with an older brother who was always with his friends and a dad who was busy playing the field in proper 1970s style, I was alone a lot, and the TV was my savior from fear and loneliness.

I surfed the channels for a while and was happy to find *Singin' in the Rain* starring Gene Kelly, Debbie Reynolds, and Donald O'Connor. I'd always thought it was a charming movie made back in the day when stars would sing, dance, and do a bit of comedy. It had aired many times when I was home from school sick with severe allergies. I loved to watch old movies that were broadcasted only on weekday mornings and early afternoons. I thought about the other people who watched these movies, and I imagined them to be old folks long since retired, reminiscing back to the time when they first saw the movie playing in a theater. For me, this movie was a comforting slice of cinema. I looked over at the phone a couple of times. I felt alone, as if I were forgotten in this cabin while the world passed by. Ashley was living without me in the city, and I was a sad puddle of misery deep in the woods, clutching onto Gene Kelly singing in the damn rain! I started to cry. I was pathetic.

I looked at the two books stacked purposefully on the coffee table with a note card on top. A tiny pebble held the note in place. I had noticed the books the night before and thought they must be the ones my mom had mentioned in her note, but I didn't feel like checking them out. The small rock, however, caught my attention. I leaned forward and picked up the smooth and perfectly round granite pebble. I could see why she kept this pebble; it was unusual to find such a round stone.

My mother and I had never been close, but we shared the same passion for art. The only time we'd connected emotionally was through art. I respected her as an artist, and she in turn acknowledged the talent I possessed. I wished we could communicate through art instead of words—I would tell her how deeply hurt I was that she'd left me as a child, and she would, hopefully, tell me how sorry she was for leaving me. *Wow, now that would be some painting!* We saw life in a similar way, though. If you placed a smooth pebble in a pool of hundreds, we would both choose the same one. This thought was comforting to me, and I always hoped she would someday turn into the motherly person I desperately needed growing up. It was wishful thinking.

Holding the tiny stone in my hand, I snatched up the note card. I was expecting to find another curt note like "Here, read these." Instead, the note simply said, "Breathe."

Breathe? I thought. *What does that even mean? Breathe.* I put the card aside and, now curious, picked up the first book. It was a book on mindful meditation.

"Okay, thanks, Mom," I said aloud, rolling my eyes and setting the book aside. I picked up the second book. It was on astral projection. I laughed. *Astral projection, what the hell is that?* Judging from the book cover and the smell and color of the pages, I thought this book had most likely been printed in the 1960s. I flipped the book over. The author was a kind-eyed woman with a gray ponytail. The back explained the book's values and how one could travel anywhere within their mind. I was intrigued by the notion of traveling in one's mind, but I set the book aside just in time for Gene's finale, where he literally sings and dances in the rain.

I spent most of the day couch-bound. My mind wandered in and out of thoughts of Ashley and what she might be doing in San Francisco. It had been over two months since the breakup, and the uncontrollable thoughts seemed more sporadic and less desperate. I could feel my heart slowly healing, but I was far from being free of her spell.

Exhausting my TV quota, I became bored and decided to explore the cabin. I noticed a piece of art I'd made in junior high hanging on the wall, a self-portrait. I stared at the pen and ink drawing of myself and noticed how sad I looked despite my carefree childhood. I didn't remember giving the drawing to my mother. It brought back memories of my younger years in Southern California. Being raised by a single parent in the late 1970s and 1980s offered a freedom and an independence most of my friends didn't get to experience. Once I spent an entire week at my friend's house without asking my dad. One day we ran into my dad downtown. He asked me if I'd been at home, and I simply told him, yes, I was just there. He looked confused but let it go. My dad wasn't a bad parent; it was just a different time. I grew up in a safe community, and let's just say, it truly took a village to raise this kid. Plus, for my dad, raising two kids single-handedly was uncharted territory at the time. There wasn't a handbook to follow except maybe the movie *Mr. Mom*. He did the best he knew how to do, and I loved him.

A photo of my mom and stepdad, Greg, building their first log cabin hung on the wall. They looked like two settlers beginning a new life out west. They'd built the entire cabin by themselves in June Lake, California. Population six hundred. It was a simple log cabin with a woodstove in the center and a loft to sleep in, just like the one on a bottle of syrup. It was rustic, and when the wind blew outside, you felt it inside.

My dad sent my brother and me there once a year for a weeklong visit. I absolutely hated it. My mom had zero patience for her children, and I often ended up with a wooden spoon to my backside. If I tried to block the blows, my knuckles would pay the price. I still hate wooden spoons to this day. I guess you could call it wooden spoon PTSD. One year my brother went without me. I think they got sick of me crying every night, all night long, and decided to let me stay home. When I cried, my mom never comforted me. Instead, she would make my stepdad handle it. Now, looking back, I realized I just wanted her to hold and soothe me like moms do; to reassure their children that everything is all right in the world. The only thing my crying got me was a tired and grumpy stepdad begging me to go to sleep. Needless to say, I was always happy when it was time to go home. When I grew older, I realized she was always happy to see me at first, but it was very short-lived. As soon as I would do something to annoy her, which was always, we would start fighting.

When I was thirteen and desperately trying to turn my mom into a real mom, I asked to live with her. After a week of that, she decided it wasn't a good idea. I would never forget her words that day: "I may be your biological mom, but I will never *be your mom*." She was just one of those people who should have never had children. She didn't have a motherly bone in her body. But she was still technically my mom, and I figured that was better than nothing.

I finished browsing the art on the walls as if I were in a museum. I approached the door to the bedroom, but I hesitated to enter. The door that was always open was decisively closed tight for my arrival. Never being great with boundaries, I slowly opened the door and entered the room. The smell of lavender filled my nose as the air rushed by. Lavender always reminded me of my mom. Whenever I visited, she would drag me to a lavender farm a few miles away. The room was nice with a puffy covered sleigh bed and Victorian prints hanging on the wall. An antique chair in the process of being refurbished sat in the corner. To my left was a blonde wood dresser I recognized from every house my mom had lived in.

A framed photo of my mom draped in fur sat perched on the dresser. It must have been taken when she attended art school because she looked about twenty years old in it. I found it striking, and being an artist myself, I thought it was beautifully done. I found it strange that I could see my mom as a beautiful woman. Most kids don't see their mothers as pretty, and if anyone says that she is, the immediate response is "Gross!" They see them as moms. I'd never viewed my mother as "Mom," so I guess it wasn't that strange. I looked at her youthful face in the photo. Her expression held wonderment of her life ahead. She hadn't met my father yet when the photo was taken. I wondered what she was like back then. She seemed so happy in the photo. What happened to her that made her so cold and disconnected from emotion or empathy? She had told me that her father was abusive, and she ended up disowning her family at an early age, never speaking to them again. *She must be in so much pain*, I thought.

I looked in the mirror above the dresser and compared my facial features to my mom's. I had her Scandinavian traits. She was blonde with light blue eyes and pale skin. I looked a lot like my mom, except my eyes were green and my hair was dark. I remembered a photo my grandmother showed me of my mom when she was a child. Her hair was in pigtails, and if you covered up her hair with your fingers, it looked just like me. Our mouths were quite different, though. Her lips were thin and tight like she was pissed off all the time, and I inherited my dad's full lips. The kind of lips women pay doctors for.

Next to the photo were three note cards just like the one she'd left for me on the coffee table. They were lined up purposefully, and each one also had a pebble on top. I leaned forward with my hands at my sides. I read what they said, being careful not to breathe too hard so I wouldn't inadvertently move them.

The first card read, "Live in the now." The second stated, "You only lose what you cling to," and the third read, "Be free wherever you are."

These quotes clearly rang true to my situation, and I wondered if she had left them for me to see, knowing I would breach the bedroom door. Or if they were simply written mantras to keep her strong and moving forward, leaving her past deeply behind.

Next to the dresser was a large bookshelf. I browsed the titles, finding a collection of art and reference books, and a typical mix of self-help and spiritual books you would see from a young adult living in the 1960s. I knew she was a practicing Buddhist who occasionally hosted monks here at her artist's retreat. On one of the bookshelves was a stack of the same three-by-five note cards. Wanting to know more about the person who created me, I quickly sorted through the deck, finding many quotes like the other three. *Why those three?* I wondered. I searched for a card that said, "Fucking get over it," her favorite saying, but it wasn't included in her stack of wisdom.

I put the cards back and looked around. I noticed an old fly-fishing pole hanging above the bed. My stepdad was an avid angler and had a large collection of fly-fishing gear, but I still thought the placement of a fishing rod in a bedroom was odd. The pole reminded me of the many fishing trips we'd taken to June Lake. Those trips were the only good memories I had of that place. I loved fishing on a beautiful lake. I loved it as a kid, and I still loved it now, but living in Southern California inhibited me from mountain lake fishing. An unfamiliar glimmer of excitement pierced through my jaded brain with the thought of fishing while I was here. It had been two months since I had felt excited about anything. In an instant, I decided, *Tomorrow I will fish.*

The afternoon soon turned into evening, and the dark sky became unnerving. The night landscape outside my cabin oasis transformed into moving shadows and unknown creatures. I turned on every light inside as if some force field would protect me from the monsters outside. However, it only made my situation worse, for I was now unable to see anything lurking outside in the darkened woods. I found a large flashlight next to the door. I switched it on and slowly cracked open the door, scanning the woods for the terrible unknown. I wasn't used to being so isolated and alone. My mind started to play tricks on me, and my imagination ran wild with fear. I knew deep down there wasn't anyone in the woods watching me, but my mind was intent on making my night one of paranoia and discontent. I thought of my mom and could hear her voice, "Get over it, Jason."

I decided to settle my nerves with a little TV time and some food. I baked a frozen pizza and grabbed a beer. I took a bite of the steaming, cheesy slice but found that my mind still didn't want to allow my stomach its nourishment. I set my slice down and picked up my beer. *I guess I'm still on the broken-heart diet*, I thought.

My mind drifted to thoughts of Ashley living in the big city, surrounded by friends and, more importantly, guys. I wondered if she thought about me. I wondered how she had the strength to be so cold and not talk to me after spending so many years together. I jumped, startled as the phone shrilled, cutting through the fog of my despair. I assumed it might be Ashley, but I quickly realized she didn't know I was staying here. Still hopeful, I scooted across the leather couch and snatched up the receiver. "Hello?" I said in a careful, soft tone.

"Dude! What's up?" It was my friend Matt calling to check on me. I was a little disappointed it wasn't Ashley, but I was happy to hear a familiar voice—or any voice, for that matter.

"Hey!" I said. "What's up with you?" It had been almost twenty-four hours since I'd talked to anyone, and honestly, I was having a hard time dealing with the solitude. There is something to be said about being surrounded by friends and family.

"Not much. So, how's the cabin?" he asked with enthusiasm.

"It's…well, it's fine," I said, unsure of how I felt.

"Fine? Dude, you need this, you'll see. Just find some mountain babe and get your mind straight!" He laughed.

"Yeah, right. I'll just start walking through the woods looking for a mountain woman. So, how's things in SoCal?"

"Forget SoCal. SoCal is SoCal, it's the same. You haven't called her, right?"

"Nope! I swear I haven't called, and I'm not going to."

"Good. Don't call her," he ordered.

"I won't, I won't."

"No, really, don't call her!"

"I said I wouldn't!" I barked back. "It's fucking scary here, by the way."

"Scary?" Matt laughed.

"Yeah, seriously, man. It's like a killer-is-waiting-outside-in-the-woods kind of scary."

When he stopped laughing, Matt assured me I was safe and that my mom had probably already scared off anything from coming close to her place a long time ago. A smile came to my face, and I laughed, knowing he spoke the truth.

"Remember when your mom yelled at the UPS man for driving on her property?"

I chuckled. "Of course! She made him back up the truck and leave her packages way up the road."

"Your mom is seriously fucking crazy!"

"Yes, she is, and she's all mine."

Matt laughed. "Dude, you're going to be fine. Just stick it out, and in a few weeks, you'll feel better."

"I know, I'm good, and thanks for calling," I said.

"No worries, brother. I'm here for ya. JUST DON'T FUCKING CALL HER!" he yelled. I jerked the phone away from my ear, then put it back.

"Good night, Matt." I hung up the phone. I laughed to myself, thinking about how funny Matt was and how I wished we were sitting on his deck playing a game of Crazy Eights. I was exhausted, so I lied down on the couch and let the healing, protective glow of the TV lull me to sleep.

Chapter Three

The next morning, I awoke excited. Thanks to Matt, I had a renewed sense of purpose knowing that I was here to heal and move on. Thrilled to finally go fishing, I ate a Tiger's Milk bar for breakfast and chugged a few gulps of chocolate milk. I made my way outside and into the small workshop across from the house. It was red with white trim and looked like a miniature barn. Ivy had almost completely covered the shop, and the door was stiff, reluctant to slide open against my force.

Inside, I found a dozen or more fishing poles along the wall. Below the first pole rested a tackle box filled with various fishing lures and tackle. I spotted a pole that I'd used when I was a kid. I brushed off the cobwebs, grabbed the pole and tackle box, and headed toward my VW Bug.

As I drove by Old Man Dave's house, I scanned the property but didn't see him or his dogs. I decided to head up the highway to Jenkinson Lake, a lake I liked when I was young. I stopped at the local hunting and fishing shop to get a license and some fresh night crawlers for bait. I swung open the door, and the familiar sound of the bell rang, just like the one at the general store in town. Putting on my local face, I walked up to the counter and asked for a tub of worms. A tub of worms is a small Styrofoam container filled with dirt and about a dozen night crawlers.

The store clerk nodded, slid open a cooler just behind him, and reached in for the tub. "Anything else?"

"Uh, yeah. I need a fishing license and a sixer of Bud." It's a rule that you cannot go fishing without beer.

After supplying ID and cash, I was on my way. I twisted and turned through the mountain roads to Jenkinson Lake, which was about fifteen miles from town. I'd been here a few times with my stepdad, and I fondly remembered the time he caught an enormous trout. I hadn't had much luck here in the past, but today was more about the scenery than anything else. I found the turnoff and parked my little Bug alongside the road. It was a short hike through a small grassy meadow to the lake. It was as I remembered years ago: a beautiful V-shaped lake that commanded its own postcard at the local gift shops. I stopped, inhaling the crisp mountain air, and took in the view. Morning mist hovered over the far side of the lake. I made my way along the narrow trail that wrapped around the freshwater. My favorite spot was about a half mile down the trail.

"Quit it! Put that damn fish down!" a voice shouted up ahead. I slowed my gait to a sneaking pace and peered around the bend to see who was shouting and why.

Oh no. It can't be, I thought. But there he was—Old Man Dave, "the Crow Killer"—in the flesh. It seemed he had caught a trout, but one of his dogs got to it before he could land it. Still half hiding, I chuckled as he tackled his dog and grabbed at the decent-sized rainbow trout lodged in his dog's mouth. Dave managed to wrangle it away, and still shouting, he tossed the now maimed fish into his cooler.

Clearing my throat loud enough for him to hear, I made myself known. Startled, he jerked his head in my direction. As soon as his eyes met mine, he instantly turned away. That was the first time he'd ever looked at me, at least I thought it was. I headed down the path toward Dave, who happened to be fishing in my favorite spot.

"Nice day!" I called. He didn't reply. I closed in on his camp and continued walking farther down the trail. I could've fished right next to him, but I knew he liked being alone, and I was in no mood to befriend the crazy, bird-killing neighbor. As I passed, one of his dogs was intent on claiming the trail and made it clear that I wasn't welcome anywhere near his master. I stopped, not knowing what the snarling, overfed black Lab would do. Dave shushed the dog, snatched its dragging leash, and quickly jailed the dog by securing the leash beneath his foot. I thanked him as I passed, but again, he didn't reply.

I walked another quarter of a mile down the trail and found a nice spot to dream away the day. I joyfully cracked open an ice-cold beer and soaked my bait while gazing out at the lake. The wind-kissed water sparkled in the sun, overpowering what was left of the morning mist. I basked in the shimmering sunlight and decided that this was my new favorite spot.

I felt purposeful as I fished. I was a mountain man, and I was doing just fine. Today, all I needed was this lake and a fish for dinner. Being alone in a beautiful place like this was different than simply being alone. The romance of nature overpowers fear and loneliness. I could simply breathe and be calm. This lake was definitely the place for me to be.

After a few missed bites and four cans of beer in the same number of hours, I decided to call it a day, as much as I didn't want this day to end. I feared leaving this spot would make my mind race back to thoughts of Ashley. Thoughts that would surely bring back the pain. Sighing, I brought in my line then gathered my beer cans before heading back up the trail. By the time I got to my old favorite spot, Old Man Dave was nowhere to be seen. I noticed a shiny, brand-new fishing lure that he must've dropped. I picked it up and stowed it away in my tackle box.

The lake reminded me of the time I took Ashley fishing. We were just out of the honeymoon phase, having had our first fight. I wanted Ashley to meet my mom and stepdad for some reason. I was still hoping my mom would just snap out of the spell she was under and want me to be in her life as her son.

Ashley and I decided to make a trip out of it by joining my mom and stepdad on their yearly fishing trip to June Lake, where years before, they'd built their log cabin. I had delusions of grandeur that my mom would love Ashley, and she in turn would love my mom back. I replayed the fantasy in my head of my mom hugging me and saying how sorry she was. We would both cry, then laugh and live happily ever after; all would be good. Wishful thinking. In reality, Ashley hated fishing, and we fought the entire time. At one point, my mom and stepdad passive-aggressively began using fishing sayings like "Throw that one back" or "Not a keeper" to get their point across. They were cruel to make fun of her only because she didn't enjoy fishing. The last straw was when my stepdad childishly suggested that we use her as bait. As they both chuckled at his gibe, Ashley had finally had enough. She jumped up and threw her fishing pole on the ground and stormed off.

"Mom! Why can't you be nice?" I shouted. "Would it kill you to think of me, just once?"

"She's a tart," my mom snidely replied. "Don't say I never did anything for ya."

As I turned to make haste after Ashley, I muttered, "Yeah, you never did do anything for me, that's the problem."

Our trip was ending that day, so my mom's timing was perfect. The good news was that we had driven our own car to the lake. The bad news was that driving back to Southern California was a six-hour drive, and Ashley was pissed. After about four hours of total silence, I tried to break the tension. "Well, that went well."

"Yeah," she said. "That went *really well*. I'm fucking bait! What's wrong with them?"

"I know, I know. They can be protective." Once the words came out of my mouth, I instantly regretted them.

"Protective?" she fired back at me. "From what? Do you seriously need protection from me?"

"No! No, that's not what I meant. I'm sorry. Let's just drop it."

"Fine! You and your fucking crazy family can fuck off!" Ashley jumped in the back seat, and aside from a few yeses and noes, she didn't speak to me the rest of the trip home. A few days later and back in our familiar environment, the nightmarish trip began to fade. Over the next couple of weeks, I made her laugh by occasionally saying, "Hey! You wanna go fishing?"

Shaking from my reverie, I made my way back to my little VW Bug. The sky started to turn gray, and it was raining hard by the time I pulled off the main street and drove down the dirt road to my mom's place. I struggled to see through the foggy windshield even though the inadequate wipers were doing their best to keep up with the downpour. As I passed Old Man Dave's place, I remembered the fishing lure I'd found. I thought to stop and return it, but the fear of approaching his house with its many "Trespassers Will Be Shot!" signs changed my mind.

With a splash, I pulled up to my mom's cabin. Not prepared for the rain and wearing a light flannel shirt, I dashed from my car, holding an old newspaper over my head. As I approached the cabin, I stopped dead in my tracks. The hair on my neck stood at attention while I stared at the opened front door of the cabin. My heart raced, keeping time with my thoughts on what might be happening. I slowly dropped the paper from above my head, barely noticing the rain hammering down on me. I stood for a few moments, waiting to hear or see something from inside the cabin. Silence. I turned quickly, looking left then right to see if anyone was around. I saw nothing. I slowly crept up to the cabin and peeked into the doorway. I stopped and listened again, but there was nothing. I looked down and saw that the floor was wet from the rain. The door must have been open for some time. Thinking I must not have shut the door all the way and the wind probably blew it open, I courageously shouted, "Hello? Hello!" Nothing.

I headed inside and made a quick but cautious check to find nothing amiss. I closed and locked the door, after peering outside one last time to make sure no one was lurking about. It was only late afternoon, but the storm and towering trees shut out the daylight. The forest was once again dark. I tried to distract my fear by turning on the TV, but nothing piqued my interest. I looked down at the two books my mom had left for me. "Hmm…astral projection and mindful meditation," I said as I picked up both books and settled back on the couch. *Talk about light reading*, I thought.

My mom might not have been a particularly good mother, but she was gifted when it came to otherworldly arts. She had given many psychic readings throughout the years to her friends and developed a small following due to the accuracy of her readings.

After looking over the books again, I decided to try the astral projection one, not knowing what it was all about. I turned off the TV, and as I started reading, I immediately found the concept interesting. The book stated that through meditation and concentration, one could send their energy to another place. The book talked about the ability to send energy to and receive energy from a person just by thinking of them. And that it was possible for people to respond to your thoughts of them.

This got my attention, as I'd always believed that all people have their own path in life. Along this path, we meet people for a reason, and situations occur to help us acknowledge that we are on the right one. For example, you think about someone you haven't talked to in a long time, and the next thing you know, the phone rings and it's that person. I had noticed throughout my life that weird little things like that happened to me a lot.

When I was a kid, a friend of my dad told me that there is nothing random in the world and things happen for a reason. She said you could always tell if you were on your path by the coincidences surrounding you. I was too young to comprehend what she was speaking of, so I simply dismissed it. She was a hippie. As I got older, I understood what she meant when unexplained things started happening to me.

For instance, when I was twenty, I had an accident and almost died. I had broken up a fight, and one of the guys stabbed me with a knife in the right side of my chest. I felt a sharp pain and looked down to see blood seeping through my shirt. I fell to the ground, my body sputtering like a plane that had lost its engine. I could barely breathe, and when I coughed, I tasted blood. I was terrified, and in that moment, I was convinced I was going to die. Suddenly, like the switch of a light, everything changed. It was as if my mind was beside me, or outside my shaking body, and I was no longer afraid. I was calm. In fact, I felt wonderful, as if I was sitting in the warmth of the sun. An overwhelming sense of love filled me. I heard sirens in the distance quickly getting louder, getting closer. The sound caused my mind to snap back into my failing body. It was as if the sound gave me hope.

I was fortunate to have survived a pierced lung and nicked artery. I woke from surgery to find a nurse cutting off my blood-soaked jeans. With a gravelly voice, I told her to wait. She came to my side. "Please don't take my socks off," I pleaded. She looked confused, and I beckoned her to come closer. I whispered, "My girlfriend painted my toenails." She giggled and left them on. *Thank God.* But my relief was short-lived. The nurse came back with ten other colleagues. She smiled as she pulled off each sock to reveal my glittered, crimson toenails. The nurses had a good laugh at my expense, and I cursed myself for letting Ashley paint my nails. I remembered her saying, "Oh, come on, no one will ever see them." *Yeah, right.* Coming close to death had changed my life, and normal coincidences that happened to me became magnified. It was as if I could feel the universe guiding me on my path. I guess the hippie chick was right.

I continued reading the book. It explained it would take many hours of practice to achieve astral projection because the mind is like a running motor. It said that one must slow down their thoughts to achieve mind travel. The book included lessons to follow and practice sessions to achieve projected travel. The author placed a lot of emphasis on meditation, on becoming grounded and mindful. I read the chapter on mindful meditation and the first lesson.

The book said to close your eyes and breathe in through your nose, counting one, one thousand; two, one thousand. Then exhale and count one, one thousand; two, one thousand; three, one thousand; four, one thousand. The book recommended practicing this breathing exercise until it could be done easily and with a calm mind for several minutes. I closed my eyes and tried to breathe deeply, but my mind raced with erratic thoughts. "This is bullshit," I said, opening my eyes.

My nervous body wasn't ready to accept this quiet reflection. Abandoning the meditation but still curious, I read on. I skipped ahead to where the author wanted me to imagine a gate with a latch. I closed my eyes to try again, but I only saw static until fleeting thoughts crowded my mind. I tried to focus and see a gate, but I couldn't slow down my brain. I was frustrated within minutes, and again, I gave up. When I leaned forward to place the book on the coffee table, I saw the note card that said, "Breathe." *Yeah, thanks, Mom. I'm breathing and projecting and whatever!* The rain pounded the cabin's tin roof. I couldn't think. *How can anyone meditate with all this noise, anyway?* I turned the TV back on and tuned out for the rest of the night.

Chapter Four

I awoke to a rain-soaked world. The smell of midmorning sun hitting the wet forest was a refreshing and wonderful welcome to a new day. I ventured outside and into the woods. The terrain around the cabin was flat and home to giant pine trees growing out of a fern-covered earth, green and pulsing with life. The ground was soft from layers of pine needles that had fallen each season for years. I wandered for about a mile until the forest stopped at a rocky outcropping that led down to a deep valley and the river below. The river was huge, but from way up here, it looked like a stream. I sat on the rocks that loomed over the basin. I looked out over the rolling hills and mountains that seemed to go on forever. I felt the same serenity as I had at the lake the day before. As my mind and body began to calm, I decided to close my eyes in hopes of finding the latched gate mentioned in my mom's book.

Okay, inhale, one, one thousand; two, one thousand. Exhale, one, one thousand; two, one thousand; three, one thousand; four, one thousand. I felt calmer than yesterday, so I continued. *One, one thousand; two, one thousand—what the hell is that?!* I was startled by a crunching noise. I opened my eyes and jerked my head around. It was just a falling pinecone. *C'mon, Jason, get it together.*

I was jumpy being in the forest alone. All I could think about was the story my mom told me about a mountain lion that mauled a kid just up the road from the cabin. It had happened only a year ago. I wondered if they ever caught it, and not wanting to find out, I decided to leave. I managed not to get lost on my way back to the cabin, and with the sun now shining, I decided that I would go back to my new favorite spot on the lake. *Maybe today I will catch a fish,* I thought.

I grabbed a few Tiger's Milk bars and was soon winding back down the mountain road to Jenkinson Lake. I parked my car and walked through the meadow, stopping at my old favorite spot. I thought about Old Man Dave and the lure I'd found. I thought to try my luck here but decided I liked my new spot better and moved on.

For the second day in a row, the lake did not disappoint. The water was like glass and reflected the towering landscape. I baited my hook and cast my line. Sitting in this perfect spot, the sun caressed my face, causing me to close my eyes. I felt relaxed. With my eyes closed, I no longer saw just static. Instead, I saw shimmering colors. The lake seemed to calm my frantic mind, giving birth to a rainbow of color.

Okay, I thought, and with a deep breath, I began to count. *One, one thousand; two, one thousand. Exhale, one, one thousand; two, one thousand; three, one thousand; four, one thousand.* I was surprised to be able to repeat this for about five minutes. Despite feeling a little light-headed from the deep breathing, I felt good and focused hard on a gate. Soon the melding colors dissipated, revealing the gate. *This is so weird!* I thought. *I see a gate!* This was different than simply thinking of a gate. I saw a gate that I hadn't thought of. I wanted to see a gate, but I hadn't envisioned any particular one in my mind. This was *my* gate! I could see it! It was old and made of wrought iron. It had a circular window also lined with decorative wrought iron. The gate reminded me of an entrance to a medieval castle's garden. Thick, crawling ivy covered the iron latch, suggesting it hadn't been opened in a long time. The gate and the wall to the left and right of it were covered in ivy, forgotten to the ages.

I found it difficult to stay focused on the gate. My mind kept racing as my excitement grew, releasing adrenaline. I battled thoughts of Ashley along with fears and loneliness. I continued trying to focus, but as soon as my gate came to mind, random thoughts would creep back in, over and over. The book said this would happen and to just go with it; the more you practiced, the less the thoughts would interfere.

I jerked from my inner struggle to my outer as my soaking bait found a taker. I jumped up as my fishing pole lurched hard against my surprised grip. I pulled up on my pole, securing the hook within the fish, and after a few fast reels, I landed a beautiful three-pound rainbow trout. "Yes!" I shouted as I rushed to retrieve the fish. You could never celebrate too soon when it came to fishing. I had seen many a fish lost to premature celebrating, but not this one. This fish was dinner. In an instant, not only did I catch a fish, but I was smiling. Today was a good day.

I placed the fish in my ice-filled cooler and thought about my gate. It was still vivid in my mind, as if I'd physically been there before. I stowed away my fishing pole and sat down, staring into the shimmering lake. I closed my eyes for round two. This time, I instantly saw the mixing of colors I'd seen before. As I started to breathe deeply and count, I quickly focused on the gate. *There you are*, I thought as the gate came into my mind's eye. I imagined I was standing about ten feet from it. The vivid green ivy was everywhere. It was greener than in real life, almost otherworldly. Like the book directed, I practiced on visualizing the gate until I could see it clearly without any intruding thoughts. For now, my gate was clear but only for moments. The intrusive thoughts snaked back in, distracting me from my goal, but I was intrigued by the progress I'd made in such a short time.

I sat for several more minutes, trying to control my mind. I felt a strong breeze whip across the lake and hit my skin, causing goose bumps to rise on my arms. I opened my eyes, and for a moment, the world looked slightly different. The trees appeared to vibrate with electricity, maybe from the solitude or the deep breathing. I wasn't sure, but something had changed. This sensation seemed to happen just after I tried to meditate. It was a good feeling, and I wanted to feel this way all the time.

Grabbing my gear and fish-filled cooler, I headed back to the cabin, excited and looking forward to reading more. On the drive back, my thoughts turned to Ashley. The feeling of anger had started to subside, and the need to call her had slowly decreased. I felt like I was where I was supposed to be and that maybe I was here to learn something important. I recalled a conversation I'd had with my friend Kelly about relationships. She thought that a failed relationship was meant to help one learn and evolve in preparation for one's final relationship. At the time, her theory meant nothing to me because I could only think about getting Ashley back. But now, I was curious. *Did all this happen just so I would come to my mom's cabin and read the book on astral projection? Is it all connected?* I felt hopeful for a moment and was eager to read more of the book. I knew my gate was there, and maybe, just maybe, I might find my way, my path, just beyond the gate.

I hurriedly put away my fishing gear so that I could resume reading where I'd left off. I had found a cure for my despair in the form of a book. It was a treasure hunt, and I was looking for the next clue. I sat in my usual spot on the couch, and with book in hand, I flipped to the dog-eared page. It was the first time in my life that I happily sat in a room alone without the television on.

The book instructed me to imagine a gate with a latch. This would be the gate to my special place, the book said. It could be any place I wanted—the beach, the mountains, wherever I wanted to be. I could go to this place no matter where I was and feel safe and calm. The lesson further described the necessary steps to find my special place. After I could see my gate clearly, I was to visualize myself reaching out to the latch and opening the gate.

I set the book aside and adjusted myself, getting ready for the next step. I closed my eyes, and to my surprise, I quickly saw my gate in my mind's eye. The green ivy was as saturated as before. With each breath, I focused more on the gate. I focused on the window of the gate and imagined what my place would look like. The more I focused, the clearer and sharper the gate became. I noticed some aged, cracked wood beneath the ivy, and I moved my focus to the rusty latch. I took it slowly, like the book said to do. The lesson said to take each step slowly as if you were painting a picture and you had to paint every detail of the image. I needed to notice everything and study it intently.

Staring at my gate, I wondered why I saw it the way I did. Why was my gate old and covered in ivy? What did this mean about me? I began imagining what my place would look like on the other side of the gate. I imagined lush pathways through a forest. It wasn't like the forest outside my mom's cabin. It was a tranquil, coastal forest that led to a private beach. I caught myself moving too far ahead and directed my focus back to the gate. I took a deep breath and imagined myself slowly walking toward it. I understood why the author said to move slowly. If I imagined myself simply walking up to the gate, the detail would be lost, and it would turn into a fleeting image. To keep the detail, I needed to move slowly. I breathed in and out deeply again and again, only taking a step after the initial step was stable and my mind's eye could stay focused. I was now within reach of the gate. I gazed at the latch for a long time, focusing on the rust and imagining how the latch would open. It needed to be pushed down to release a lever, freeing the gate to swing open. I focused on the hinge and saw how it would open inward, away from me. I wanted to open it so badly, but it was too soon. I ended the session by closing my mind's eye and slowly opening my eyes to the physical world, the cabin.

I felt so calm, as if I'd been asleep. I sat still and quiet for several minutes. My mind started actively thinking about the place beyond my gate. I wondered why I imagined a coastal, forested beach and not my favorite spot by the lake. The book mentioned that your special place would come naturally and without effort because your inner self had already been there, and your physical self would need to focus and meditate to go there. My body slowly came alive, and with a growling stomach, I changed my focus to the delicious three-pound rainbow trout waiting for me.

I cleaned the fish and dressed its soft flesh with salt, pepper, lemon slices, and a dollop of butter. I wrapped both fillets in a tinfoil sarcophagus and placed it inside the preheated oven for fifteen minutes. This was the full-proof way my dad had taught me when I was a kid. Lucky for my brother and me, my dad was a great cook who had been taught by his mother. When he was a young, traveling surfer, he had hopped a plane to Hawaii and spent some time as a short order cook at a diner. Combining what he learned from his mother and the diner, he had succeeded in providing nourishing meals for me and my brother.

The smell from the oven filled the room as the fish and butter steamed to perfection. I was hungry and determined to put the pounds back on that I'd lost on the broken-heart diet. Not to mention, these mental exercises were exhausting, reminding me of how I'd felt when I was in school. I would get so hungry simply from studying.

With three beeps, the oven announced its job was done, and I hurried to save the perfectly timed fish from being overcooked. I sat happily in front of the TV with my steaming tinfoil pouch. Using my fork, I tore at the foil, exposing the tender white flesh of my catch. I lifted the plate to inhale the visible steam. My eyes closed, and the smell of lemony butter filled my senses. I gently flaked the fish and broke off a piece, bringing it to my salivating mouth. It was incredibly fresh and delicious. My hunger switched into overdrive as I devoured the entire fish quickly. I was stuffed, and it felt good.

It had grown dark outside. I double-checked the doors were locked before settling on the couch for the night. While channel surfing, I thought about my day, the fish, and of course, my gate. I was excited to read more about astral projection. I looked over at the phone and thought about calling Ashley, but my compulsion faded, and my attention reverted to the television.

Chapter Five

I woke up the next morning with a horrible cramping in my gut. I knew the feeling and wasted no time rushing to the bathroom. My body wasn't ready for an oversized portion of rainbow trout after eating only Tiger's Milk bars for the past two months. After spending quality time on the pot, I made some oatmeal and toast in hopes of settling my stomach. Though my appetite was back, I ate my breakfast slowly. The oats and dry toast went down smoothly, so I decided it would be a good idea to hit the store. My newfound hunger needed sustenance. *I don't think I'll ever eat another Tiger's Milk bar again*, I thought as I grabbed my jacket and slipped out the door.

The morning sun peeked through the clouds, but the air felt heavy and wet. *Hope it doesn't rain*, I thought as I walked to my faithful car. My eye caught movement in the woods. I stopped and scanned to see what it was. Far off I could see the silhouette of a deer. It was deep in the woods. Beams of morning light filtered through the trees, and as the deer walked, the streams of light revealed the animal's honey-colored fur before it disappeared back into darkness. I watched it move slowly in and out of the sunlight until I could no longer see it.

The deer reminded me of how close to nature I was. My thoughts drifted to the mountain lion and the mauled kid, and I suddenly felt extremely nervous being out here alone. My stepdad's voice echoed in my head. He'd said that because of the mountain lion scare, the police had told locals to carry a flashlight at night but to point the light backward over their shoulder instead of illuminating the path in front of them. Apparently, mountain lions only attacked people from behind, and if you held your flashlight backward, they would think your back was your front. It seemed to make sense at the time, but now I thought, *is it better that a mountain lion attacks you from the front? I guess it would be better to see it coming...but wait! You wouldn't see it coming because your damn flashlight would be pointing backward!*

Chuckling to myself, I opened the door to my car. I drove through Camino and its one-light intersection and hopped on the highway to

Placerville, which was about ten miles away. Placerville was an old mining town, but it was the place to go if you needed a real grocery store. It had a rich history stemming from the gold rush. It was a charming town, lined with western buildings and historical sights. I drove down Main Street and took in the colors and sounds of the tourists and local townsfolk. I felt a little strange being around so many people after being isolated in the woods for a few days. I could count on one hand the number of people I'd seen. Not to mention, I hadn't really talked to anyone in a few days either. I found that the more time I spent alone in my head, the less I wanted to talk to anyone.

I pulled up to Safeway and went inside. I filled my shopping cart with all the items I'd missed and been unable to eat for the past two months. I overloaded the cart so I wouldn't have to make another trip out here. Fully stocked up and checked out, I drove back up the highway to my personal oasis, my little cabin that with each new day I was ever more grateful for.

As I pulled off the highway and made my way down the single-lane road, I passed Old Man Dave's place. He was outside, head down, and intently raking pine needles as if to rid them from the earth once and for all. I was in a good mood and decided to mess with the old guy. After all, we had history. When I as a kid I would cut through his property to get to my mom's house quicker. He'd always shake his fist and yell, "This is private property!" I'd just laugh and wave back as I ran. I honked my car's horn as I passed him. *Beep, beep, beep!* I was curious to see if he would look up, but he didn't waiver from his mission. I immediately felt bad. I wondered if I would ever be that guy: one who only needed a few dogs in his life. *He's gotta have some kind of story*, I thought. *Maybe he just needs to find his gate,* I smirked.

I pulled up and unloaded my bounty. I spied the woods for deer or mountain lions but saw none. By the time I was inside, the skies had darkened, and it began to rain. I had planned on fishing, but the rain dampened that idea. I decided to read more, hoping that I would be ready to open my gate. I opened my book, unfolding the dog-eared page.

To gain access to the world beyond my gate, I needed to open the latch, I read. To do this, I was prompted to concentrate harder than before, visualizing my hand grabbing the handle and opening the gate. I focused on how the handle worked and which way the gate opened. Each tiny detail was of utmost importance. The author stressed the necessity of going slowly to avoid losing any detail, which would result in an unclear experience. The point of projection, the author said, is to make it so real every time you go to your place that you reach the ability of actually going there in your mind. I felt that I was ready to open my gate.

I closed my eyes, and counting with steady breaths, I inhaled through my nose and exhaled out my mouth. I began to relax, and my racing thoughts slowed, becoming somewhat controllable. *There it is my gate!* After concentrating on this gate so many times, I began to feel as if I were truly there. I stared at the handle, figuring out how the latch worked and which way the gate would open. I moved forward, within reach of the gate, and ever so slowly extended my hand out in front of me. I focused on my hand in great detail. It was easy to do because I already knew what my hand looked like. I wiggled my fingers and turned my hand over, examining my palm and its lines. *Okay. Let's open this gate.*

I refocused on the handle, gently resting my hand on it. It seemed so real I almost expected to feel the iron beneath my fingers. I pressed down on the handle, and my imagination took over as the rusty handle squeaked. With a victorious clang, the latch opened. The gate fell free as I gently pushed it open. The vines stretched like spiderwebs before breaking, allowing the gate to fully open. I peered into the world beyond. It was as lush and verdant as I expected. A narrow path led through a grove of large pepper trees, their branches drooping and brushing the ground.

I closed the gate behind me, making sure the latch was securely in place. I looked down at my bare feet and thought it strange, considering I hated being without shoes or socks. I always wore big, clunky combat boots. My mind felt at ease in this place, and I started to feel my surroundings. The ground was warm on my bare soles, and the smell of honeysuckle filled the air. It reminded me of being a kid in the summer. I loved that smell.

The path was lined with tall grass and wildflowers. I now understood what the author meant when she stated that everyone has already been to their special place. It was as if my mind put all the good memories of my childhood in one special place, my place. There were bees hard at work, buzzing from blossom to blossom. The path went forward and then seemed to bend to the left, out of sight. I moved along the path slowly, not getting ahead of my imagination. The smells and the colors were palpable, abundant, and vivid. Passing the large pepper trees that shaded the ground below, I carefully stepped along the path. The trees opened to a field of grass and flowers waving in the wind. The bees struggled to navigate the gusts. Up ahead, I saw a small footbridge over a small creek. Wispy clouds stretched across the blue sky.

I approached the bridge and walked halfway across then stopped. To my right, there was a small pond filled with shimmering water. It was a perfect pond. I wondered if there were any fish in it. I turned to my left and saw that the stream snaked through a narrow valley and disappeared in the distance. At the end of the bridge, the path curved to the right and traveled uphill. I followed the dirt path, which eventually turned into a sea grass lined path of sand that led to the coastal bluffs. The warm sand felt good between my toes, and my feet sank deeper into the sand with each step.

As I made my way up and over the path, I caught sight of an expansive, sparkling ocean. The aquamarine water spread before me for miles and miles. I continued down the path to the beach, where I stood and drank in the beautiful scenery. I truly felt as if I were at the beach, not imagining it. Feeling the warmth of the sun spreading over my head and shoulders, I sat down and simply stared out at the sea. I sat for a while, and soon my mind created a beautiful pink sunset just like the ones I remembered from home. As the sun went down, I decided to head back.

When returning to the gate, the book mentioned that it was just as important to go as slowly as I had when I began the session. I stood and turned then walked up the sea grass path and down the other side. The bridge was to my left, and I stopped in the middle again to stamp each detail into my memory. I crossed the wind-kissed field and entered the pepper tree grove. The grove was dark but in a good way. Walking beneath the pepper trees felt like being inside a protective dark room where you would go in search of solitude. It had been too long since my life was quiet.

I continued walking along the path until I found the gate. As I approached the gate, I thought of something I hadn't thought about before. I'd spent so much time discerning what might be on the other side of the gate that I never considered what would be there on the way back. I needed to imagine a landscape because I didn't want to open the gate to nothingness. I focused and opened the gate, conjuring up a long cobblestone road leading as far as the eye could see. Tiny farms dotted the landscape way off into the distance, so far away that no one would ever venture up this road. It was forgotten to them but not to me. This was my road, my gate, my bridge, and my beach.

I closed my mind's eye and, with a deep breath, opened my eyes to the physical world. My body tingled, and I felt extremely light-headed, as if I'd been floating and asleep for hours. I felt rested and relaxed. I felt great. I stretched my arms above my head and yawned. I picked up the book and thinking about where I'd just gone, I finished reading the chapter. The book advised me to visit my place twice a day until it was second nature. I read the title of the next chapter: "Taking Flight." *Oh shit!* I thought.

I looked at the time and was surprised to see that I'd been away for almost a full hour. I'd meditated before, but only for a few minutes at a time. There was something unique about this type of meditation. In a way, it was giving my sad, codependent life meaning again, and I was grateful. I wanted my envisioned place to be as familiar as any other place in the physical world, and I wanted to be able to access it at any time I needed to escape the chaos in my life. My special place was saving me, and I wanted it to be real, not just a thought.

The rain had stopped, and the sun pierced through the late-morning cloud cover. I decided to go fishing as previously planned. I made a couple of peanut butter sandwiches, grabbed a few beers, and took off to the lake.

As I approached the turnout for the lake, I was surprised to see Old Man Dave's car parked alongside the road. It had been raining most of the morning, so I hadn't expected to see anyone else at the lake. I shamefully recalled honking at Dave, and again, I felt bad. I wondered if he would say anything. I made my way through the field and began down the trail. There he was, silhouetted by the shimmering water now steaming from the sun. I stopped and watched for a moment. He sat still, staring across the lake. I was curious to know what he was thinking about. I could tell he was in deep thought because his casted fishing line was drooping.

I cleared my throat extra loudly to make myself known. He startled, most likely not expecting to see anyone out here as well. He snapped out of whatever deep thought he was in and shifted his posture as if a teacher had reprimanded him for slouching. I wondered why his dogs weren't with him today. I decided to continue walking, respecting his obvious desire to be left alone. As I approached, I remembered the lure he had left behind. I paused and quickly kneeled to open my tackle box. "Sorry to bother you, but I think you left this here."

He turned to observe the shiny lure dangling from my extended hand. "Not mine," he grumbled.

"Are you sure? I found it right—"

"Not mine!" He hissed, cutting me off midsentence.

I stood with my hand still extended for about fifteen seconds, not understanding why he didn't want his lure back. I didn't want to force the issue, and as I turned to walk away, I said aloud, "No good deed goes unpunished."

"What was that?" he shouted as if I'd said something nasty.

I turned and replied, "No good deed goes unpunished."

"Oh," he said calmly, knowing that my words held no salt.

I walked back over to the old man and tossed the lure at his feet. "Here, just take the damn lure. It's yours anyway." I turned and again walked away, mumbling, "Why wouldn't you want your lure back? It's, like, a five-dollar lure. It doesn't make any sense."

As I rounded the cove and disappeared into the trees, I forced the encounter out of my mind and focused on the possibility of catching another fish for dinner. I reached my spot and quickly baited my hook, not wanting to miss out on a single passing fish. I cast my line taut and studied the tip of my pole for movement. My hand gripped the pole gently, waiting to pick up on the slightest vibration. The warm sun on my face felt good, and I closed my eyes. It was as comforting as my grandma caressing my forehead when I was sick.

She was the closest thing I had to a mom, and I was thankful for her.

My closed eyes filled with color that quickly turned into a daydream. I instantly saw my gate. I didn't fight the illusion because the feeling was comforting and inviting. I walked through my gate and down the path easily. Crossing the bridge and walking up and over the bluff were quick and effortless. I stood on my beach, breathed in the salty air, and listened to the seagulls squawking in the distance. The gentle, incoming waves lapped at my toes, and I felt the cool water of the ocean. I looked at the horizon, noticing that the sun was again close to setting. I stared for what seemed like hours across the flat sea until a breeze flipped my hair into my eyes, forcing a blink. This time I wasn't jarred from my vision because of a fish. Instead, I was interrupted by the sound of Old Man Dave clearing his throat with a cough and grumble.

Shaken from this blissful state of mind, I winced as I opened my eyes and was instantly stabbed by the glint of light reflecting on the lake. I blinked a few times, priming my sensitive eyes to the world. Old Man Dave was walking toward me. I stood in a defensive position. *Who knows what he's capable of? After all, he does shoot crows. Maybe this will be the day he snaps and decides to use me as bait just like my stepdad wanted to do with Ashley.* He continued to walk toward me, not caring to make eye contact.

"Can I help you with something?" I asked as he approached.

"Well, yes. This aint mine, like I said. You found it, so it's yours and that's only right." He stood, hand extended, holding the lure I'd previously thrown at his feet.

"Oh, well, thanks."

"It's only right," he said again.

"Okay, I'll take it." I extended my hand.

His eyes, still unable to make contact with mine, darted left and right. His face was rough and unshaven, and you could tell from the few scars across his forehead and the one right next to his eye that he'd seen some terrible things. His darting eyes were bright blue and seemed to glow in the reflecting light. He looked to be in his sixties and still had a full head of closely cropped gray hair. As he dropped the lure into my waiting palm, I noticed a faded tattoo on his freckled forearm. It was a military tattoo I'd seen years before when I was about thirteen.

My best friend Aaron and I were into everything military. In fact, we both wore army fatigues and made up ranks for each other. We hung out at the army-navy surplus shop in our town. It was called Bushwhackers, and the owner was a Vietnam vet. That was where I'd seen the tattoo before, on the arm of the owner. I remembered asking him about it, and he'd explained that he was in the marines and his whole platoon had the same tattoo.

Holding the lure, I said, "So you were a marine?" His eyes met mine, and the blue intensity seemed to look straight through me. As quickly as he looked at me, his eyes darted away again, returning to the left-right pattern.

"Who told you that?"

"Your arm did." I pointed to the faded US Marines insignia on his arm. His eyes quickly looked at his arm, and his other hand covered it as if he'd forgotten it was there and didn't want anyone to see it. "Sorry," I said. "I didn't mean to—"

"No, no, that's okay," Dave said. "It's just been a long time since I heard them words spoke."

I told him about the army-navy store owner's tattoo and about my friend, Aaron. He listened intently to every word as if he longed for another life. A life he'd lived but was now forgotten by everyone but himself. The tattoo and the scars said so much. What he must have gone through and what he must have seen.

"You want a beer?" I quickly flipped open my cooler, snatched up a beer, and forced it into his hand before he could say no.

He looked at the beer, seemingly unsure what to do. I was sure this was the first conversation he'd had with another person in years. "C'mon! Have a beer and take a load off." I pointed to a tree stump and motioned for him to sit.

"Well, I guess it aint going to hurt none," he said as he sat down.

I reeled in my line and grabbed myself a beer and cracked it open. "Cheers," I said, raising my beer to the old man.

He grunted with a nod and raised his can just enough to reciprocate.

I took a swig from my ice-cold beer. "So, you were in the war?" This being the only thing I could think to talk about besides fishing, I thought to go for broke.

"Yep, I was there," he said, now staring at the lake.

I bit my tongue and didn't ask all the questions I had racing through my head about the war. We sat without speaking for a few minutes, and I cast my line out.

"Any bites?" he asked, as if finding his tongue and remembering he could speak.

"Not today. I did, however, catch a three-pounder yesterday."

"Three-pounder, huh? That's pretty good."

I chuckled. "Yeah, that is pretty good." As soon as I started to say another word, he downed the rest of his beer and crushed the can beneath his worn work boot.

"Thanks for the beer," he said, now standing and handing me the crushed, cold can. He turned and walked away.

Before he could get too far, I said, "Dave, right?"

He stopped and turned. "What?"

"Your name. It's Dave, right?"

"Yup!" he said as he again turned and walked on. He must have recognized me because he seemed unfazed that I knew his name.

I shouted, "Mine's Jason!" He didn't stop or respond. My attention now refocused on my fishing. The encounter with the old man ran through my head—the scars, the tattoo—and I thought about Aaron, my childhood best friend. I wondered what he was up to.

I fished for the rest of the day, not catching anything. When I passed the old man's spot, he had already left. I drove back to the cabin and to my book. Thinking of my path, I felt that I'd met Old Man Dave for a reason. For what, I wasn't sure, but it was for a reason, and the lure was the catalyst bringing our paths together. I would need to take it slow, just like my gate. I knew if I pushed too fast, I wouldn't learn what I needed to from him.

I sat at the window, eating the last peanut butter sandwich while staring into the forest, thinking of why I feared it at night. I thought about Old Man Dave and the army-navy shop owner, both who had been in a war. I tried to imagine the horror they must have faced and how silly I was for being afraid of the dark. I felt childish. The Viet Cong wasn't trying to kill me. Sure, there might be a bear or a mountain lion out here, but what were the chances? I decided I would go into the forest that night and face my fear. I was sick of being scared, and my mind was the enemy that I needed to conquer.

A few hours later, after a steaming bowl of Top Ramen and a second beer for courage, it was time to head out. The TV flickered with commercials and nonsense. I looked out the window and only saw black. I tried to remember the pretty moss-covered trees and the ferns at their feet that I knew were there only hours before. I forced myself to put on my shoes and jacket and ventured out the door into the darkness. The air was damp, and there was a steady sprinkle just like the night of my arrival. I went back inside and put on a rain slicker that I found hanging in the mudroom. *Okay, Here I go.*

I stepped out across the front deck and onto the soft ground. The pine needles crunched beneath my feet, seeming to be much louder at night. I stood and stared into the darkness, looking left and right, noticing the forest was still. All I could hear was the light sprinkling of rain patting the hood of my slicker. I flipped on my flashlight and slowly scanned the forest. To conquer my fear, I decided to take fifty steps straight into the forest then return home. I knew if I walked in a straight line, it would lead me directly to the rock outcropping overlooking the valley. That spot was far more than fifty steps away, so I felt safe enough. I began stepping and counting, often looking over my shoulder at the cozy, lit cabin as if I were swimming away from a boat and didn't want to go too far.

Twenty-five, twenty-six, twenty-seven…I counted, walking on pine needles that crunched with each step. Like a Scooby-Doo character, I stepped as lightly as possible, hoping not to stir anything awake. My fear seemed silly, but it was a true fear, so I guess I was silly.

Forty-seven, forty-eight, forty-nine…fifty! I stopped and was still. I turned and saw the cabin several yards away. The lights were bright in the dark forest, beckoning me home. I imagined I was a bear or a killer watching the cabin from the forest. It made me feel better. *Why would anyone be way out here?* I thought.

I turned and stared into the darkness of the woods. I could see only about five feet in front of me. I looked up at the sprinkling rain hitting my face and noticed the massive limbs of the pine trees. They reached out above me like huge umbrellas. Standing there was surreal. It had only been a week since I'd arrived, and I never imagined I would be standing in the forest alone at night. In a way, I had Ashley to thank for this experience. I was on a journey both physically and mentally. I missed her, I loved her, but I no longer needed her. I stood, embracing my thoughts and the stillness of the night for a while. Without fear and without counting, I walked the fifty steps back to the cabin.

Chapter Six

I slept late into the morning, enjoying a sense of peace I hadn't had for some while. Later, with a bowl full of Cheerios in my belly, I put on my shoes and decided to retrace the fifty steps I'd taken the night before. I quickly arrived at the spot where I'd stopped last night. I looked around and up, thinking that the more I did this, the more comfortable I would feel in the woods at night. I just needed to visualize the forest at daytime to encourage myself at night. I decided I would venture into the forest each night, taking fifty more steps each time until I made it all the way to the rock outcropping that overlooked the deep valley. It would become my rite of passage. Standing there alone in the forest, I felt both excited and scared. For the first time, I knew I was going to be okay.

I walked back to the cabin and went inside to read the next chapter, "Taking Flight." I wondered what the title meant as I flipped to the new chapter. The book explained how one could travel to another place on the planet just by concentrating hard enough. Though this would not be as easy as creating a gate to your special place, once you mastered this type of astral projection, you could go to a specific place and even call on someone. If I wanted to contact Ashley, for example, all I needed to do was to go to her in my mind and she might hear me. This seemed crazy to me. I'd experienced the phenomenon when you thought or talked about someone and they called you immediately. You know the old saying "Your ears must be burning." This was kind of the same thing but much more intense.

The first part of the lesson in projecting was to imagine a tube of light coming from the top of your head and flying up through the air. That seemed simple to me, as I'd already created a gate and an entire landscape. The author further explained that moving slowly would be crucial in keeping the vision sharp.

The lesson went on to say that when you are traveling in the energy-tube form, you will move over larger areas much faster than walking down a path. The author stressed the importance of flying slow and visualizing real landmarks below to help you stay focused, find your destination, and travel back home again."

I put down the book, and with confidence, I closed my eyes and began breathing deeply. My brain immediately wanted to go to my gate and the beach, so I needed to refocus my attention to my head. I imagined a beam of light the same size as my head protruding upward. Goose bumps prickled my arms. I envisioned the tube with a translucent light extending about four feet out from the top of my head. The book instructed to extend the tube of light out and then bring it back in, each time extending it farther and farther until you had ultimate control over the tube of light. I found it interesting because it was similar to my plan of taking another fifty steps each night in the forest and repeating the same steps during the day to help me see at night.

For almost an hour, I practiced extending my tube of light four feet out then four feet back. This was strange behavior, as I was impatient by nature. With each projection, I began to feel more control over the light until I could easily extend it with detail and retract it quickly. I was on the right track, but I still wondered if it would work. I calculated 136 miles from here to San Francisco. I wondered how long it would take for me to learn to project my light all the way there and back. For the time being, I was satisfied with my four-foot adventure and decided it was time to go fishing.

I didn't see Old Man Dave's car at the turnout. I grabbed my gear and headed to the lake. As I approached Dave's spot, my old favorite spot, I decided to stop and fish because he wasn't here, and I didn't feel like walking the distance to my other place around the lake. As soon as I cast my line, I caught the first of several fish I would catch within the hour. *The fish are biting today!* I thought excitedly. I put the best of the rainbow trout in the cooler for dinner and let the others go. I took a break and unwrapped a sandwich and cracked a beer. *Now this is the life*, I thought as I sat on the shore of the mountain lake. This was exactly what I needed at the time, and for now, it was good enough.

I finished my lunch and was about to head home when I noticed Old Man Dave walking toward me. "Hey, Dave. I hope you don't mind me fishing here."

"It's a free country," he said as he unfolded his canvas, aluminum framed chair and sat. He quickly reached into his cooler and grabbed a beer, popping the top. He took three big gulps, as if priming his brain for the big hunt, then placed his beer in the homemade wooden cup holder that he'd fastened to the right arm of his chair with zip ties.

"Nice cup holder," I said.

"It works."

"That's all that matters, right?"

He seemed a bit more easygoing than before. I assumed it had something to do with the conversation about his tattoo or the guy who owned Bushwhackers. Whatever it was, it was comfortable. I was intrigued to learn about Dave and his story.

"You gettin' any bites?"

"Bites? How's this for a bite!" I flipped open my cooler, revealing my beautifully sized rainbow trout.

"Looks like dinner."

"Yep. That's just one of six I've caught so far."

"Wow, better than yesterday, aye?"

"That's for sure," I said. The small talk was great. I hadn't spoken to anyone since Matt's call, and it felt good to communicate with someone, even if it was with a grumpy, bird-killing old man. We fished for a while, catching only a few more, and as the sun got low, the fish stopped biting. We surrendered and cracked open a couple of cold ones.

"So, you're Barbara's son, right?"

"Yeah. You know my mom?"

"Well, she is my only neighbor," he answered, like my question was stupid.

"No, I know, but she told me you never talk to her."

"Maybe she doesn't talk to me." He shrugged.

I immediately thought about my mom chasing away the UPS guy. "That's a good point." I laughed.

"So, why are you up here, alone?" he asked.

"What do you mean?"

"Well, you're a young man staying alone at your mom's cabin, fishing every day like an old man."

I laughed. "Fair enough." I told him about Ashley and why I was staying at my mom's. Dave didn't seem interested in my story of lost love.

"So, what's up with shooting the crows?" I asked. He seemed a little upset about my question, so I said, "I don't mean to offend you. I'm just curious why you don't like crows."

"I don't shoot them. I use blanks to scare them off because they mess with my cat."

"The birds mess with your cat?" I laughed. "How does that even happen?"

"If you must know, my wife's—I mean, *my* cat doesn't see well, and the birds for some godforsaken reason peck at him and chase him."

"I didn't know you have a wife."

"I don't," he snapped. "Not anymore."

"You mind me asking where she is?" I asked carefully.

"She passed on."

"Oh. I'm sorry. I didn't mean to pry."

"You sure have a funny way of not prying."

"Sorry. I just haven't talked to anyone in a week and *trust me* when I say that's a miracle in itself."

"Actually, that doesn't surprise me. The longer you don't talk to people, the less you want to," he said.

"I guess that's true. Do you mind me asking your wife's name?"

The old man shifted uncomfortably, dropping his head, and after a long pause and a sigh, he said something.

I didn't hear him and asked again.

"I said Jenny is her name, *was* her name," he said a little louder.

I wanted to know more about Jenny and how she had passed, but I knew I needed to tread lightly so he wouldn't get scared off. I decided to change the subject, hoping to earn his trust. "So, did you get drafted?" I asked.

"Yup. I never did have much luck with gambling, but I sure did win that lottery."

"Man, that must have been a scary letter to receive."

"It wasn't Publishers Clearing House, that's for sure."

"My dad got drafted—well, kind of," I said.

"How do you *kind of* get drafted?" he scoffed.

"Well, my dad's name is Don Romero, and he received a draft notice in the mail, but the address was wrong. The address was two streets over."

The old man seemed intrigued by this story. "What did he do?"

"Well…he walked two streets over, knocked on the door, and asked if a Don Romero lived there. The woman said, 'Yes, that's my son.' So, my dad handed her the draft notice, apologized, and walked back home. He got lucky, I guess."

"I'll say." Dave shuddered. "So, what got you interested in army gear?"

I looked at him squarely and said, "Rambo."

With his head down, Dave's shoulders shook, and with a cough, he burst into laughter. "Ha-ha-ha! Rambo! Rambo! Ha-ha-ha!" He laughed so hard I stood up, startled.

"What's so funny about Rambo?" I said defensively, then relaxing, I laughed at myself.

"Sorry, boy, it's just I never thought that's what you would say. Rambo, ha-ha-ha! That's a good one."

"Yeah, I saw Rambo, and the first thing I did was buy some camos and jump off the roof of my house into a tree. I fell *all* the way down."

"Boy, are you sure you're right in the head?"

"Well, not really." I laughed.

"Did you ever think about serving in the military?"

"Well, I kinda did."

"Wait a sec. First, your dad *kind of* got drafted, and now you *kind of* served in the military? How does one *kind of* serve in the military?" With bated breath, he said, "This ought to be good."

"Well, I'll tell ya. My best friend Aaron and I were hanging out at Bushwhackers—you know, the army-navy store I told you about yesterday?"

"Yeah, yeah, I remember." He motioned for me to continue.

"Well, we were hanging out there, and I noticed a pamphlet about being a Young Marine. I picked it up and showed it to Aaron; he smiled and suggested that we join the Young Marines. You know, camping, hiking, drilling—that sort of stuff. It seemed like a fun thing to do. The pamphlet said it cost two hundred dollars for a whole weekend of adventure. So, we took the flyer to our dads, and after they agreed, they signed us up."

I settled into my chair and began to recount the story to Dave. I remembered my dad driving us to the El Toro Marine Corps Air Station, where he dropped us off at the Young Marines camp. Aaron and I were so excited to learn how to be soldiers, camp, and maybe shoot a gun. There were a lot of kids there, at least forty of them. A man in full camo waved at everyone to gather around. His name was Sergeant Willard, a name I would *never* forget.

Sergeant Willard greeted the parents with a big smile and stated that their kids were in the safe hands of the United States Marines and to pick us up at 1600 hours on Sunday. He laughed at the confused expressions of our parents' faces and translated the time in laymen's terms as four p.m. Everyone laughed, then he told us to say our goodbyes. I gave my dad a quick hug and waited for the fun to start.

As soon as our parents were gone, the sergeant filed us into a single line. I noticed that the tone of his voice had slowly started to change. He pointed to a dirt clearing about the size of a football field about three hundred yards away and barked, "Okay! My name is Sergeant Willard. Your parents are gone, and now you belong to me! Get your disrespecting asses down to that lot now! I mean now! Run! Run! Run! Run! Run!"

I was startled by the sergeant's sudden and abrasive tone, so I ran in a full sprint with Aaron at my side. I looked over at him and saw pure terror in his eyes. Huffing and puffing, we all made it down to the dirt lot, and by the time Sergeant Willard walked up, we were still trying to catch our breath.

"Okay, let's fall in. That means you!" Sergeant Willard shouted. "I want four lines here." He scratched four lines in the dusty red clay several feet apart. All of us rushed to find a spot in line, bumping into each other.

"Okay! You, here! You, here! And you, here!" Sergeant Willard continued shouting as he put us in line one by one until we were all in a clean formation of rustled nerves.

"What's my name?" Sergeant Willard shouted.

A couple of kids softly said, "Sergeant Willard."

"I *said*, what is my Goddamn name?"

Everyone shouted, "Sergeant Willard!"

I looked over at Aaron, who was about four kids up and one row to the left of me. He was short for his age and had cropped hair. He was wearing multicolored Converse shoes and a shirt that read, "Kill Gaddafi."

Aaron looked back at me, searching for some answer as to why we were in this predicament. Unfortunately, Sergeant Willard caught him looking at me.

"Who do we have here?" Sergeant Willard said as he made his way toward Aaron, who was still looking at me. I tried to signal for him to turn around, but it was too late. "I *said*, who are you?" Sergeant Willard shouted in Aaron's face.

"I'm Aaron," he said softly as he stared at the ground.

"Aaron with the clown shoes," the sergeant said. "Where did you get those shoes, Aaron? At the clown store?"

"No, I…uh…"

"I don't care where you got your silly clown shoes, Aaron." Sergeant Willard continued to shout in poor Aaron's face. "So, let me guess. You want to kill Gaddafi in your cute clown shoes, huh?" I could tell that Aaron was on the verge of tears. "Well, at least you have half of it right," Sergeant Willard shouted. "Eyes forward, Aaron!"

"Yes, sir," Aaron said in his tiny, high voice.

"What did you say? I can't hear you!"

A couple decibels louder, Aaron replied, "I said, yes, sir!"

"It's sir, yes, sir!" Sergeant Willard shouted. "Say it, everyone! Sir, yes, sir!"

Everyone shouted, "Sir, yes, sir!"

"Repeat!"

"Sir, yes, sir!"

Sergeant Willard made his way through the lines of terrified kids, teaching each one to stand straight while the others observed and followed suit to avoid getting yelled at as he passed by.

"So, you think you little worms can get away with disrespecting your parents and making their life hell? Well, I'm here to tell you that you are wrong!"

At this moment, my stomach dropped, and I began to sweat. I realized Aaron and I had made a huge mistake, and we were stuck there for the entire weekend.

"By the end of this weekend, you are going to wish you never crossed me or your parents. You will respect me and your parents, am I clear?" Sergeant Willard shouted.

"Sir, yes, sir!" was heard by all in unison.

Sergeant Willard turned to greet another soldier who was making his way over to us. Aaron quickly looked back at me and mouthed, *WTF!* I shrugged my shoulders as if to say, *I have no idea.*

We had thought we were in for a fun-filled weekend of adventure and war games with fake guns and maybe a game or two of capture the flag. Boy, was I wrong! I should've read the pamphlet a little more thoroughly. Now I knew why my dad was laughing when he dropped us off. After reading the brochure, our dads probably thought it would be funny to let us go through with it. *Yeah, real funny*, I thought. Now we were in a disciplinary camp for troubled kids, which Aaron and I were not. Well, not really.

Sergeant Willard and the other guy walked back to us. "Okay! Listen up!" Sergeant Willard said. "This is Corporal Mike! Now Corporal Mike likes to exercise. He likes to run and do push-ups and all sorts of fun things you weaklings have never heard of. So, if you would be so polite to offer your attention to Corporal Mike, you might learn something. Are you ready, Aaron?" Sergeant Willard pointed out Aaron's shoes to Corporal Mike, who giggled to himself. Aaron, already standing stiff as a board with fear, tried with all his might to stretch just a little more at attention.

"Boys, I'm Corporal Mike. I don't yell as much as Sergeant Willard, but you will hate me more, *I promise.*"

The exercises started soon after his introductions and seemed to last forever. Corporal Mike called a few marines over as we were doing push-ups. They literally kicked dirt in our faces. It was one of the worst things I'd ever been through. After about two hours of doing torturous push-ups and pull-ups and running, we were taken to an enormous helicopter hangar. It was amazing. They led us through the hangar and into what looked like a huge bathroom. I hoped they were going to let us pee.

"Okay, strip!" Sergeant Willard shouted. We all looked around for someone to save us, but there was no one. "I said, strip!" One kid started crying, then another one. "You will strip and shower before chow! Do you piss-ants need any help?"

In unison, everyone immediately started shedding their dirt-covered, civilian clothes. I'd never been naked in front of a group of other guys, not even in gym class. I looked around at all the kids' frightened eyes. We were all naked, standing with our hands covering our genitals, waiting for the next order.

"Now, all of you get in the shower. You have exactly five minutes to clean yourselves and get out!"

We hurried into the next room, which had about twenty showerheads lining the wall. I wanted to hurry and get it over with, so I ran to the first stall and turned on the shower. I expected the water to be cold, but no, it was scalding hot. I spied a bar of soap, grabbed it, and began aggressively washing myself. I was done in thirty seconds flat. I carefully ran back out the door only to find myself standing alone in front of Sergeant Willard, Corporal Mike, and another soldier, all of whom were laughing at the display of scared, naked kids.

"You done?" Sergeant Willard asked.

"Sir, yes, sir!" I shouted as loud as I could, knowing if it was anything less, I might be hog-tied or worse. I was directed to a large plastic bin that held sweatpants and sweatshirts marked with USMC.

"Put these on and stand over there."

I felt mud running down my face. In my haste, I'd forgotten to wash from the neck up. I swiped the mud with my hand and tried to mix it into my hair so I wouldn't get sent back to the shower. As soon as everyone was clean and dressed in a new wardrobe courtesy of the USMC, we were filed into a line and marched over to the mess hall for food. I was so hungry I began to salivate. The mess hall was huge and filled with soldiers of different ranks. Each kid was given a tray, a plate, and a fork.

"Whatever you put on your plate, you must eat!" Sergeant Willard shouted. That was fine by me. I was so hungry I could eat a horse. It was cafeteria-style like grade school where line cooks and servers plopped food on your tray. "All you need to do is point to what you want."

I instantly focused on a large tray of chicken fingers and pointed excitedly. I loved chicken fingers, so I asked the soldier for a second helping. He obliged. After our trays were full, we were directed to the lunch tables.

"Okay. Clear your plates, and not one crumb left behind!" Sergeant Willard barked.

No problem, I thought. *I will mow through these chicken fingers before you can say "chicken finger."* I happily picked up a fried chicken finger and stuffed the whole thing into my mouth, letting my teeth do the rest. As soon as my taste buds kicked in, I was in for a rude awakening. *What? This isn't chicken.* My fast chewing screeched to a stop. My mouth was full of some unrecognizable, undercooked whole fish. I say *whole* because it included the head, tail, eyes, and guts. It was a sardine or local grunion of some sort. Although I liked the taste of fish, this fish was not right. It was repulsive, and to my horror, I now had a mountain of them looming in front of me. My mouth was stuffed full of this disgusting catch of the day. I started to gag and felt a hand rest on my shoulder. Sergeant Willard stood behind me.

"Looks like somebody enjoys your little fish heads." He smiled at the cook, who was still slinging food to other Young Marines. "How are them fishy fish sticks, son?" he said to me.

With all my strength, I closed my eyes and swallowed down the slimy, undercooked kipper snacks. "I…well, I thought they were chicken fingers, sir," I said pleadingly. I hoped he would take pity on me and understand that it was clearly a mistake.

Sergeant Willard just laughed. "Well, you better gobble up them fishes like a seagull, and I mean *all* of them." He grinned and walked away to mess with another kid.

I looked around and noticed that everyone was staring at my mountain of fishiness. Their eyes were full of pity, but they redirected their focus back to their own plates of much less disgusting slop. Envious, I looked down the row and saw Aaron sitting right next to Sergeant Willard. His head was down, and he was stuffing some sort of potatoey thing into his mouth. The sergeant was talking with Corporal Mike and another soldier, pointing at Aaron's shoes. *Why did he even wear those here? He has combat boots!* I thought. I felt bad for him, but I felt even worse for me.

I grabbed the nearest mustard bottle and doused my pile of food in hopes of masking the taste of fish. I started in one after another, barely chewing and gulping them into a hard swallow. In between gags, I was able to get down about seven of my ironic Chickens of the Sea. I began to panic, thinking there was no way I could eat another seal treat, but I was saved. Sergeant Willard abruptly stood up and ordered us to deposit our unfinished meals in the trash. I guess we were running late and needed to leave. He didn't need to tell me twice. I jumped up, spun around, and dashed to the trash can a few steps away and happily tossed the contents of my plate into the bin. I even spat a few times to get out whatever remnants were left in my mouth.

After dinner, we were led outside and marched in a single-file line back to the open dirt area where our parents had dropped us off. With each step my stomach gurgled, and fish bile rose into my mouth. I held it down, as there was no way I was going to vomit in front of everybody. We stopped at the patch of dirt where tent kits were neatly laid out in two rows.

"Okay! This is where you pick a buddy and build a tent," Sergeant Willard said. "You got ten seconds to pair up now!"

I instantly searched for Aaron. I hadn't spoken a word to him since we'd arrived because we'd been separated from the get-go. I saw Aaron up ahead looking for me. I ran over to him, and we almost hugged in desperation.

"Dude! What the hell is going on?" I said.

"I don't know, but we need to get the hell out of here!"

"Yeah, this is definitely not what I thought it was going to be."

"Didn't you read the pamphlet?" Aaron asked.

"Well, sort of," I said.

"Dude, that guy is such an asshole, and he keeps teasing me about my shoes."

"Yeah, I noticed. Why did you even bring them? You have combat boots."

"I don't know! They're comfortable, and I didn't think we signed up for a detention camp for asshole kids!" he said pointedly.

"I know, I know. I'm sorry. Let's just get our tent made and try to make the best of it. At least we'll be together for the night." As soon as I said that I heard it.

"Oh no, no way!" Sergeant Willard said as he walked straight over to us. "You guys look like trouble."

"Sir, we came here together—we're friends," I pleaded.

"Oh, I'm sorry. I didn't mean to ruin your little buddy camping trip," he said. "Clown Boy! You over there." He directed Aaron to the far side of the tents. "Fish Boy! You stay here."

Most of the other guys had already paired up, so I picked up a kit. At least I would have my own tent, or so I thought. As soon as I started to put my tent together, I heard Sergeant Willard marching straight for me. Behind him was a severely obese kid who looked very unhappy to be there. I'd seen him before during our regimen of forced exercise. He'd almost passed out a few times. I'd thought they were going to kill him.

"Okay, Fish Boy, this is your bunkie, Sloppy Joe. You two get that tent made and do it right!"

I sighed, looking at Joe. His eyes were glossed over, and there were visible signs that he had been crying recently. As Sergeant Willard moved on to some other poor souls, he left us to our task of building a tent.

"Hi, I'm Jason."

"Hey," he said in a depressed voice.

"How'd you get the lucky name of Sloppy Joe?"

"Sergeant caught me with spaghetti sauce on my face."

"That would do it, I guess." I didn't explain Fish Boy to him, as I assumed everyone already knew. "Have you ever put up a tent?"

"Sorry, no." He looked down at his feet.

"No worries, I think I know how to do it." To my surprise, I made quick time of the tent and started laying the bedrolls inside. I realized that there was barely enough room for two skinny kids, let alone one misplaced kid and one troubled, three-hundred-pound Sloppy Joe. I looked over at Joe standing there like an ocean buoy swaying in the current.

"Hey, Joe. How does it look?" I said, looking for some kind of attaboy.

"Um, it looks good," he said, glancing over.

"You want the left or the right?" I joked.

"Uh, I'll take the right," he said quickly.

"I was kidding, but okay, you can have the right." *Great*, I thought, *I'm at a military detention camp, Aaron is nowhere to be seen, and my new friend Sloppy isn't the most social kind of guy. It's going to be a long weekend.*

I felt bad for Aaron. It had been my idea to sign up for this mess. A new idea popped into my head...*I should just go and tell Sergeant Willard what happened and ask if I can call my dad to pick up Aaron and me.* I made a beeline to Sergeant Willard, who had just finished yelling at another kid. I thought I should catch him in between rants.

As I approached, he shouted, "Okay! Everyone over here. Fall in and listen up! Some of you may think you can just sneak out of here tonight. Get this straight! You are surrounded by fields and barbed wire. If the coyotes don't get you, I will. If I get you, you will wish the coyotes got you first. So, if anyone gets any bright ideas of making a run for it, do yourself a favor and don't. And before you ask, no! You cannot call your parents."

Damn! It was as if he'd been in my head. Or more likely, I wasn't the first kid who'd thought of calling his parents in hopes they might have mercy on him and pick him up.

"Your parents signed an agreement of no contact," Sergeant Willard explained. "That means exactly what it sounds like. You can't call them, and they can't call you. You are mine 'til 1600 Sunday. That's four p.m. for those of you wussies who don't know military time."

My head hung in defeat, and I abandoned any hope of being saved.

"Okay, everyone, sack up. That means beddy-bye time."

Nooo, I thought. *It's only, like, seven.* I usually fell asleep around ten.

"You've got ten minutes to get in and button up. Now move!"

I saw Aaron several tents away. He was still struggling with his bunkmate to put their tent together. I hurried over to save them. Aaron looked up at me, his face red with frustration, and signs of tears were growing by the second. I had seen Aaron freak out before, and this looked like it could be a doozy.

"Hey," I said, kneeling by his side. "Let me help you."

His bunkmate approached and said annoyingly, "Hey! So that's fucking funny!"

"What's so funny?" I shot back.

"Is it true that you guys wanted to come here and begged both your dads to send you?"

"That's Dusty," Aaron said, rolling his eyes and validating my correct diagnosis of obnoxious.

"So, Dusty…why are you here?" I asked with authority as if I was better than him because I wasn't a troubled kid.

"I lit my house on fire," he said proudly. He laughed as if he wanted to do it again.

"You lit your house on fire?" I said in disbelief. "Why would you do that? Was it an accident?"

"No, my stupid mom took my bike away, so I lit the house on fire," he said easily as if his actions were normal.

I looked at Aaron, who looked at me dumbfounded. We just started laughing.

"I gotta get back to my tent," I said.

Aaron smiled. "I saw your bunkmate…at least you won't get cold tonight!"

"At least he won't set the tent on fire if I snore! Good luck, Aaron." I walked away quickly. When I approached my tent, all I saw were two feet sticking out. I kneeled and lifted the tent flap to see that Sloppy Joe had already claimed his spot on the right side. I squeezed into the sliver of space left for me. I was literally pushed up against Joe's side and pinned against the side of the tent pole.

"Move over," Joe said. "You're touching me."

"Are you serious? Do you see how much room is in this tent? If I could move over, trust me, I would. It's not my fault you're three hundred pounds." Joe said nothing. I felt guilty about the fat comment, but what did he expect? "Dude, I'm sorry."

"I'm not three hundred pounds. As a matter of fact, I'm only two fifty."

"You're right, Joe. I'm sorry. Let's just try to go to sleep." Joe was silent. I could hear other kids talking and some laughing. I wished I were in a laughing tent. I wondered what Aaron and Pyro Dusty were talking about.

"Okay! Stop your yapping," Sergeant Willard shouted. "Lights out! That means go to sleep."

Everyone was quiet. A few people giggled, someone farted, and far off someone else said, "Asshole!" Lucky for him, his comment fell on deaf ears. About two hours passed, and I was still wide-awake.

"Joe?" I whispered.

"What?" he whispered back.

"You asleep?"

"No."

"Why did you get sent here?"

He didn't reply right away. "My dog died," he finally said.

"Wait. Why would you get sent to a detention camp for that? Did you kill your dog?"

"No, I loved my dog. He was my best friend. I buried my dog in the backyard, but when my stepdad got home, he got so angry he told me to dig it up. When I refused, he started doing it himself, and well, I hit him with the shovel I was holding."

"Dude, are you serious?" I tried to convey my emotion in a whisper.

"Yeah, my stepdad called the cops, and I was arrested and taken to juvie."

"That fucking sucks, man."

"When I got out the next day, I found out that he dug up my dog anyway and took it to the dump. I *fucking* hate him. I wish he were dead," Joe said, fully crying.

"What was your dog's name?" I asked, trying to calm him down.

"Ranger."

"Ranger. That's a cool name. What kind of a dog was he?" With a name like Ranger, I envisioned a German shepherd or maybe a Rottweiler.

"He was a Chihuahua."

Trying hard to restrain my laughter by holding my hand over my mouth, I said, muffled through my fingers, "A Chihuahua?"

Joe hesitated, then giggles bubbled out of him in answer, knowing that the name was a ridiculous fit for his little dog. "Yeah, I really wanted a Lab, but my mom's friend needed a home for her dog, so we got her Chihuahua. I was so disappointed at first, but after a little while, he became my best friend. Every day after school, he would wait at the front door to greet me. He liked me for me and didn't care that I was fat or dumb."

I couldn't help but think that Joe was bullied at school and probably didn't have much in the friends department. I felt bad for him, knowing that I had Aaron and without him I would be lost in the world.

"Maybe you can get another dog," I said, trying to reassure Joe.

"I don't want another dog. I want Ranger." With that, Joe shifted his bulk and muttered, "Good night."

I lay awake thinking about Joe and his dog, and how unfair it was that he was here. I was fortunate to have Aaron as my friend, and I hoped he was faring well with Pyro Dusty. After about an hour, my eyes went heavy and I fell asleep. This hellish day was finally over.

The next morning, I awoke alone in my tent. I was shocked that Sloppy Joe hadn't woken me up when he'd gotten out of the tent. I rubbed my eyes, trying to wake up, when I heard, "Everyone! Fall in!"

I scrambled to find my shoes and frantically tied both laces. I popped out of the tent, my eyes stabbed by the light of the rising sun. Like a disturbed anthill, all the other kids ran around gathering their shoes, putting on shirts, and running toward Sergeant Willard, who was waiting impatiently at the end of the tents.

"Fall in!" He shouted again. I looked over my shoulder and saw Aaron pop out of his tent and dart toward Sergeant Willard. We all stood at attention and awaited our morning orders.

"Okay! Apparently one of you snot-nosed kids decided to leave our camp last night and is still missing. Do any of you know anything about this?" I was in disbelief that a kid managed to escape. *Where did he go?* I wondered.

"Who was bunking with Joe?" Sergeant Willard shouted.

My head perked up. *Joe? Does he mean my two-hundred-and-fifty-pound buddy, Sloppy Joe?* I raised my hand and spoke. "Me, sir!"

"Fish Boy! Front and center."

I rushed up the rows of delinquents to stand at attention before Sergeant Willard's feet.

"What do you know about this?" he demanded.

"Uh, nothing. I don't know where he went. He wasn't in the tent when I woke up."

"He told you nothing about his plan to run away?"

"No, sir. He told me about his dog and why he was here, and then we went to sleep."

"Okay. Fish Boy, you wait here. Everyone else, follow Corporal Mike to the mess hall for morning chow."

Now that I was alone with Sergeant Willard, he asked me again about Joe's escape but in a faker, softer tone. I stated that I didn't know anything except that Joe was really upset last night over losing his dog. I told him the whole story about his dog, his stepdad, and the shovel.

A sheriff's patrol car pulled up and parked on the gravel road. The deputy exited his car. Sergeant Willard told me to stay put before he walked over to the deputy. I overheard them talking about Joe. He was still missing. Then I heard it…the glorious news! Sergeant Willard told the sheriff that he needed to call the parents to pick up the kids so that he could help in the search. *Is it true?* I thought. *Are our two days of hell turning into one? Are we going home today?* Sergeant Willard walked back over to me, and I stiffened up my already attentive stance.

"Okay, Fish Boy. I want you to double-time to the mess hall and tell Corporal Mike to meet me back here, now!" He stormed off, back to the deputy who was talking on his radio.

When I arrived at the mess hall, all the other detainees' eyes were on me, anticipating any news I might have. I saw Aaron and went straight for him.

"Dude, we're going home! We are going home because of Sloppy Joe, the kid who escaped. They're calling all our parents to pick us up early."

Aaron's face lit up as he quickly turned and passed the good news to the others. It spread like wildfire. I hurried over to Corporal Mike and relayed the message. He got up and immediately left. As soon as he did, the rumbling of excitement boiled over as everyone started praising Joe's escape. A woman quickly walked over to us and settled us down.

"Boys, my name is Sergeant O'Malley, and I want you to get up and follow me now."

I was hungry, but I wanted to go home even more. We all fell in line and followed her across the field, through the hangar, past the dreaded showers, and back to where our parents had dropped us off.

"Okay!" Sergeant O'Malley shouted. "Fall in and line up!"

We rushed into perfect form and stood at attention. She told us to wait here until she got back. We waited for about a half hour before a few more sheriff cars pulled up and parked at the registration office across from us. There was chatter among the ranks about what possibly happened to Sloppy Joe. I thought about his story and worried about him. He seemed nice, and like Aaron and me, he didn't deserve to be here. But he'd managed to escape...*I guess he wasn't so sloppy*!

Another hour passed before Sergeant Willard appeared from the office and walked over to us. As he neared, the group became silent and everyone immediately stood at attention.

"Okay! I have an announcement to make. Due to unforeseen circumstances, you are going home today." I could feel the excitement among the lines. "Your parents have already been called, and most of them are on their way to pick you up. Those of you whose parents we could not get a hold of will remain in the registration office until they arrive."

I prayed that my dad was on his way. I looked over at Aaron. He had a huge smile on his face. I replied with the same grin. I heard tires rolling over gravel, and a few cars pulled into the parking lot. The last car in line was my dad's.

Sergeant Willard shouted, "You will wait to be dismissed when your parents arrive. Do not leave without being dismissed!"

As soon Aaron saw my dad, he had different plans. He took off running, and I didn't wait to see what Sergeant Willard was going to do. I took Aaron's lead and ran after him.

Sergeant Willard yelled, "You two, stop!"

Nothing was going to keep us from getting into my dad's car and getting the hell out of there. We made it to my dad's still running car and jumped in. "GO! GO! GO!" we shouted. My dad looked at us, wondering what all the fuss was about, and as I looked back, I expected Sergeant Willard to be chasing after us, but he wasn't.

"What's wrong?" my dad asked. "Don't you want to stay and play Rambo for another day?" Chuckling, he put the car in drive.

We told my dad our horrible tale, how terribly we'd been treated and how much it had sucked there.

My dad laughed and said, "You should've read the pamphlet more carefully. Lesson learned, boys."

As we drove home, I thought about Joe. I imagined he got away and was adopted into a nice family who loved him and bought him a black Lab named Ranger II.

When the story of my adventure in the Young Marines concluded, Old Man Dave was out of breath from laughing. "The best part was the fish!" he said. "Man, you really had a go of it, didn't you."

"Well, I'm sure it was nothing in comparison to your experience in the military."

"No, I think yours was worse." He chuckled.

"So…did you get that scar in the war?" I asked cautiously.

The old man's chuckle silenced. He stared for a few moments then spoke. "Yep, it was a nasty place, for sure. I was probably about your age. We were on patrol taking sniper fire all day, picking us off one at a time. We were scared out of our wits. Each step felt closer to the bullet with your name on it. Suddenly, everything went black. Next thing I knew, I woke up in a hospital in the U.S. I'd been shot in the face and was in a coma for more than a month. After patching me up, I was given my walking papers and told that I was only one of three guys in my platoon who survived that day. Anyway, that's where the scar came from."

Old Man Dave looked agitated and fidgety, so I said nothing. We both sat silently for a while reflecting and staring into the shimmering lake. After some time, I finally spoke up. "You definitely had it worse."

"Yeah, perhaps." He sighed.

"On the other hand, if you tasted that fish, you just might have chosen to get shot in the face!"

Dave's laugh returned, and I felt relieved. "Anyway, I better get back home," he said. "I don't feel much like fishing anymore."

"Oh okay. I hope it wasn't something I said."

"No, no. I just lost the taste for it is all. Maybe I'll see you tomorrow." He grabbed his pole and tackle box and walked away.

I tried to imagine what he went through in the war. He must have been so scared. *He's lucky to be alive*, I thought. I wondered what his wife was like. My grumbling stomach reminded me that lunch had worn off and trout was for dinner, so I also decided to pack up and head home.

Chapter Seven

After I'd been at the cabin for a week, it was becoming familiar and comfortable to me. My fear began to dissipate, and I was enjoying the solitude. I looked at the calendar on the wall, noticing the thirtieth was circled, and in cursive, the word *home* was written. In only five days, my mom and Greg would return from their trip across Europe. I'd never traveled anywhere outside California. When I graduated from high school, I'd wanted to take my girlfriend to Bali using the money I'd saved, but my dad had insisted I use it for college. I thought about the experiences I might have missed out on, then chuckled to myself, thinking I could just astral project myself to Bali once I mastered it.

I stared out the window intently as I shoveled Cheerios into my mouth. It was a beautiful day, and I decided to walk through the forest to the outcropping. The clouds were like feathers across the sky, and the river below was wild and rough. Hawks were sailing in the wind, and the forest seemed alive. I began looking at everything differently, seeing things in a fresh, new way. The meditation and visualization were helping me focus on the details around me, making me feel in tune with the energy of everything. It felt good to be connected to something larger than myself.

I sat alone for a long time enjoying my surroundings. Back home, in Southern California, there were too many people and things moving about. There was a lot of hustle and bustle all around, and it seemed impossible to just sit silently without any kind of distraction. Here, I felt at peace in my special places. The lake, the forest, my gate, my bridge, and my beautiful beach. All these were mine; real or imagined, they were mine alone. It seemed so simple and perfect. In only a short week, my life somehow seemed completely changed. I'd been through so much pain, and my body and mind were exhausted. I was grateful for this time and my special places.

A sudden and rapid chill raised bumps on my arms, and the forest became alive with gusts of cold wind. I looked up, noticing the hawks were gone and the sky was turning gray. It appeared that a storm was fast approaching. I headed back through the forest, stopping at the spot I'd visited the night before. I marked it with a river rock I'd found in the pocket of the rain slicker I was wearing. It was most likely a rock my mom had picked up along a creek or by the lake. It looked like the pebbles I'd found holding the note cards in place back at the cabin. After I placed the rock, I retreated to the cabin before the rain began.

I hung up my jacket in the mudroom and was surprised to hear the phone ring. I knew it was Ashley before I picked it up. I didn't know how, but I knew it was her—I could feel it.

"Hello?"

"Jason, is that you?" It was her. *I knew it, I knew it!* My heart raced along with my mind as I hesitated to speak. Her voice instantly brought back so many memories of love and pain. I composed myself, taking a deep breath. "Jason are you there?" she asked again.

"Hey. Yeah, it's me."

"What are you doing up there?" she asked in an almost condescending tone.

"What am *I* doing? Really?"

"Well, yeah. Why are you at your mom's?"

I thought about it for a second. I didn't want to tell her that I was here because I was a mess, and everyone had told me I needed to get away from the memories of her. I wouldn't tell her that. "Well, I'm just here."

"You're just there?"

"Yeah, I'm just here," I said, defending my answer. "Is it okay with you that I go to my mom's place for some peace and quiet?"

"Yes, of course. I was just worried about you, that's all."

"Worried?" My voice raised. "Why are you suddenly worried about me?"

"Can't I worry about you?" she insisted. "I haven't heard from you in a couple of weeks, so I called Matt. He told me you were there, and I just wanted to make sure that you're all right." Though I was hearing the voice I'd longed for, I knew the other side of that voice, and it held a sharp edge. It was the same voice that had left me alone in a puddle of grief.

"I'm fine. I'm doing really well."

"You don't sound like it," she said.

I rolled my eyes. "Well, I guess you know me better than I know myself." I was annoyed by her questions. "So, what's up?" I said, short and to the point.

"Like I said, I was just seeing how you're doing."

I paused, taking a couple of deep breaths, composing my rising emotions because I just wanted to scream at her for what she had done to me.

I wanted her to confess her mistakes and beg me to come back. But as I spoke, something more powerful than my ego and hurt came over me. "Look, Ashley. What's done is done, and I accept that now. I'm really okay, and you don't need to worry about me anymore."

"Oh okay. I was just thinking about you and wanted to hear your voice, that's all." I could hear in her voice that she felt bad, but she didn't know how to tell me how she felt.

"I think about you as well, so I guess we're even."

She laughed at that and breaking the tension, she mentioned that she'd seen a 1959 Chevy pickup truck that reminded her of the one I owned back in Orange County. The one she'd lent me seven hundred dollars to buy. It was a junker, but I had restored it, and we'd taken many road trips in it together.

"Remember when we drove the truck up here to my mom's in the middle of summer? It was over a hundred degrees outside."

"Yes, I remember! God, what were we thinking?"

"I don't think we were." I laughed. "I think we were stupid in love and nothing else mattered at the time." The phone went quiet for a moment. Then she spoke.

"So, what are your plans?" she asked. I hadn't thought about my future since she'd broken it off. The last plans I'd made were moving to San Francisco with her. Beyond that, I had nothing.

"Well, I'm going to be here until the thirtieth; that's when my mom gets back."

"Wait, you are there all alone?"

"Yeah, why?"

"Uh, nothing. It's just not like you to be all alone, especially way out in the woods. What do you do all day?"

"I pretty much just fish every day and walk in the woods."

"Oh, that sounds nice. Are you catching anything?" she asked, as if she really cared about how many fish I'd caught.

"A few. It's really pretty here, and I'm just, well, I'm just *being* here."

"You sound all Zen."

"Zen? Why would you say that?"

"I don't know, you just sound a lot calmer…it's a good thing," she said reassuringly.

"I guess it is." I thought about asking her about the city and if she was seeing other guys. You know, the normal interrogations to find out information that would send one into a tailspin. I thought better, bit my tongue, and didn't ask her anything personal.

"So, are you going back to Orange County on the thirtieth?" she asked.

"Not sure, why?"

"Just curious."

"Well, I thought I would move right next door to you in the city," I joked. She laughed and said that wouldn't be so bad. My mind ached from that response. Even jokingly, it hurt. I dismissed the thought of being close to her again, and as much as my mind struggled to find a way to direct this conversation to us getting back together, I refrained. I realized I couldn't force us together anymore, and I was feeling okay with it. "Actually, I'm thinking of visiting Koji before I head home. He lives in SF now."

"Oh wow. So, you'll be here in the city."

As if I had to ask permission. "Well, yeah. Is that okay with you?"

"Of course! What part of the city does he live in?"

"He said he lives in the Castro District. Do you know it?"

"The Castro?" she said loudly.

"Yeah, I think so. Why, is it a bad area?"

She laughed hard. "No, no…it's, well, it's the *gay district*, that's all."

"Isn't San Francisco full of gay people?"

"Well, yes, but the Castro is like the Disneyland of gay people."

I laughed. "Just what is the Disneyland of gay people? Are there, like, rides with disco music and rainbow Ferris wheels?" It felt good to laugh with her.

"The Castro is just famous for historically being a gay neighborhood."

"Well, Koji isn't gay, so I guess it's not *all* gay." Koji was a good friend of mine whom I'd met doing work for a snowboard company back in Orange County. He was half-Japanese and one of the best people I knew. He was incredibly generous and an all-around great friend. His hair was long, down to his waist, and he had a face like a lion. As weird as it sounds, he reminds me of a lion for some reason. A Japanese lion. He moved to San Francisco after getting a job working on comic books. It was right before Ashley and I broke up, and knowing my situation, he offered me a couch at his place. I declined because I didn't want to be a downer around him or anyone else. "Anyway, I think I might visit him if his offer is still good."

"Cool. The Castro is only about three miles from where I live." The phone went silent again as both of us gathered our thoughts. "Would you like to see me when you get to the city?" I sensed hesitation in her voice, as if she was worried that I might say no, or even yes.

"Um, I guess. If I have time. I'm not sure how long I will be there, but if I get a chance, I'll call you and we can get lunch or something."

"That sounds good."

"All right. I guess, good night and, well, good night," I said, unsure how to end the conversation.

"Yeah, you, too. It was nice hearing your voice, and I'm glad you're doing good."

"Thanks."

"Okay, bye."

"Bye."

I hung up the phone and sat there gathering my thoughts and replaying the conversation in my head. I felt like I'd just gotten out of a job interview, worried that I'd said the wrong things. *Why do I care so damn much? Why does she have such a hold on my heart?* I thought. It did feel good that I was finally able to just talk with her instead of us screaming at each other.

I hated how our relationship had turned into a chess match for power. For the first time since I'd met her, I realized I didn't really like her as a person. I'd always been so jealous in our relationship and thought I was just being insecure. But thinking back, there were so many things she did purposely to make me jealous. She craved attention and chaos and liked to push my buttons. It was as if she enjoyed trying to make me insane, to get any type of reaction from me. On numerous occasions my friends, including hers, would ask me why I put up with her behavior. She liked to flirt with guys in front of me, and she would go out to lunch with her ex-boyfriends. If I brought it up, she would dismiss me by saying they were "only friends." I just dealt with it because I loved her. But after much thought, I started questioning if I was ever in love with her. I think I was too busy trying to win her attention. Whatever it was, I was now on the road, alone and feeling fine.

With the conversation still reeling in my head, I called Matt to vent. He picked up on the first ring.

"Dude! What the fuck!" he said.

"What's wrong?" I answered.

"Nothing, I was literally just about to pick up the phone and call you when it rang, and I saw your name on caller ID. Weird shit, man."

"Yeah, that's weird, but not as weird as the conversation I just had with Ashley."

"What? You asshole. I can't believe you fucking called her," he scolded me.

"I didn't call her. She called me thanks to you."

"Please tell me you didn't beg," Matt said, knowing that was my usual MO.

"No, I actually didn't say much really. She was just checking up on me. By the way, just when were you going to tell me you talked to her?"

"I wasn't," he fired back. "That's the whole point...you not talking to her."

"Well, it might've been nice to know."

"Well, now you know." He laughed. "How'd it go?"

"We just talked about nothing really. I told her I might go to San Francisco and visit Koji when my mom gets back."

"What did she say to that?"

"She asked if I wanted to see her, and I said I might *if* I had time."

"'If I have time,' you said that?" It was obvious he didn't believe me.

"Yup. I didn't want to set something up that I couldn't commit to."

"Am I talking to Jason Romero, the same guy who drunk dialed her over and over until she threatened you with a restraining order?"

"I know, right? But I've been doing a lot of soul-searching here, and I'm sort of seeing things in a different way." I thought about telling Matt about the book I was reading on astral projection and the special place beyond my gate, but I quickly changed my mind. I wasn't sure why, but I wanted to keep that to myself for now.

"Good for you, man. You deserve way better than her."

"Why, thank you, kind sir," I answered jokingly.

"Have you met any mountain women yet?"

"Nope, not yet, but who knows." I laughed.

"All right, you let me know if you do!"

"You'll be the first to know."

"So, listen," Matt said. "If you end up visiting Koji, you should call that girl Amy. You know, the cute girl I hung out with when I went up there with John." John was a close friend of Matt's from Los Angeles. Matt was a bit of a social butterfly and had friends all over the place.

"Who's Amy?"

"Dude. Amy's the girl who sent me the package of funny tchotchkes from Chinatown. You remember. You told me that she seemed cool and that I should date a girl like that instead of my usual...let's see, how did you put it? Oh yeah, whores."

"Oh yeah, I remember that. She did seem cool, and you should've dated her."

"She lives in San Francisco, and I live here. Even if I wanted a nice girl, I would get one down here," he said. "But seriously. She's super cool. And she lives with two hot chicks with big boobs!"

"Right. I'll just give her a call and schedule some breast exams," I said.

"Exactly."

"I'm not sure how long I'll be there, but give me her number just in case, I guess. Hold on, let me grab a pen." I wrote down her number along with *Amy, Matt's friend in SF* on a note card.

"So, you up there until the thirtieth?" he asked.

"Yeah, then who knows, maybe SF or back to Orange County. I'm not really sure yet."

"All right, then. You sound awesome, and congratulations for not being such a pussy on the phone!"

"Thanks, I think," I said. "Well, it's starting to rain hard here. I better get a fire going before it gets too cold."

"Right on. Talk to you later."

"Thanks, man." I hung up the phone.

It always felt good talking on the phone or hanging out with Matt. We were close, and our friendship was effortless and always fun. He's a great guy. Super funny and has that type of personality that everyone loves. We'd met as teenagers when we both skateboarded on the same team. He was an exceptional skater, and I was just okay. Chicks were always chasing him, and he usually juggled a few at a time. I, on the other hand, was always looking for a long-term girlfriend. Once, I brought a girl to his place for a BBQ, and by the end of the night, she ended up with him. Oddly enough, I didn't get upset. She obviously wasn't long-term material. Regardless, Matt had always been there for me and had helped me through troubled times. He was one of the best people I knew, and I was grateful for his friendship.

The rain was coming down in buckets, so I decided to call off my nightly march into the forest and stay inside instead. I built a fire in the potbelly stove, and soon the cabin was glowing with warmth and light. I was mentally exhausted from talking with Ashley, and after a PB&J for dinner, I fell asleep on the couch.

That night, I had a dream about a girl. This was a girl I'd never met, but in my dream, we were in love and lived together. The dream was so vivid. When I woke up, I felt a longing sadness. I could see her face and remember the feelings I had for her. It was as if someone I knew had died, and even though I knew she wasn't real, I felt heartbroken. I laughed as I stood and stretched. *Great, not only am I heartbroken in real life, but I am in my dreams too…Perfect.*

Chapter Eight

Though it was still raining, I grabbed a banana, put on a rain slicker, and began my walk into the forest. I counted another fifty steps before arriving at the stone I'd placed on the ground the day before. I ate my banana and sat down, protected by the rain slicker. I looked around while I ate, and when I was done, I laid the banana peel ceremoniously to my side. I stared straight ahead, toward the rock outcropping in the distance, and closed my eyes. I could hear every drop of rain hitting my slicker, each tiny sound of pitter-patter, tap, tap. I commenced my breathing exercises, and soon, I felt light-headed, which meant I was in my headspace.

I imagined the tube of light leaving the top of my head and extending four feet out and then back in, just like before. I recalled reading in the book that one could harness energy from living things such as trees and use them for power. Apparently, trees have a lot of energy. The book explained that trees were like living power plants of energy that one could focus on and transfer their energy from the roots to your center. I decided to try and tap into the trees surrounding me. I focused on the forest around me and imagined tree roots deep and strong. I imagined the roots emitting a stringy light vibrating toward me. The light entered me and flowed up into my heart. I filled my body with the light until it reached my head and streamed out of the top like one of those spotlights used for grand openings of restaurants or clubs. I could actually feel the energy and see the light. Excited, I reminded myself to go slow and tried to focus on the light tube as it shot up and into the rain-filled sky. It was difficult at first because the light was erratic, having a mind of its own. But the more I breathed and focused, the clearer and more precise it became. I visualized the light tube twisting and turning through the forest. I imagined it flowing out over the rock outcropping, down the steep hills and cliffs, and dipping into the roaring rapids hundreds of feet below. I retracted the light, following the same course back to me. In my head, it looked exactly like a long-exposure photograph I once saw of skiers wearing headlamps at night. The light snaked down the mountain through the photographer's lens and looked just like my tube of light twisting through the trees.

I opened my eyes. I decided to go to the rocks. I stood at the ledge and looked down the valley at the rushing water. It was surreal and amazing to feel like I'd just been down there. In reality, I knew I hadn't been down at the rapids, hundreds of feet below, but then again, maybe I had. It sure felt like it.

My mind wandered, and I thought about Old Man Dave. I sat down and decided to try and send my light through the forest to his house. I closed my eyes and focused. I imagined I was now streaming my light through the forest back to my mom's cabin and down the road to Dave's house. It was as if my face was at the front of the light tube flying through the forest.

Like the book said to do, I focused on landmarks and details that I knew were there, and I built on that to steady my flight. I tried hard to keep steady and soon approached Dave's house. I'd only seen one side of his cabin, which housed various broken-down cars outside. I approached the cabin from high up, in fear that he would see me and possibly shoot me down like the crows. His cabin was dark except for one light. I circled the cabin and tried to piece together what the rest of it would look like. I approached the illuminated window and imagined Dave sitting in a worn recliner with his dogs vying for attention at his feet. I envisioned his television playing endless reruns of a game show like *Wheel of Fortune*. His old cat was sitting next to a heater vent by the wall, trying to absorb the heat. I felt bad and excited at the same time. I exited the room and went back outside. Even though it was all in my imagination, I still felt like I was invading his privacy. I pulled the light back to me as if I were fishing and reeling my line back in.

I opened my eyes, curious to compare what I'd envisioned with reality. Heading back to the cabin, I thought of possible excuses to visit Dave. I remembered that I'd brought my old Vietnam-era army jacket with me. It was in the trunk of my car. I pulled the jacket out of my car, shook it out, and put it on. I drove down the road and slowly pulled into the driveway of Dave's property. I was hesitant to drive closer, considering he wasn't expecting me, and I didn't know how he would react to an uninvited guest. I was heading into uncharted territory. I decided to honk my horn, signaling my arrival, but nothing happened. Thinking he may not have heard, I honked a few more times. Nothing.

As soon as I decided to turn around and leave, the garage door rolled up, and Old Man Dave appeared. I took a step out of my car and waved my arm as if holding a white flag. To my relief, he waved back. I took that as an invitation to proceed. I hurried from the car and jogged through the rain to the open garage.

Under the shelter of the garage door, I said, "Private Romero, reporting for duty," giving my best Young Marine's salute to Dave.

His annoyed expression changed, and without skipping a beat, he said, "You want some half-cooked sardines?" We both laughed.

"Not much for fishing weather. I stopped by to show you my old army jacket that I bought at the store I told you about the other day."

"Yep, that's what we wore."

"Not so great in the rain, though," I said.

"You got that right."

The garage was what you might expect from a guy like Dave. There was an American flag on the wall and some medals encased in a frame. Various tools and little baby food jars full of nails, nuts, and bolts were scattered on top of a workbench. It reminded me of my grandfather's garage that I used to enjoy exploring when I was a kid. Dave's walls were adorned with posters of girls on cars and a few taxidermy deer heads.

"Nice place," I said, giving his man cave my stamp of approval, whatever it was worth.

"It is what it is," he replied, walking over to the far end of the garage to grab a couple of beers from his refrigerator. I was happy he was receptive to my intrusion. He handed me a beer.

"Thanks, and sorry for the intrusion."

"No bother. I aint doin' nothing anyhow. Might as well drink a couple of cold ones."

"Amen to that! So, how long have you lived here?" I asked.

"I'd say about twenty years now."

"Wow. All the way out here for twenty years?"

"It's not like it's the moon." He gestured for me to sit.

The well-worn 1970s wicker patio set seemed out of place in Dave's garage. The clam-shaped, high-backed chair creaked as I took a seat. There was a hole in the center of the glass tabletop that once held a shade umbrella. From the looks of Dave's place, he didn't seem like the kind of guy who threw things away. Dave sat down across from me and took a big swig of his beer.

"I've just always lived around a lot of people," I said, "and this kind of solitude for twenty years is hard to imagine."

"You get used to it. Soon you find that you prefer it. I wouldn't be caught dead living in the city with all them rats crawling all over each other." Dave shuddered.

"That, my friend, is a perfect example," I said.

Dave chuckled. "So, where are you headed after your mom gets back? You gonna go get that girl back in the city?"

"Not sure. I really need to think about it for a while. My mom will be back on the thirtieth."

"Well, you got yourself a few days to work it out."

"Yeah, I guess." I was only half done with my beer when Dave grabbed another two. I quickly downed the rest of mine and accepted the other.

"You're gonna need to keep up, son." Dave laughed as he sat down and cracked open his second beer. "Here's mud in your eye!"

"What does that even mean?"

Dave stared down blankly and then, after a moment, laughed and said, "I have no idea."

We quickly downed our beers. With liquid courage, I felt comfortable enough to ask Dave about his wife. I really wanted to know how he'd met her. "So, how long ago did Jenny pass?" I asked cautiously. My question got his full attention, and he seemed to freeze in both mind and body.

"Well"—he cleared his throat—"it's been almost ten years now."

"That's quite some time."

"Yep."

"Have you ever thought of meeting someone else?"

He smiled. "If you knew Jenny, you would know how silly that question is. But since you never had the pleasure of meeting my Jenny, I'll tell you about her. It's a kinda funny story, you see. I met Jenny before I went to the war. She was a nurse stationed at Marine Corps Base Camp Pendleton. You probably know the base, being from Southern California."

"Yeah, I know it."

"When I was drafted, we had to report to the marine base for a physical. Well, I waited in line all day, and they poked and prodded us like lab rats. Jenny was one of the nurses checking vitals, and by gosh, I saw her from a mile away. There was just something about her. Not sure how to explain it, but she seemed to exude this bright light, and I was the only one in the room who could see it. When it was my turn, I nervously sat down at her station. I'll never forget her sparkling eyes and her beautiful smile. Her hair was a honey brown that she pinned up in a bun. And her figure, well, you know what I mean…she was curvy in all the right places. I was gobsmacked. She looked down at me, noticing my dazed stare, and asked if I was okay. She noticed my Southern drawl when I answered her, and she asked where I was from. I told her I was from Memphis.

"Then she said, 'Okay, Dave. I am going to listen to your heart and lungs,' and she placed a stethoscope on my chest and listened. 'Are you feeling all right, Dave? Your heart is beating very quickly,' she said.

"I said, 'Yes, ma'am. I feel great, except there is this one thing…'

"She asked, 'What's that?'

"'Why, I believe you have stolen my heart!' I said.

"Jenny laughed. 'I don't know about that, Dave, but I am flattered just the same. You are all set,' she said. She handed me a paper and directed me to follow the line. Still in a daze, I stood and reluctantly walked away, falling into line with the other recruits."

"So, what happened next?" I asked.

"Patience, boy, I'm getting to it." Dave grabbed two more beers and continued his story. "I left the base and went home. I couldn't stop thinking about her, but unfortunately, I also knew I was about to ship off to war. I needed to put her out of my mind and do my job as an American. A few weeks later, I received my papers instructing me to report to Camp Pendleton for deployment. I was both scared and excited. I knew several of the folks going with me, and I felt a sense of belonging and camaraderie. Stationed at the base, we were ordered around, hollered at, and rushed from here to there…you know what I'm talking about." Dave winked at me.

"Very funny," I said.

"We all settled in, and after only a week, we were officially trained killers of all sorts. I tell ya, it don't take long to get trained as a killer." Dave laughed ruefully. "Anyway, our sergeant informed us that we were heading out in the morning, overseas. Some guys started hollerin' how they were gonna kick some ass, but most of us just got quiet and scared. I thought about that nurse I'd met and how I wished it were a different time. I could still see her face, her eyes staring at me, and that big smile of hers…man, she sure was pretty.

"We packed up and piled into the bus that would take us to our ship docked at the San Diego harbor. We drove down with several other buses transporting other soldiers, officers, and medical staff. I looked out the window and noticed a bus approaching on the side of ours. Lo and behold, sitting right there in the bus next to ours was my little nurse. She turned her head and saw me gawking at her. She smiled big, waving at me, and I smiled back, bigger. Man, I wanted to jump over and plant a big one right on her. Our buses were side by side, stopped in traffic. I struggled to pull the window down, and she did the same. I yelled across to her. 'Hey, there! Remember me?'

"She hollered back, 'How could I forget you!'

"I yelled over to her, 'Hey, I don't know your name!'

"'It's Jenny,' she told me.

"The traffic started to clear for Jenny's bus, and as it jutted forward, I stuck my head out the window and locked eyes with hers, thinking it was the only thing that would save my life and bring me home. She didn't look away until her bus was too far ahead, breaking our connection.

"After we reached the harbor, we were shuffled onto a ship. I hoped I would encounter Jenny, but after a week at sea and meeting all the nurses, they told me she was stationed on a different one. I made a vow to myself that I would find her when I got home from this stinking war."

"Wow! So, did you see her when you got over there?" I asked.

"Nope. She was stationed on a medical ship while I was fighting in the bush. Just six months into my tour, I got shot in the face, and well, you know the rest."

"You woke up from a coma in the VA hospital."

"Yes, that's right, but that's when things got really interesting. After I woke up, I stayed in Illinois for a few months to complete some physical therapy before they shipped me back to California. I got a Purple Heart and a first-class ticket on Uncle Sam's dime. Where this gets interesting is when I got off the plane in San Diego. You see, they bused us wounded back to the base for medical discharge. During the drive, our bus got stuck in traffic, and you'll never guess what happened."

"What?" I asked.

"I glanced out at another military bus idling next to ours and—"

"No!" I said. "No way…it was Jenny?"

"Yup. It was her, sitting just across from me. I never believed in fate until that day. I banged on the window, hollering, but she didn't see me. I managed to pull the window down and shouted her name repeatedly until she noticed me. I saw that she was crying. Tears ran down her cheeks, but when she saw me, her face lit up, and she laughed, crying a different kind of tears. Just as we reconnected, that doggone bus started pulling away. At least this time we were both going home instead of to some stupid war."

"I sat in my seat, trying to calm my pounding heart just like the first time we'd met. I didn't know her, but I knew I was going to. When my bus finally pulled up to the base, I noticed that all the other buses were already parked. Pushing people out of the way, I ran down the aisle and out the door. There she was waiting for me, still wiping tears from her smiling face. Though we really didn't know each other, it felt like we'd been torn apart and finally reunited. I walked up to her, nervous as all hell. She grabbed both my hands, kissed them, and then she hugged me. She trembled and cried in my arms. I didn't talk or move…I just held her. I never wanted to let go. She pulled away and calmly looked up at me. With her finger, she traced the scar running down the side of my face and rested her palm on my cheek.

"She said, 'I thought you were dead.'"

"I said, 'Dead? Why would you think that?'"

"She said, 'The day I met you here…well, I was taken with you, and I wanted to remember you. I wrote down your information from your medical charts and found out which platoon you were with.' This made me feel pretty damn good, knowing she'd been thinking about me all this time."

"I was a bit taken with you as well," I said. "If it weren't for this damn war, I would have asked you out directly," I told her, assuring her that the feeling was mutual.

"She told me she was on a hospital ship where they received several fallen soldiers, and when she saw they were from my platoon, she searched for me, fearing the worst. I wasn't among the soldiers on the ship, so she asked the medevacs what happened to my platoon. They told her my entire platoon was wiped out and that some of the bodies were still missing in action. She said, 'I don't know why, but I was devastated. I didn't even know you, but I felt like I lost someone dear to me.'"

"I looked at her and said, 'I'm right here. I'm not dead.' I told her what had happened, about being shot and being in a coma for over a month. We sat on a bench at the base and talked for hours in the California sun as if we were in a hurry to find out everything about each other. We discussed the bus and how strange it was that we'd parted in the same way we were brought back together. Well, that was that. We got married a few months later."

"Wow." I gulped the last of my third beer. "That is an amazing story. Why was she back at the camp so soon?"

"Her mom died. She was going home for the funeral. That's why she was crying on the bus when I saw her."

"I can see now why you never remarried. I mean, how can you top that?"

"You can't."

"No, I guess not."

We sat talking while our beer buzz slowly wore off. I was hoping Dave would invite me inside. I wanted to see if his living room was anything like I had envisioned when I astral projected to his home, but he didn't. Dave told me he would be out of town for a couple of days and that he wanted to go fishing when he returned. I could tell by his drooping eyes that he was tired. I thanked him for the beers and the story and went back to the cabin. I was a bit foggy from the beer, so I decided to lay down on the couch for a bit.

I woke up what must have been hours later to a pitch-dark night. I flipped on some lights and made another PB&J for a late snack. I was feeling refreshed from the nap and sandwich, so I decided to walk some steps into the forest. I opened the front door and stared out into the darkness. The trees looked like giant, angry monsters bending in the wind, creaking and moaning. *A storm for sure*, I thought.

It wasn't raining hard, just a sprinkle, but the wind was alive and making itself known, so I donned the rain slicker and headed out. As I counted my steps, I thought about Dave and Jenny and their amazing story. I felt bad that she was gone, leaving him all alone. He seemed like he was just going through the motions until he died and could be with her.

Ninety-eight, ninety-nine, one hundred. I made it to the spot. It was dark, and I didn't have my flashlight, but I could see the white pebble I'd placed on the ground. I looked behind me and could see the cabin's light flooding into the darkness. It felt like the cabin was a spaceship and I was on a tether exploring space. I turned back and stared out into the dark. I proceeded, *one hundred one, one hundred two, one hundred three…*until I reached the one hundred fiftieth step. I stopped and turned to see if I could still see the cabin, but all I saw was darkness. It was quiet, the only sound was the pitter-patter of tiny sprinkles on the hood of my jacket. I felt completely alone in the middle of the woods, and the fear in my gut raised its ugly head. I wanted to run back to the cabin, but instead, I thought about Dave's story again. I wondered if there was a Jenny out there for me. I thought about Ashley and how I felt so disconnected from her, as if the spell she'd put on me was now broken. I also thought about Koji and how excited I was to see my friend. I wondered if I was being drawn to the city in search of my Jenny, my soul mate. My fear subsided, replaced by the confidence of being on my path. My curiosity grew with the decision to project my light tube to San Francisco to find my soul mate instead of trying to get Ashley back. *We're done*, I happily thought. *I'm going to circle my light around the city and ask the universe to help me find my Jenny.*

I sat at the point of my one hundred fiftieth step. Though I was still a little scared of the dark forest, I closed my eyes and breathed evenly, deep into my abdomen, through my nose, and out my mouth several times. I quickly fell into my familiar meditative state. I pulled from the powerful energy of the surrounding trees and focused the energy through my body and up into my head. My light tube shot out of the top of my head, to the treetops, and streamed above the forest. I zipped back to my mom's cabin and looked down as I passed. I could see my VW Bug parked at the end of the path, and I could see my light flooding into the forest. I followed the road from high above and soon passed over Dave's house. I followed the mountain roads that I knew so well, twisting and turning high above the dark apple orchards and shooting over downtown Camino.

I traveled over the main highway to Placerville and followed the cars and trucks driving below me. I focused on landmarks that I knew so that I wouldn't get lost or lose focus. I'd made this trip so many times I knew it by heart, so it wasn't difficult to think of waypoints along the road to keep me on course. In a short time, I arrived in Sacramento and turned right, heading toward Berkeley and over the famous windmills you could see as you got close to San Francisco. I flew high above the windmills and crested the coastal foothills to see the city alive with twinkling lights. Like Peter Pan, I flew through the night sky in search of Wendy.

I headed straight for the Golden Gate Bridge and buzzed over the top, looking down at the tiny cars in traffic waiting to pay the toll. *No toll for me*, I chuckled to myself.

I circled the city repeatedly until my light tube blanketed the entire city with my light. I focused hard, calling to that person who might be there for me. I told her I was coming and to wait. I imagined what she might look like, and I talked to her as if I already knew who she was. And I hoped she was waiting for me too. When the city was completely on fire with my energy, I headed back the way I came. I soared over the windmills, up the freeway, and past Sacramento to Placerville and then Camino, finally taking a right at Dave's house. I slowed and imagined I was looking down at myself sitting in the forest. I could see the light emanating from my head. I slowly ascended through the trees and into my waiting body.

With a few breaths, I opened my eyes to the dark forest. My body was numb and tingling. I was amazed at how real it had felt. I'd seen trolley cars, taxicabs, and people laughing. My life felt purposeful for the first time. Thanks to the books and note cards my mom had left me and Dave's story of finding his true love, I'd never felt more on my path than I did at this moment.

The walk back to the cabin was a bit unnerving because I thought I heard something rustling around. I didn't have my flashlight, and though I was terrified, I acted as if I wasn't scared. As soon as I could see the warmth of the cabin's light, I quickened my stride, feeling as if I was being followed by something ominous and invisible. I made it safely inside and closed the door. I looked back into the forest to see if there were any creatures, but of course, I saw nothing. The dark, windy forest had turned silent, and I admonished myself for giving into fear so easily, knowing my mind was just playing tricks on me.

I retreated to the couch to watch my nightly TV. I reached for the remote but stopped midway. What was once a form of comfort now didn't feel needed at all. Instead, I sat quietly and thought about the mental flight I'd taken to the city. I chuckled to myself, thinking that I was fishing for my soul mate using light and energy instead of bait and a pole. It seemed I could easily project from the safety of the cabin, but for some reason, the ritual of walking through the forest, facing my fears, sitting, and meditating held more power within the act. The trees also seemed to make it easier for me to focus and project my light, drawing from their energy.

That night I simply sat, keeping my mind still. It was odd just sitting still, alone. It was a new and strange sensation that felt good. I was in control of my emotions and no longer running away from my life. I was living it and feeling it. I was alone, and I was okay.

I woke up the next morning with only one thing on my mind: circling the city again with my light. Outside, the wind was howling, and the limbs of trees were bending to its will. Unfazed, I grabbed a banana and headed out into the forest to resume my meditation. My mom would be home in a few days, and I was on a mission to find my Jenny. I spent the morning sitting on the rocks, looking over the river below. I meditated, visiting my gate and beach. I spent most of the day practicing my astral projection and flew to the city several times, circling it with my energy. Each time I flew to the city, I was able to capture more and more detail. Before I knew it, it was late afternoon, so I headed back to the cabin. That night, I ventured to the point of my two hundredth step and continued in my mind to the city just as I had during the day.

The weather was the same for the next few days and so was my routine. My gate, my beach, and the city had become almost second nature to me. My mom was returning home tomorrow, so this would be my last night in the forest alone. I was sad to be leaving soon, but I knew I couldn't stay forever.

The storm had finally passed, and the moon was full. It was a perfect last night to be in the woods. I could see the roaring water below in the moonlight, and the forest seemed to be alive with energy from the moon. I sat on the rocks, closed my eyes, and flew to the city one last time. I imagined the full moon shining over the Golden Gate Bridge, and I concentrated harder than usual. I called to her with every ounce of my soul. The city radiated with my light. Astral projection had seemed silly to me when I first started reading the book, but now it had become very real. I thought about the coincidence of summoning a call from someone out of the blue just by thinking of that person. *If that worked,* I thought, *then why not with a stranger...someone you were destined to be with?* Well, I was sure going to find out. I stopped my session. I needed to get back so that I could call Koji and reserve his couch. As I headed back to the cabin, I stopped and picked up the pebble I'd left there days before. I decided to keep the pebble with me as a reminder of my travels in the forest.

I dialed Koji's number and left a message letting him know I was heading his way in a couple of days. That night I slept poorly. I tossed and turned with anxiety about seeing my mom. I knew I would have to spend the next twenty-four hours with her. I still held so much anger toward her, and I wasn't looking forward to seeing her. It only took about a day of putting up with her cold and passive-aggressive tone to break our biological bond and result in a massive blowout. One of the biggest issues I had with her was not that she didn't participate in my life but that she insisted that she did. The last time I brought it up to her, she just cried until my stepdad yelled at me as if I was only trying to hurt her. As I tried to fall asleep, I accepted my fate of never being able to talk with her about my feelings or our past. I would need to learn how to be okay with her limitations as a mother.

Chapter Nine

I awoke to the sun beaming into the cabin. My mom wasn't due until the late afternoon, but I still hurried around the cabin, cleaning up after myself and disposing of the beer bottles that had collected on the kitchen counter. I was anxious, and I could feel my nerves rising by the hour. I finished cleaning the cabin and decided to drive down to the lake. I wasn't going to fish; I just wanted to walk around the lake and clear my head. Soon I would be leaving this beautiful place and venturing into the big city and into the unknown. I wanted to visit the lake one last time to take a mental snapshot of it.

The lake was a mirror, and I was glad I had decided to make this last trip when I saw what a beautiful day it was. It was postcard perfect. After a few hours of wandering around the lake, I headed back. As I rounded the last turn to my mom's cabin, I was surprised to see her pickup truck in the driveway. I immediately felt uneasy. I headed up the path to the cabin. I stopped at the open front door because I no longer felt like I could just walk in. I knocked and hollered, "Hello?"

My mom appeared quickly around the corner with a big smile. "Why are you knocking?" she asked, giving me a half hug.

"I didn't want to startle you. How was your trip?"

"It was fine but exhausting." She proceeded to rank the places they had visited by the rudeness of the foreigners. She loved to do what she called, "sports judge people." To that, I would always say quietly under my breath, "Look in the mirror." Hypocritical was an understatement when it came to good ol' Ma.

"Hey, Jason!" my stepdad, Greg, said, appearing from the bedroom and embracing me with a bigger hug than my mom had given me. "How are you doing?"

I perked up. "Actually, I'm doing great."

"Good," he said.

"It's about time," my mom said before disappearing into the other room.

I ignored her comment, as it was nothing new to me, and my skin was pretty thick at this point.

"What's been going on with you?" Greg asked.

"I've pretty much been fishing and doing some hiking."

"Jenkinson Lake?" he asked.

"Yep."

"Catch anything?"

"Yeah, a couple, but then the rain came for a few days. It finally stopped today. I just got back from the lake."

"Sounds great. Maybe we can go tomorrow," he said.

"Well, I was planning on heading to SF tomorrow. I'm just waiting for Koji to call me back."

"You're not going to chase that little tart, are you?" my mom scolded from the other room.

I sighed. "No, Mom. I'm going to Koji's for a couple of days. That's why I'm waiting for him to call me back."

"Yeah, whatever you say," she said.

I couldn't blame her for not believing me; the old me would've been stalking Ashley for sure. But I was not the old me anymore. I was the new and improved me.

"Barbara, leave him alone," Greg said, coming to my defense.

"I'm just saying," she quipped.

"As a matter of fact, Mom, I talked to Ashley a few days ago, and I don't have any plans on seeing her," I said.

"You called her?" Greg asked.

"No, she called me here."

"What did she want?"

"She was just worried about me, I guess. Since I hadn't called her for a few days, she assumed something was wrong." I laughed.

"She's still a little tart," my mom said mostly to herself but still loud enough that I could hear.

"Let's just say I'm pretty much over Ashley and I'm excited to move on."

"Sounds like a plan," Greg said, giving me a pat on my shoulder. "To Koji's, then?"

"Yeah, I guess. I'd like to check out the city. I spent so many months planning on moving to SF. Just because Ashley changed everything doesn't mean I shouldn't at least see what it's like."

"That's true," Greg said. "Just be careful not to fall for her shit."

"I know, I know." Greg was a good guy, except when he blindly defended my mom. On several occasions, I had talked to him about my problems with Ashley, and he'd been supportive, offering me good advice. I would call to talk to my mom, but she would lose patience and inevitably pass the phone to Greg. Greg was well-meaning and often accepted my tearful rants. I looked at him as more than a stepdad. He was also a friend. He did have his asshole moments, but who didn't? I had more good memories of him than bad. He had taken me fishing many times when I was a kid. We had a lot in common, and even though my mom wasn't the greatest influence in my life, at least Greg was a decent guy.

By the time they had unpacked and settled back into their home life, it was late in the afternoon. Greg cooked hamburgers, and we ate in front of the TV.

"So, Jason, does Koji know you're coming?" my mom asked.

"Well, not exactly. I called and left a message."

"So, he doesn't know you're coming, then."

"I think I just answered that," I said, feeling an argument coming on. I instantly thought about my beach and discretely started focusing on my breaths, in and out, which calmed me. Instead of taking her bait, I backed off. "I'll call him again tonight. I will make sure that I get a hold of him before I go," I said calmly.

"I just don't want you getting stuck in the city and finding your way to Ashley's door, that's all."

"Mom, I'm not going to Ashley's. I don't really care about her anymore, and I have no intention of getting back together with her."

"I guess we will see…"

"Barbara, leave him be," Greg said. I think he felt sorry for me, knowing how my mom treated me, and he knew that I longed to have a nurturing mother. He defended me on these little things but would never dare to challenge my mom on her mothering skills or lack thereof.

With perfect timing, the phone rang. Greg snatched it up. "Hello? Yeah, hold on." Handing the phone to me, he said, "Koji."

I grabbed the phone, looking over at my mom and smirking. She just rolled her eyes and continued eating her meal.

"Hey, man!" I said.

"What's up, bro?" Koji asked with the same enthusiasm.

"Not much…So, is it cool if I come by tomorrow?"

"Yeah, for sure. My roommate is out of town for a few weeks, so we'll have the place to ourselves."

"Nice." Koji gave me his address, and we made plans for my arrival the next afternoon.

"See you then, bro," Koji said.

"Yeah, thanks a lot."

"No worries."

I said goodbye and hung up. I was excited that all was good and that it was still okay for me to stay at his place.

"Well, there you go," my mom said sarcastically.

"What do you mean by that?" I fired back.

"Just sayin'…there you go."

That night Greg and I watched a golf tournament, and my mom disappeared into her room. I slept in the guest room for the first time since my arrival. The bed was comfortable, and I wished I'd slept on it from day one. I slept great and woke up early feeling refreshed. I got up and dressed, excited for my trip to the city.

When I walked into the living room, my mom was at the table shuffling through a stack of index cards. She looked up at me and motioned for me to sit down at the table. I knew what she was going to do. She was not a great mom, but when it came to the universe, she was on the mark.

"I had a dream about you," she said, still shuffling her cards.

"You did?"

"Yes, I did."

"What was the dream?" I asked, curious.

"I dreamt you were in San Francisco."

"Oh. Let me guess…I was chasing Ashley."

"No. You were happy and not with Ashley." When my mom said she'd had a dream, she didn't mean a dream in the usual sense. Her dreams were more of a meditative state or a psychic reading of sorts. She had meditated about me and my future, and she was now going to reveal her findings. I had my guard up but was also curious to know what she saw. I felt close to her whenever she did my numerology or anything metaphysical for me. It was the only time she seemed positive and, well, nice. She was serious when it came to her abilities and expected me to take it as seriously.

"Do you *want* your reading?" she said as if she would be just as happy not to share it with me.

"Yes, I do. Sorry."

"I received some very clear things for you to hear."

"Okay," I said, almost nervous to hear what my future held.

"You are going to San Francisco and you will stay there."

"Am I going to live with Koji?"

"No, I see you living with girls."

"That sounds good to me!" I laughed.

She looked at me pointedly. "Shall I continue?"

"Yes, please, go on."

"I see you working with someone in antiques, but I also see you making something or manufacturing something…but that part's not clear. You will have a partner in this business. You will meet someone with long, dark, and curly hair. This person will be close in spirit to you. This could be your soul mate."

The hair on my neck stood up when she told me this, and I wanted to share everything I'd been doing while she was away. I wanted to tell her about my special place, about walking in the woods, and even about Old Man Dave. I held my tongue in fear she might ruin this for me. Even though she'd left the books for me, she had a way of contradicting her intentions and turning a positive experience into a negative one. Instead, I sat quietly and listened to her reading.

"Her hair came in very strongly. It's curly, but not kinky…more like ringlets or spirals. She has a furry black-and-white animal. I'm not sure if it's a cat or a dog, but it has long hair and is obviously black and white. Not like a black cat with a white spot, but more like a cow with even black-and-white areas."

"Okay," I said, wondering why she was being so specific on that point.

"She lives in a gray-and-white apartment with a bay window. And the strange thing is, you already know this person." She looked at me, waiting for me to reveal a name to confirm her findings.

I shrugged. "I don't know who that could be, especially not in SF. Are you sure I know the person?"

"Yes, very sure."

"Is there anything else?"

"Yes…she will be the mother of your child."

I sucked in my breath. I could hardly contain my excitement, and I wanted to share my astral projection and my mission to find my soul mate with her.

"Is that it?" I asked.

"Yeah, pretty much. Here ya go," she said, handing me a piece of paper with my future written on it in black and white.

"Thanks."

"It's good to see you, Jason." She smiled.

"You too, Ma."

"It's been a long time." She stared at me, looking me over as if she was comparing my face to the last time she saw me. Generally, when she looked at me like this, she would say one of two things about my appearance. She would either say that I looked good, which meant she approved of my current hairstyle or clothes. Or she would say, "So, this is the new style, huh? Hmm…," meaning she didn't approve.

"You look skinny. Are you eating?"

"Yeah, I am now."

"Good. You need to put on a few pounds."

"I know. I will. Thanks for the reading."

"It is what it is," she said, meaning it was up to the universe. "Did you read the books I left for you?"

I wasn't prepared for the question. "Uh, yeah, I did, actually. I read part of the astral projection book."

"What did you think?"

"It's pretty interesting." I refrained from telling her about my journeys. I still wanted to keep it to myself. I wanted to share with her, but I was worried she would say I was doing it the wrong way. Because of the lessons I'd learned during my stay at the cabin, I would never be the same, and I wanted to thank her, but I just couldn't find the words. Instead, I walked over and hugged her, holding her tight. She stiffened the harder I hugged her. I waited for her to relax and receive my love, but she wouldn't. I released her and walked away. I refused to let her inability to accept my love get me down.

"I better get packed," I said, disappearing into the guest room. I was excited about my future adventure. I wanted to leave right then and there. The energy of being close to my mom was strange. I felt such an innate connection to her, but her energy harmed me and caused too much emotional distress, which made me want to leave as soon as possible. I reviewed the psychic reading in my head. I thought about the mystery girl with the curly hair and wondered if she was truly my soul mate.

I'd been alone for more than a week, and even though I was perfectly happy in solitude, the cabin didn't belong to me, and my mother was home. I said goodbye to Greg and gave him a hug. My mom gave me a ride to the mechanic in Camino to pick up my car. I'd dropped it off the day before for a tune-up and oil change. As we drove down the dirt road from the cabin, we approached Dave's place. I was surprised to see him outside raking pine needles. *He must have returned early or not have left at all*, I thought. As we started to pass, I expected him to turn and wave at me. I waited, but nothing. I reached over and honked my mom's horn to get his attention. He didn't turn. I wondered why he wouldn't say goodbye. My mom shouted at me for honking at Dave.

"What the hell do you think you're doing? Don't honk at Dave! Why did you do that?" she shouted.

I wanted to tell her that I knew Dave and that we'd had beers, fished, and talked about Jenny. But I realized something and understood why Dave didn't turn to wave. Though he and I had become friends, that was then and this was now. He wanted to be left alone, and the wall I'd broken down was only for a moment. A smile formed on my face as it dawned on me that Dave was raking the exact same spot he'd raked days earlier. He did say goodbye to me. That was his goodbye.

"What are you smiling for?" my mom asked, still mad, as if she was protecting Dave from my immature behavior. "That guy wants to be left alone and doesn't need you bothering him like that."

"I guess you're right, Mom. I should never have honked at him." I laughed, thinking about the first time I honked at Dave and how it led to a quick friendship.

"Just what is so funny?" she insisted.

"Nothing. I just think that guy is an asshole," I said, still laughing. "I mean, what a jerk! He can't even wave to us. Who does that?" I couldn't stop laughing.

My mom just looked at me strangely. "Well, maybe he has a reason for not wanting to wave."

"Yeah, you're probably right."

We winded through the mountain roads and soon arrived in Camino. I saw my little Bug waiting for me outside the mechanic shop.

"Thanks for letting me stay at your place," I said with one foot out the door of my mom's truck. "It really did me some good, and I appreciate it."

"Okay, be safe and call us later to let us know what you're doing." She started to tear up, but this was usual. She always teared up when I left, and I never understood why she could cry but not want to be my mom. I surmised it was some sort of guilt, and I was done trying to figure out why she was the way she was. It was time for me to let go and become a man without his mom. Today was my new start, and in that very moment, I decided I was moving to San Francisco.

Part II

Chapter Ten

My little Bug hummed along the highway. I looked up at the blue sky and imagined I was flying above. I took a mental note as I passed each landmark that I'd used for navigation during my many spiritual flights to the city. I was filled with excitement and anticipation when I saw the Golden Gate Bridge looming ahead. It was beautiful and bigger than I remembered as a child. As I crossed the bridge, the cars began to back up. All of these people were heading to the city for different reasons. We all moved together to the hills of San Francisco, like a line of ants heading up one big anthill. I looked up at the huge cables and towering supports. Just yesterday, I was flying, twisting and circling above the giant bridge, but today, I would pay the toll just like everyone else.

I found myself immediately lost as I exited the bridge, taken aback by the hustle and bustle of the city. My heart raced as I tried my best to navigate the winding one-way roads. I discovered trying to find my way and not crash was proving difficult, so I gave up and simply went with the flow of traffic. I was swept up by the current of cars and finally spit out in downtown San Francisco's Market District. Resolved I would eventually get to where I needed to be, I drove around the district, taking in the sights until I found a parking spot and stopped. I needed to find a pay phone to call Koji and see if he would come save me.

I walked a couple of blocks and found a phone being used by a homeless person. I patiently waited for him to finish his entertaining yet obviously imaginary conversation. I noticed his cardboard sign read, "Vietnam Vet." I immediately thought of Dave, and I quickly reached into my pocket to peel a dollar bill from my meager roll of funds.

The man looked over at me and the dollar in my already extended hand. He hung up the phone and approached me.

"Here ya go," I said with a smile.

"Bless you," he said, snatching up the dollar. He grabbed the phone again and continued with his imaginary conversation.

Well, that didn't work, I thought. I hoped by giving him a dollar he would move on, but no, so I did.

I found another pay phone on the next block. I picked up the receiver and wiped it against my shirt before inserting some coins and dialing Koji's number. He answered, and I was happy to find that he was excited I'd already arrived. I gave him the cross streets I was parked at, and he said he would see me soon.

I hung up and returned to my car. Cocooned in my little Bug, I felt shielded from the rushing of the city. A wave of fear had come over me as soon as I had arrived. I'd been in solitude for so long I couldn't handle the onslaught of the city's energy. My anxiety level peaked, and I couldn't wait to see Koji's familiar lion face. I tried to close my eyes and breathe, but there were too many noises and distractions. I wondered how much harder it would've been to meditate here in the city as opposed to the cabin. A horn beeped, breaking my train of thought. It was the familiar sound of a Toyota truck horn. Koji's Toyota truck. I opened my door and popped out like a groundhog, looking around. There he was double-parked. I waved, and he waved back, yelling at me to follow him. I nodded, and we drove out of the downtown area. After what seemed like a hundred left and right turns, we stopped at a quiet street across from a little park. I pulled in behind Koji's truck and hopped out.

"What's up, man!" Koji said as he walked toward me, extending his arms for a hug.

"Dude! How are you!" I said as we hugged. Koji's smile was infectious, and out of all my friends, you could tell he was genuinely kind just by the way he looked at you. "I'm here," I said, throwing my arms up as if to say, *I give up*.

Laughing, Koji said, "Let's grab your shit and head up." We grabbed my one duffel bag and climbed up the long stairs to his flat. It was a typical San Francisco Victorian apartment building, old and full of character.

"Thanks for letting me stay," I said as we entered the door to his flat.

"No worries, dude. I'm super busy with work right now, so you're somewhat on your own, but I'll give you a key."

"Right on, that's cool." The flat had cherry-stained hardwood floors and antique wall sconces illuminating the hall. I could imagine when they were oil or gas lamps back in the 1800s. The history of this city was amazing and could be seen in the details everywhere. We walked to the back of the flat, which opened into a large living area.

"Here's your room," Koji said. He laughed and tossed my bag on the couch.

"Better than most I've had." I sat on the couch, holding my bag as if it were a life preserver.

"You want a beer?" Koji asked, already pulling two from the fridge.

"Yes, please! I need one after that trip."

"So, dude. What's up with Ashley?" He handed me a beer. "Does she know you are here?"

"No, well, not really. I told her that I might visit you, and she asked me if I wanted to see her. I told her maybe."

"Maybe? You said maybe? Am I talking to the same Jason who is in love with this chick who totally destroyed him?"

"Yeah, I know, but I've had a lot of time to work things out, and I guess things have just changed." I proceeded to tell Koji everything: arriving at my mom's, fishing, befriending Old Man Dave, and visiting my gate and beach. I even told him about the nighttime forest walks and my projected flights to the city. I was comfortable telling him about it all because I knew he wouldn't immediately laugh at me, like most of my friends would. Instead, he found it interesting.

"Wow," Koji said after my long rant. "That's quite the journey."

"You're telling me!"

"Dude, you need to meet my friend Star. She just moved here and is totally into that kind of stuff. She's an art student too. We grew up together in Mendocino."

"I don't think I'm quite ready to date."

"I thought you were looking for your soul mate?"

"Yeah, I am, but I think I need a little more time on my own."

"Well, it doesn't have to be a date...just meet her as a friend. I was invited to a BBQ at her place tonight, so you don't really have a choice."

"Tonight? I was hoping to hide on this couch for the next twenty-four hours. Sorry. I've been isolated in the woods for a while, and I'm having trouble handling all this energy of the city."

"Dude, you'll be fine."

"Right on, but I'm gonna need a few more beers for sure!"

We sat and talked for the next couple of hours, catching up on each other's lives. Koji showed me the comic books he was working on, and we laughed about the good times we'd had in the past. When it was time to go to the BBQ, I realized I had a lump in my throat from the anxiety I couldn't shake since arriving in the city. I wondered what was wrong with me. We jumped into Koji's truck, and with a fairly good beer buzz, my nervousness eased a little as we dashed and darted through the streets.

I felt the anxiety peel away as Koji's stereo blared Bob Marley's, "Three Little Birds." With both of us singing, my endorphin-filled energy erased my unease. This was my favorite feeling for sure. I almost forgot we were going to a BBQ with people I didn't know. The extent of my social interaction for the past few weeks had been with one old man and my brain. I was feeling some sort of culture shock and desperately needed to take baby steps. That, however, wasn't on the menu for tonight, and I would just have to deal with it. *So be it*, I said to myself as we arrived at a quiet street far from the buzz of the city. With beer in tow, we climbed the stairs and knocked on the door of a little house. The door opened, and a petite blonde girl smiled, greeting us.

"What's up, girl?" Koji said, hugging her and continuing further into the house. "That's Jason. He's an artist and a weirdo like you!" Koji laughed and left me behind to meet Star.

"Yeah, thanks, Koji. Like you're not an artist and weird," I said, defending weirdness in general.

"Hi. I'm Star."

"Jason." I shook her hand.

"Koji told me you were coming to visit. It's nice to meet you."

"You, too," I said, trying hard not to act nervous. "I like your place."

She laughed. "It's a dump, but thanks anyway." Star was nice, and her smile infectious. I could see why she and Koji were friends. "So, Koji mentioned you're an artist?"

"Yeah, I do graphics and, well, whatever I can," I said.

"That's cool. I'm studying photography at the Arts Academy."

"Awesome. My dad's a professional photographer. He used to be a real estate agent, but one day he just decided to become a photographer."

"Wow, that's a risky move."

"I still remember the day he told us. He told me and my brother he was going to stop selling houses and take photos," I said. "My brother cried."

"He cried?"

"Yeah. I was too young to understand, but my brother thought we were gonna be poor or something. It was strange for sure."

"Yeah, that sounds strange." Star laughed. "Well, let's head in and join the festivities."

I was happy to see only two other people inside, Star's roommates, one of which was rushing around, grabbing her coat, purse, and shoes in a hurry to leave for a date. The other roommate was nice but soon excused herself due to too many libations from the night before. We ate hamburgers, and I listened to Koji and Star talk and joke about their younger years growing up together. They were truly connected and seemed more like brother and sister than friends. I was happy, and it felt good to be around such great people.

After a while, Star asked if I wanted to see her unfinished art installation she was working on for an upcoming show. Grabbing my hand, she led me down to the basement, which she used as a photography studio. She had camera equipment, backdrops, and what looked like a makeshift darkroom in the corner. On strings, she had large portraits of people's faces in black and white hanging from clothespins.

"These are amazing," I said. They were. I loved most anything creative.

"You really like them?"

"Yeah, totally. They're really cool." The faces were unique. Each subject wore a black stocking that covered their hair, emphasizing a large, illuminated face.

"Would you like to help me with something?" she asked.

"Help you with what?"

"I need one more face to complete my project." She was smiling with her hands together in prayer position, hoping I would accept. "Please? You would be great!"

"I would? Why?"

"You have a nice face."

I blushed. "Well, since you put it that way, I guess."

As soon as I said yes, she immediately squeezed my head into a black stocking and tucked my hair into it, revealing only my face. I looked at her, and our eyes locked a few times. I hadn't been this close to a girl in a long time, and I was nervous. I was attracted to her, but for some reason, I knew she would only be a friend. She sat me on a stool and flipped on hot, bright lights to either side of me, making me squint.

I felt very exposed and uncomfortable. "So, do I smile, or what should I do?" I asked.

"Just sit there and be yourself."

"Okay," I said, trying to think what that meant.

She took several clicks, and just as I thought she was going to give me more direction, she said, "Great, that's it."

"That's it?"

"Yep, see, painless."

"I guess," I said, laughing.

She told me that her project was to put a person in front of the camera without any instruction or direction so that she could capture their vulnerable emotion, sitting alone.

"Wow, that's pretty cool. So, my big face is going to be in the show?"

"Yep, next month. You can go if you like."

"Yeah, that sounds terrifying," I said. We both laughed.

"I understand. I'm not sure I'd like to see my own face projected that largely on the wall for everybody to see," she admitted.

"But you like doing it to others." I laughed. We went back upstairs and found Koji in the backyard, sitting by a fire he made in a pit.

"Hey, you two," he said. I grabbed a beer, and we joined Koji by the fire.

"So, Koji, did you let Star take your face photo?"

"He wouldn't let me take one." She scowled at Koji.

"What? Koji, I just sat in front of that camera. You're her best friend, and you haven't done it?"

"Not gonna happen," he said proudly, puffing out his chest.

"Dude, that's ridiculous! Why?"

"He's chicken," she teased.

"Say whatever you want. I'm not doing it," he said.

"What a jerk," I said jokingly.

"Exactly," Star agreed.

Changing the subject, Koji blurted out, "So, Jason. Tell Star about your flying through space."

"Wait, what?" she asked.

"Dude! What the fuck! That was private."

"Oh yeah, sorry, I forgot."

"You forgot? I just told you not four hours ago *and* that it was private."

"Dude, I'm sorry…it's just that Star's into all that mystical stuff and I thought you could tell her about it."

"No, it's okay," Star said, glaring at Koji. "It's obviously something he doesn't want to share."

I thought about sharing, but it was private, and honestly, I was having too good of a time to go over it again on the same day. Explaining it to someone else was almost as exhausting as doing it physically. "Thanks. Maybe another time?" I said and smiled at Star.

"Deal," she said. She clinked her beer to mine.

I was getting the hint that she was possibly attracted to me and that I should ask her out, but I couldn't get over the strong feeling that we would be friends and nothing more. We sat and talked for a while, and then Koji and I left, heading back to his flat.

I was exhausted from a full day of traveling and partying. I plopped down on the couch and must've fallen asleep. I awoke to Koji talking loudly on the phone. I was curled up under a soft, blue blanket. I got up and used the facilities. I looked in the bathroom mirror and pulled my hair back with my hands and wondered what the photo Star took of me would look like. I already felt embarrassed.

Koji was obviously busy, so after eating a bowl of cereal, I decided I would go for a walk around the neighborhood. I went into Koji's room/office and motioned to him that I was going out. He grabbed something from his desk and tossed it to me. It was a key to the front door. I smiled and gave him a thumbs-up and headed outside.

Chapter Eleven

It was a nice day. The white, puffy cloud kind of a day where kids search the sky for animals. I missed the forest and the lake, but I was glad to be in the city. The streets were filled with people, and I struggled to navigate against the current. Like fish, some went upstream and some down, effortlessly slipping by one another without trouble. I, however, was not and found myself jamming up the flow and causing roadblocks as I moved upstream. I looked up and noticed a huge banner hanging across the street. It read "Castro Street Fair." I thought of Ashley and our conversation about the Castro, so I stopped to look around. There were a lot of rainbow flags, but I didn't feel like I was in the middle of a gay pride parade. Then I saw it, a guy wearing a rainbow, G-string leotard, roller-skating. I watched him snake up and down the sidewalk, in and out of people, then spin around in circles before he headed back to where he began, starting over. He was wearing 1970s-style headphones and periodically blew a little gold whistle in time to whatever music he was listening to. *Well, I guess she was right*, I thought, laughing to myself. This must have been a usual sight because I was the only one paying attention to the roller-skating wonder.

I browsed the shops and wandered down to the park across from Koji's flat. I sat beneath a huge tree and looked around at the surrounding, bustling sidewalks. I wanted to meditate but was self-conscious that people would stare at me and think I was a weirdo. Then I thought about the guy on roller skates and how nobody paid him any attention. I closed my eyes and took some deep breaths. I tried to picture my gate, but it was hard to do. I couldn't get control of the racing thoughts in my brain. The noises from the city were filling my senses and creating a barrier. I sat and continued to breathe. I slowly inhaled and exhaled a count of four seconds each. I sat for about ten minutes, and soon, my mind calmed. With each slow breath, I became calmer and more in control of my mind. The surrounding sounds of the city diminished, and my mind, along with my gate, opened. I found my way down the path and across the bridge, stopping to view the valley before walking up and over the bluff to the beach. The sky was beautiful, and the tide lapped at my feet as I stood at the shoreline. I looked out at the horizon, thankful I could make the trip. I stayed for a while before retreating to the gate. The far-off farms were still there, and the forgotten road remained untouched. I closed the gate and opened my eyes to the physical world. The sound and energy of the city flooded my senses once again. I looked around and was relieved to see that no one was staring at me meditating in the park like some hippie. Getting up and walking away, I admonished myself for caring about what strangers thought of me.

I headed back to Koji's to find the door locked. I fished the key out of my pocket and went inside and noticed a note with my name on it lying on the couch. I picked it up and read.

Hey, dude, I'll be back tomorrow. Sorry, there's no food. Here's Star's number. Call her.

I was in the city, and I was on my own for the night. As soon as I crumpled up the note, the phone in Koji's room rang. I wasn't sure if I should answer it, but I thought it might be Koji calling me. I rushed over and snatched up the phone. "Koji's room, Jason speaking."

"Hey! It's Star."

"Oh, hey! What's up?"

"Is Koji still around?"

"No, sorry. He left already."

"Oh darn. I was hoping to catch him before he left for Mendo."

"Mendocino. That's where he went?"

"Yeah, he went to help our friend move. I mean, well, he's kind of my boyfriend and I wanted Koji to take something to him."

"Oh right. Yeah, well, yeah…," I said, fumbling my words.

"He lives in Mendo still, so I don't see him much."

"Yeah, I know what that's like."

"So, hey…I was thinking—"

"Be careful with that," I said, cutting her off, trying to be funny then regretting the stupid joke.

"Right," she said, kindly accepting my humor. "I'm going to a little restaurant near Koji's house tonight with a few friends for dinner and thought you might want to join us."

"Oh. Well, yeah, I think that sounds good," I said, feeling unsure about committing to something social with people I didn't know.

"Okay. Well, if you want to come along, no pressure. We'll be at Harvey's. It's on Castro Street. Our reservation is at seven. If you can't make it, no worries."

"Yeah, okay. I'll try to make it, thanks."

"All right. See you when I see you," she said.

Sitting alone on the couch, I thought of Ashley, and I wanted to call her. I'd been distracted by Koji and Star, but now that I was alone and only a few miles from her, my mind began to obsess on it. She had to know I was here, and she'd mentioned that she wanted to see me when I arrived. I reached for the phone and dialed her number. It rang once, and a man's voice answered. I quickly hung up. My body tingled with anxiety, and waves of regret filled my brain. *Why did I call? Why did I hang up? Damn it!* I said to myself. *She's going to know it was me.* I'd called her so many times late at night, harassing her and angry at how she had treated me. I wondered who the guy was. My brain thought the worst, of course. I slumped on the couch, pained all over again. The past still stung, more than I thought it would. I couldn't hide from it, and it haunted me, waiting for the perfect opportunity to strike. Its strike bit hard and deep. I felt stupid and thought about calling Matt. I knew exactly what he'd say, so I decided to save myself from his tongue-lashing.

I left the apartment and headed to the store for provisions. I grabbed a case of Top Ramen and a twelve pack of beer. *Breakfast, lunch, and dinner of champions*, I chuckled to myself. I also bought a carton of eggs. A friend of mine had enlightened me on the art of ramen. He had told me to sprinkle red pepper flakes and crack an egg into my cooking ramen at the last minute. This simple addition turned ordinary ramen into a gourmet delight. I also grabbed a newspaper to check out the classifieds just in case I decided to stay. I wanted to see what types of jobs were available. I had about two hundred bucks and was waiting for another thousand from a graphics job I had completed back in Southern California. If I was going to stay here, I needed to get a job.

My evening was spent eating ramen, drinking beer, and reading the classifieds. Finding no graphics jobs in the paper, I began looking for a copy job. I had experience working at Kinko's in Laguna Beach. Fortunately, a few copy positions were available. I circled them with blue ink. After a couple of beers, I glanced at the clock and realized it was after eight. "Oh shit!" I said, jumping up and running to the bathroom to run a comb through my hair. I grabbed my coat, and with the help of my liquid courage, I hurried out the door.

I rushed up the street, passing bars and restaurants now full of cheerful patrons. *There it is!* Harvey's was packed. As I opened the door, Star and two other girls were on their way out.

"Hey!" she said, hugging me. I hugged back hard as if to say, *I'm sorry for not showing.*

"Sorry, I totally flaked and just realized what time it was." I smiled apologetically and acknowledged the two girls standing behind her.

"No worries, really. We are headed to a party if you'd like to come with."

I could tell she was being polite and that it was kind of a girls' night out, so I declined. "No, that's all right. I need to look through the paper for a job." It was the only thing I could think of.

"Oh? Are you thinking of staying here?"

"Well, maybe. It depends."

"I hope you do." She smiled.

"Thanks. I hope I do too."

"Okay. We are off to party down, so have a good night! Oh, wait, I forgot. Tomorrow is two-for-one happy hour at the Toronado in the Lower Haight. It's a brewpub. I was thinking of going. Maybe you and Koji want to meet up?"

"Yes! That's my kind of happy hour. I'm in."

"Great! I'll touch base with you guys tomorrow."

"Yeah, okay. Great!" I said goodnight and went back to Koji's. I was feeling pretty good again, and my disappointment about calling Ashley began to wash away. I spent the rest of the night fighting with the antenna on Koji's antiquated television. I managed to dial in one local channel, and not being able to sleep, I watched it late into the night. I listened to people walking outside and others partying, arguing, talking, and laughing in apartments surrounding me. I had learned so much about energy from my mom's book and specifically how some people are more susceptible to other people's energy. I began to think I was one of those people. I could always read people's emotions easily. I was sensitive and emotional, almost to a fault. It was a blessing and a curse, being this way. It had made me a thoughtful person, but it also drained me emotionally from taking on other people's feelings. I was looking forward to hanging out with Star and drinking some beers. She was such a positive person, and in the short time I'd known her, she made me feel warm and welcome in this big city.

J.C. Romero 92

Chapter Twelve

The next day I woke up late, feeling like I could fall right back to sleep. I was exhausted. I got up and switched off the TV, which was still on from the night before. I showered and made another bowl of delicious Top Ramen with egg. After breakfast, I stepped outside and sat in the sun on the front steps. I watched people walking up and down the busy street. After being so isolated, it was like watching fish for me. I wondered if I could fit in here or if I would rather be isolated like Old Man Dave.

I noticed a guy walking by. He nodded at me, so I nodded back. He walked a few more feet and turned his head, nodding at me again. Thinking it odd and not knowing what to do, I nodded once more. He stopped and stared at me, smiling and nodding his head a third time. Both irritated and confused, I nodded hard, as if to say, *Okay, hello!* The man began walking over to me.

"Can I help you?" I asked.

"Hey," he said softly.

I wasn't sure what to do. Thinking he must've been a little off his rocker, I quickly stood up and looked down at him. He just stared up at me, grinning like a wolf.

"Can I help you?" I said crossly.

"Oh. My mistake, sorry," he said, turning and scurrying down the sidewalk.

What the fuck was that all about? I thought as I went back inside. The phone was ringing, but I couldn't get to it before the answering machine picked up. I heard Koji's voice telling me that he and Star were on their way over. I folded my blankets and did my best to clean up, earning my keep. I was still cleaning when they walked through the door.

"Dude, you don't need to clean my place."

"Yes, I do."

"Hey again," Star said.

"It feels like I just saw you," I said, smiling. "How was Mendocino?" I asked Koji.

"You know when you go to help someone move and they haven't finished packing yet?" he said. I laughed, saying yes. "Well, that's how it was."

"I told him to have everything ready," Star said, apologizing for her boyfriend's behavior.

"Well, at least you showed up on moving day," I said.

Koji shrugged his shoulders. "That's true, bro."

I sat on the couch. "So, something weird happened here today."

"What?" Koji asked, sounding concerned.

"I was sitting outside soaking up some sun, and this guy walked by and nodded his head. Well, I nodded my head to say hello. Then he did it two more times. I was like, what the fuck, dude? Then he walked over to me, smiling, and was like, what's up? It freaked me out, so I yelled at him, and he ran away."

Koji and Star started belly laughing.

"What's so funny? Did I miss something?" I asked.

They couldn't stop laughing.

"No, really, what the hell, you guys?" I said, demanding they let me in on their inside joke.

"Oh my God, dude!" Koji managed to say. "He thought you wanted him, ha-ha-ha!"

"What? How!"

"Star, you tell him. I can't stop laughing!"

Star, now in control of her laughter, said, "Okay. So, my friend is gay, and apparently if two guys nod at each other three times, it means you want to hook up."

"Oh shit!" Now I was laughing. "I was just being polite."

"Dude, you almost had yourself a new friend," Koji said, still laughing.

"Ha! You're so funny, Koji. Is there anything else I should be aware of before I start interacting with the general public of San Francisco? Secret handshakes or types of winks?" I joked.

"Take it as a compliment." Star smiled. "You could have gotten laid."

"Yeah, very funny. So, the head nod is out, and the wave is in?"

"Not unless you want a friend," Koji said, still laughing.

The phone rang and broke up our laugh fest as Koji went to answer it. "Are you serious?" Koji said to the person on the phone. "Yeah, I got it. Yeah, yeah, I know. Okay, later." Koji hung up the phone, his expression annoyed, and announced that he had to finish a superhero poster that needed to be done by tomorrow.

"How much of it is done?" I asked.

"I kind of flaked on it, and now the guy needs it to go to print early.

Looks like I'm bowing out of the Toronado festivities."

"That sucks, dude," I said.

"Are you sure you can't go for just an hour?" Star asked.

"There's no way. I'll be pulling an all-nighter for sure."

"We could just hang here," I suggested.

"No, you guys go. I need to work."

"Well, right on. What do you say, Star? You want to show me this place?"

"Definitely, let's do it," she said, getting up.

I got a quick lesson on the SF transportation system on the way to the Toronado. Star told me where the Muni subway stations were and where the different buses went. Most of the city buses were electric and ran off long rods that stretched from the back of the bus, connecting to the overhead street cables. They looked like giant bumper cars at a carnival, and periodically the cables would spark in an arc like a Tesla coil. Occasionally, the cable rod would get disconnected, and the driver would have to get out and reattach it.

We arrived at the Lower Haight District, which shared the famous name with its twin, the Upper Haight, but was missing one key ingredient, Ashbury Street. Haight-Ashbury was a cross street made famous by the hippies of the 1960s and, of course, the Grateful Dead, who at some point had resided there. The Lower Haight was less famous, less touristy, and a little seedier but had cool shops and bars. The Toronado was packed. And when I say packed, I mean there were people sitting on the floor in small groups as if they were picnicking. I'd never seen anything like it. We shuffled in and soon were in a line surrounded by noisy, beer-drinking patrons. I was okay at first, but soon the noise started to swirl in my head, becoming a loop of dizzying sounds.

"Are you okay?" Star asked, noticing my obvious agitation.

"Yeah, yeah, I'm good. I just haven't been around this many people in a long time."

"We can go somewhere else," she said, touching my arm.

"No, I'm good. I'll be fine." Honestly, though, I wasn't so sure. We got our beers and, with a little luck, acquired a table for two in the back. We sat and fell into an uncomfortable silence. The voices of the bar filled my head again. I tried to fight them off, but they melded together and started to race along with my heart. For some reason, my only response was to laugh, but not in a good way. It started as a giggle but quickly grew into a full-blown laugh attack. I couldn't stop. I seriously couldn't stop laughing. Star just stared at me with the strangest look on her face.

"Are you sure you're okay?" she asked, visibly concerned.

"I'm not sure. I can't stop laughing," I said, still laughing.

"Why not?" she asked, beginning to giggle herself.

"I'll be right back," I said, and rushed toward the exit sign, watching my steps so I wouldn't crush any of the hands of the people sitting on the floor. The cool outside air felt good. I began deep breathing, drinking in the crisp air. I walked about a block and paced back and forth, trying to calm myself down. *What the hell?* I thought. *Why can't I stop laughing?* I could only surmise that it was a reaction from being around so many people all at once after being so isolated at my mom's. I was so sensitive to the energy that it caused me to overload emotionally, and the result was uncontrollable, nervous laughter. Slowly, I began to calm down and decided I needed to regain my seat across from Star.

I walked back into the bar, sat down, and smiled at her. "Wow, that was weird," I said, embarrassed.

"Are you feeling better?" she asked, her eyes searching my face for signs of my well-being.

"Yes, I'll be fine," I assured her. I recounted my experience being isolated in the woods at my mom's cabin, my breakup with Ashley, and my encounters with Old Man Dave. After I unloaded the whole story, Star was quiet for a while, which made me more nervous. "Sorry. I didn't mean to vent so hard," I said.

"No, it's fine. I'm just amazed by your story and about poor Dave and Jenny. Are you going to call Ashley again?"

"I'd like to say no, but I know better. I know she's not the one for me, but I just can't let it go…if that makes any sense."

"It makes perfect sense," she said, reassuring me that I wasn't crazy. Changing the subject, Star held up her glass and said, "Here's to new friends and good beer. Cheers!"

With a smile, I raised my glass and met hers with a clink. I felt at ease with her, and she opened up to me, talking about the situation with her boyfriend and a bit about her past. She also mentioned some embarrassing stories about Koji, which I couldn't wait to use on him. We decided to end the night, and she gave me directions back to Koji's.

I made it home without a hitch and found Koji still hard at work on his poster. "How was it?" he asked without stopping his work. I told him about my embarrassing laughing fit, which made us both laugh.

"Well, I'm gonna crash," I said, leaving him to his work.

"Night," he said.

"Night."

Chapter Thirteen

The next morning, I woke up early with a fire burning intensely within me. I decided at that moment I was going to stay in the city. I realized after everything I'd been through with Ashley and everything I'd learned at my mom's, there was no way I could go back to Orange County. I felt like I was on my path. I knew in my soul I was supposed to be here. All I had with me could fit in the front seat of my car, but I didn't care. I wasn't going back to Southern California to get my things. New start, new stuff. I stepped outside and grabbed the morning paper from the front steps. With a large cup of steaming coffee, I sat at the tiny kitchen table and called about the jobs I'd circled in the classifieds. By the time Koji got up at ten a.m., I'd already scheduled an interview for noon.

"What's up, dude?" Koji stretched and yawned as I shuffled through the paper.

"Looking for a job."

"I see that. So, does that mean you're staying?"

"I'm definitely going to try. I made coffee if you want some," I said, pointing to the fresh pot sitting on the counter.

"You're my savior. I'll talk with my roommate to see if it's cool that you stay here until you get your own place."

"Really? That's awesome!"

"You would do the same for me."

"Thanks, man."

"No worries. Any job options?"

"Nothing with art, so I'm just going to try for a copy job until I can get something better."

"Right on, that's a good move."

"I have an interview at noon."

"Wow, you work fast."

"I don't want to couch surf forever."

"You saying my couch sucks?" Koji laughed.

"Well, I wasn't going to say anything, but it kind of sucks," I joked.

"Where's the job at?"

"It says it's in the Financial District."

"Oh cool. That's an easy shot straight down Market Street. The station is only two blocks from here. Try not to have another laughing fit during your interview," he teased, then disappeared into his room.

"Hey, I need to borrow a shirt!" I shouted. I hadn't planned on a job interview and wasn't exactly prepared with the proper attire. A few minutes later, Koji appeared holding the ugliest purple shirt. "Is that *silk*? I have never seen an uglier shirt in my entire life." He was holding back laughter. "Dude! What is that?" I said, amazed at its ugliness.

"It's my purple shirt," he said proudly.

"I see that. How did you happen upon this lovely shirt? Did you buy it for a Prince concert? Why is it so blousy?"

Koji chuckled in delight. "When my mom remarried, we all wore purple, and this was mine." He was way too happy with this shirt.

"God, I can't believe I'm saying this, but thanks." I put on the shirt, and it felt as ugly as it looked. The shirt was a good full size bigger than what I usually wore, and the front and back were longer than the sides. Not yet defeated, I tried to tuck in the long, billowing flaps to make it more discreet, as if a purple silky shirt could be discreet. I looked ridiculous. But luckily it was raining, so I could just cover it up with a jacket, and it wouldn't look so bad. With directions in hand, I headed out for my first job interview in the big city.

Koji said I was leaving way too early and that I had plenty of time, but I was nervous and wanted to make sure I knew where I was going. If I got there early, I would locate the office and then explore the surrounding area before the interview. I was able to figure out the Muni without a problem. I'd never been in a subway, and it felt strange descending beneath the city. I imagined how scary it would be down here during an earthquake. You could feel the cool wind rushing by as the trains sped through the tunnels. I stood at the loading area with about fifty other people heading downtown. A loudspeaker announced the Embarcadero/Financial District train. That was me. I seemed to be the only one antsy in anticipation for the train. Everyone else was comfortable and calmly reading papers and sipping coffees. I soon heard the rumble of the approaching train. I watched as the light illuminated the deep tunnel and the train appeared in the open cavern of the station. The doors opened to a packed car. It was standing-room only. I hesitated then retreated. Others squeezed in with no problem or concern. I recalled the incident at the bar with Star and worried I might have another panic attack and start laughing uncontrollably on the damn train. It was just the story I didn't want to bring home to Koji.

I decided to wait for the next train arriving in fifteen minutes. I was glad I did, because the next train was nearly empty and had plenty of seating. I hurried over to a seat and waited for liftoff. The doors beeped repeatedly, warning that the train was departing, and with a hiss, the doors all shut simultaneously. The train accelerated quickly, and soon I was traveling at what seemed like one hundred miles per hour, though it was probably more like forty. I could sense we were going downhill, and I listened carefully for the Financial District stop to be announced.

After a short five to six minutes and three other stops, I heard the call. I stood while the train was still moving, and not having my subway legs yet, I ungracefully staggered toward the door and caught a hand bar for support. My hand slipped down the bar. *Ew, gross!* I thought. The hand bar was slick with slime. I could only imagine how many people touched it in a day. All that germy grease and grime polishing it every second. It was disgusting, and unfortunately for me, I was one of the lucky ones who thought about those sorts of things. The train slowed, and the doors opened with a ding. I quickly stepped off and followed the arrows to the stairs leading up to the city.

The buildings towered above me, and though it wasn't even noon yet, it seemed like it was early evening, since the tall buildings blocked out most of the sun. The bustling street was alive with taxis and buses, and people were everywhere. The people here were different than the ones in Koji's neighborhood and the Lower Haight. These were businesspeople, rushing to and from meetings and lunches. They were everywhere like busy ants constantly moving in a line with purpose.

I was an hour early and only a block from my destination. I found the location of where I needed to be for the interview and then decided to get a coffee. As I stood in line at a Starbucks, I realized that if I wanted anything in the city, I'd have to wait in some sort of line to get it. After receiving my caffeinated mocha drink, I walked the streets. I couldn't help but notice a homeless lady screaming at the people walking past her. They all ignored her as if it were an everyday occurrence. They didn't even avoid her; they just passed by, keeping on with their business.

I walked up Market Street for a couple of blocks and found a few antique shops along the way. The shops were huge, unlike the small-town ones back home. I walked in one and was amazed at all of the old treasures filling the shop. I thought about my mom's prediction and wondered what in the world I would do in the antique business. I browsed the vintage assortments until it was time to head back for my interview.

Though I was twenty minutes early, I still went in. The inside of the building wasn't what I expected. The position was copying legal documents, and I assumed it would be in a copy shop like a Kinko's, but it was completely different than I imagined. The job was located on the ground floor of a large building that looked like a dungeon with rows of copy machines. The room was dim, and you could see the strobing light from the copy machines moving back and forth like the car from *Knight Rider*. I made my way past a dozen machines roaring away. The guys running the machines seemed to be in a real hurry to make their copies. They looked as if they were trying to will the machines to work faster than they were capable of and worrying that at any moment the machine would jam with paper. The dreaded paper jams were the worst for a copy person. When I'd worked at Kinko's and dealt with customers in a big hurry, the machine would never fail to jam. I thought it was the universe telling us to slow down.

I found the office at the long end of the machines and knocked on the door. The guy I'd talked to on the phone was Steve, and he'd seemed nice. I was excited to meet him and tell him how much experience I had with Xerox machines. The door swung open, and a guy with messy hair and a loosened tie snapped, "What!"

"Steve?" I asked.

"Yeah. Oh, you must be Jason."

"Yes, I am. It's nice to meet you," I said, holding out my hand to shake with the firm handshake my father had taught me, not too soft and not too hard.

"Have a seat there. I'll be right with you," he said with a kind smile. He was on the phone with someone who was obviously in a hurry, and I guessed it was either a client or Steve's boss because he was assuring the person that he'd have whatever they wanted done on time. He hung up the phone and sat behind his cluttered desk. "So, you made it," he said, looking me over.

"Yes, I found it no problem." I tried my best to hide my hideous purple silk shirt that was trying to steal the show from beneath my jacket. "You sure have a lot of machines here."

"We duplicate for many of the legal offices located here in the Financial District."

"Which type of machine do you need me to run?" I began listing off which machines I was familiar with, but he cut me off.

"Well, not yet. I really need a runner right now."

"Oh, I thought the ad said machine operator."

"It does, but I filled that job yesterday, and the only other position available is for a runner."

"Okay. What does a runner do?"

"A runner picks up legal boxes from and delivers them back to law offices around the Financial District. It's easy once you know your way around. You pick up the boxes, the papers get copied, and the next day, you deliver them back."

"That sounds easy enough. Will I be able to move into a machine operator position later?"

"Definitely, but let's see how you do as a runner, and we'll go from there."

"So, I got the job?"

"You got the job, congratulations."

"Great. When do I start?"

"Honestly? You can start now if you'd like. My other runner called in sick, and I'm super shorthanded."

"Baptism by fire," I said jokingly.

"Pretty much." Steve smiled. "I'll get Josh to help you with your fist run, and then you're on your own. It doesn't look like you have anything to store, but there are lockers over there for employees." He pointed in the general direction of the lockers.

"No, I'm good to go." I stood at attention as if waiting for my mission.

Steve poked his head out of his office door and yelled, "Josh! Josh Henry! My office, now!"

Wow, his tone changed quickly, I thought. *I sure hope he never yells at me that way.*

Within a minute, a tall, lanky guy came rushing into the office. "Yeah, boss?"

"Josh, this is Jason."

"Hey, what's up, man," Josh said. He noticed my purple shirt and smiled.

"Hi." I wasn't sure if I should shake his hand or not.

"Jason is our new runner, and he starts now. I need you to deliver McMurphy and Douglas and show him how it's done."

"Uh, I'm working on Jones, Peters, and Tate." These were obviously names of law firms with the partners' last names.

"I don't care if you're working on a card for your mom for fucking Mother's Day!" Steve snapped. "Take him to deliver McMurphy and Douglas, now! Do you think you can do that?" Steve was pretty much yelling at Josh.

I thought, *Big red flag...what have I gotten myself into?*

Looking defeated, Josh turned to me and said, "Let's go, new guy."

I hurried after him past the machines and down a hallway to a room with stacks upon stacks of legal boxes. Each stack loomed like the buildings outside, and in between them, we walked like giants.

Josh quickly found the neatly stacked legal boxes labeled McMurphy and Douglas in large black letters. "So basically, all you do is grab one of these hand trucks," he said as he wheeled over one of five well-worn hand trucks from the corner of the room. "I'll wheel the first one, and then when we get back, you can get the next delivery." Josh made quick work of the heavy stack of boxes. I felt bad that Steve had yelled at him. There was a sign on the wall that read "FIVE BOX MAX!!!" Josh ignored this rule, stacking six boxes on the hand truck. With one hand on the top box and the other on the hand truck handle, he tilted the boxes toward him and rolled them forward with ease, as if he had done it a hundred times or more. "Follow me," Josh said, busting through a double door that led outside, using the boxes as his battering ram.

The air rushed in as we went out onto the busy streets of the Financial District. Josh walked at a fast pace. Obviously, he knew where he was going.

"Do we always deliver to the same places?" I asked. I was worried, not being familiar with the city, and I didn't want to get lost.

"Pretty much. We have about twenty steady clients, and a few random ones pop up here and there. McMurphy and Douglas is our busiest client."

"Does Steve always yell at you like that?"

"He's just pissed at me because I gave my notice."

"You did? Why?"

"I just can't stand it down there all day."

"So…it's not a good job?" I asked, digging for more information.

"It's not bad if you like slave labor and getting yelled at as well."

"I don't think I'll last long if Steve starts yelling at me."

Josh laughed. "Well, you better get used to it. Steve is stressed out because all the law firms keep calling and demanding that their copies get done faster and faster. Steve takes it out on the rest of us."

"Man, that sucks."

"You're lucky that you're a runner and not stuck in the dungeon."

"I guess." I'd just started this job, and I was already looking forward to quitting.

After a few blocks, we entered a high-rise building. We crossed the marble floor, and Josh pressed the button for the elevator. As we waited, men and women in business suits gathered around us, waiting for the same elevator. They all had coffees and briefcases in hand and seemed annoyed at how long the elevator was taking. I wondered if they were all lawyers and imagined the possible cases they were working on. When I was a kid, I loved watching reruns of *Perry Mason*. The show was filmed in the 1950s–1960s, and master criminal defense attorney Perry would always win his case. The funny thing was, the opposing district attorney was the same actor who lost the case every time. You would think they would mix it up from time to time, but they never did.

The elevator dinged and opened to the relief of the waiting suits. Josh deftly maneuvered his boxes into the elevator and spun around, backing into the corner to allow room for the rest of us. Everyone pressed a different number, and I looked at Josh, who said, "Twenty-two." I leaned over and pressed the corresponding button. Soon, the elevator doors opened, revealing the twenty-second floor. The room was alive with activity. I'd never been in a lawyer's office before, and my eyes took it all in. People rushed around, and a sense of urgency filled the room. I immediately thought I would never become a lawyer. Not that there was even a chance I could, but I still wanted to remind myself that this world was not for me.

"Okay, so all the offices are basically the same," Josh said as he headed over to the reception desk. "All you need to do is tell the receptionist you have a document delivery, and they'll have someone meet you to take the boxes. Then, if they have boxes to go back, they'll bring them to you."

"That seems easy enough."

"Pretty much." Josh approached the front desk. A pretty woman was on the phone. As we approached, she held up a finger, motioning us to wait. After she hung up the phone, she smiled at Josh and automatically called for someone to pick up the boxes. A few minutes later, a guy about my age wheeled up to us with a cart and quickly began transferring the boxes from Josh's hand truck to his cart. I found it funny that there wasn't any communication or camaraderie between Josh and the guy with the cart. They must have been doing this transfer for some time, since Josh had mentioned he worked as a runner for about a year. As soon as the guy finished, Josh asked if anything was going out, and the guy said no and thanked us. Without another word, Josh headed back to the elevator. I expected Josh to introduce me as the new guy to the office employees, but he didn't. This world felt impersonal and disconnected. Each person had a purpose and was doing their best to climb up the next step of the ladder. I really didn't like this job, but in my head, I heard my dad say, "A job is a job, so do your job and do it well." That was what I was going to do because I was determined to make it in this city.

We exited the building and headed back toward the office. I looked around, making mental notes of landmarks to help me find my way the next time I did this route alone. "So, how do I know where the other offices are?" I asked Josh.

"Steve will give you the addresses for the first few days until you know them by heart. They're all within six to seven blocks of our office, so it's pretty easy." Josh made a point to tell me about the good hand trucks and the bad ones. The one we were using was a sturdy one with good wheels. He warned me that a lot of the others were crappy with wobbly wheels. Josh opened the office door and pushed the hand truck inside. The smell of copy dust filled my lungs as Josh parked the hand truck and told me to report to Steve for my first delivery. He waved, wishing me good luck, and quickly disappeared into the copy room to finish working on Jones, Peters, and Tate. I thanked him as he walked away.

I walked over to Steve's office, opened the door, and poked my head in. "Hi. Can I come in?"

"Jason. How'd it go?" Steve smiled when he saw me. It seemed like he was feigning an extra-nice attitude because he was shorthanded, and I was the only runner he had. I could see right through his phoniness, and I knew it was only a matter of time before I would be on the other end of his stressful anger. Not waiting for an answer, he forged on, "I need you to deliver some boxes to a new client. The name is John Tyler, Attorney at Law, and here's the address." Steve handed me a slip of paper with the address written on it, along with a street map of the Financial District. "You might want to familiarize yourself with this map."

"Will do."

I stood there for some reason, waiting for more direction, but Steve went about his business answering the phone. He noticed me still standing there and muffled the phone with his palm and said, "Chop, chop." His voice had already turned curt, obviously annoyed that I was still standing in front of him.

With my map and address slip, I headed out of his office, through the copy room, and into the city of boxes that awaited delivery. *Here we go*, I said to myself as I hurried to find the boxes that were labeled for John Taylor, Attorney at Law. It didn't take long, and to my happy surprise, there were only two boxes. *Cool*. I ran over to the hand trucks and noticed that the truck Josh had used was gone. *Where did it go?* I wondered. I looked over at the others, determining which one was the best of the bunch, and grabbed the least wobbly cart. I rolled it over and loaded it with the two legal boxes that were heavier than I expected. I was impressed with how easily Josh had maneuvered his truck stacked six tall.

I looked at the map and quickly found the office Josh had taken me to. I used that location to help me figure out where the new client's office was. It seemed straightforward. I just needed to go outside, make a right, and turn left four blocks down, and I would eventually end up at the office of John Taylor. I was excited and nervous about my first job in the city. I had my orders, and I was about to complete my first mission. As easy as this job seemed, I wondered why there was such a high turnaround rate.

I folded the address slip and map and put them in my pocket. I rammed the doors, and they swung open just like they had for Josh. I was on my way. I headed right, and at a quick pace, I walked down four blocks. I walked among the other businesspeople and even saw other runners who had nicer hand trucks. I felt a strange sense of community, as everyone in the

Financial District was working together like a colony of bees. From the runners to the lawyers and the bankers. In delivering these important documents, I felt a sense of purpose doing my part for the financial colony. My spirit rose, and I felt optimistic about the future. I wasn't doing art, at least not yet, but that was okay for now. I knew I would get there, and this job was my starting point.

I looked for Davis Street, where I needed to turn left. I knew I had walked the four blocks, but I didn't see the sign. I reached into my pocket to grab the piece of paper with the address on it and the map, but they weren't there. *What the fuck? Where did they go? I just had them. Crap!* I calmed myself, determined not to freak out, and thought I had a fairly good mental map of the directions, so I decided to walk another two blocks, hoping to find Davis. Two more blocks and no Davis Street. I stopped a man and asked him if he knew where it was. He shook his head and moved on. *How could he not know? He obviously works down here.* I began to panic, looking left and right. I didn't know what to do. I decided to head back the way I'd come, thinking I must've just missed it. I made it all the way back to where I'd turned right...no Davis Street. *Damn it.*

I was only a block away from the copy office, and I thought to go back and ask Steve for the address again, but instead, I saw a pay phone. I pulled some change from my pocket, as well as the newspaper clipping with Steve's number. I fed the phone money and waited for the line to ring. My heart pounded out excess adrenaline. Steve answered. "Hey, Steve. This is Jason," I squeaked out.

"Who?"

"Jason, the new runner."

"What's up, Jason. Why are you calling me?"

"Well, I'm kind of lost and I can't find the address slip you gave me."

"Seriously? Where are you now?" he snapped, clearly annoyed.

"I'm only a block away, but I was hoping you could direct me to John Taylor's office."

"Hold on." A few moments later, the phone clicked. "Okay. Make a left on California. You'll run into Davis, go right. The address is 2234, suite 506. Got it?"

"Yes, no problem and sor—"

The phone hung up, cutting me off. *What a dick*, I thought, hanging up the phone. Oh well, I was back on task, and I remembered seeing California Street. I quickly headed back up, turned left, and saw Davis. *2230, 2232, there it is.* I sighed in relief and opened the heavy glass door of 2234. I walked over to the elevator, finding it already open and waiting. I wheeled my boxes inside and pressed the button for the fifth floor. A sense of relief came over me as I ascended to the office of John Taylor, Attorney at Law.

The doors opened to the reception desk, and I wheeled over. An older woman greeted me with a kind smile. "Can I help you, young man?"

"Yes. I'm here for a delivery, I mean, I am delivering these documents."

"Okay, I'll see if I can get someone up here for you."

"Thanks," I said, smiling at her.

"I really like your shirt. You don't see a lot of purple these days. Is that silk?"

I cringed. In all of the chaos, I'd forgotten about my shirt. "Oh, thanks. Yes, it's silk." The last thing I thought I would hear that day was a compliment on my clown shirt. I couldn't wait to tell Koji that I'd met someone with his mom's bad taste. I wheeled my boxes back a few steps and waited for someone to come for them. I pulled my jacket closed again and waited for about five minutes; no one had shown up. I left my boxes behind and walked up to the nice lady at the reception desk. "Hi, sorry to bother you, but is someone coming for the boxes?"

"Oh darn. They're swamped back there. Why don't you just go on back yourself. It's just down the hall after the bathrooms," she said, pointing to the hallway.

"Thanks," I said, walking back to my boxes. The hallway was lined with glass-walled offices. A large group of people were in a meeting, probably discussing their important cases. I wondered which person John Taylor was. I found the bathrooms and, just beyond, a door with the words "Copy Room" on it. I opened the door to find several people sorting through boxes of documents and filing mail. A couple of them looked up at me but quickly went back to what they were doing. Just as I was going to speak up, a guy saw me from across the room and waved me over. I wheeled my boxes through the maze of desks and stacks of what seemed to be unorganized boxes, unorganized compared to the boxes back at the copy shop. The man opened the top box on my cart and knew exactly where it was supposed to go. He quickly grabbed both boxes at once, walked them over to a desk, and sat them in front of another guy who was talking on the phone. The guy looked up for a split second to acknowledge the delivery.

The first man walked back over to me and said, "I have some boxes for you to take back for copying."

"Oh. Okay."

"They're right over here." He motioned for me to follow. He led me back through the sea of desks and displaced boxes. "Here we are. Do you need help?"

"No, I got it," I said, assuring him I could handle the job. He walked away, leaving me to it. I soon realized as I stacked the boxes that there were more than five. I counted seven. *Oh shit*, I thought. I had seven boxes. My mind flashed to the office sign, FIVE BOX MAX!!! *Josh stacked six, what's one more? I was a skater kid...I'm strong and agile. And I have great balance. If Josh can handle six, I can handle seven*, I thought.

I loaded the seventh box just to test the waters. It stacked higher than the handle of the truck. I tilted it back, and things seemed stable enough. I glanced over my shoulder, looking for a warning from the office employees, but no one paid me any mind. I tested the stability of the cart, rolling it across the room toward the door and into the hallway. Everything seemed fine. I figured the risk was worth it. I would be able to make up for lagging with the directions. If I made two trips just for one more box, I'd surely fall behind on the rest of my deliveries, and I really wanted to make a good first impression.

I carefully wheeled the leaning tower of John Taylor, Attorney at Law, down the hallway of glass-walled offices. I noticed one guy giving a presentation. He glanced over at me and stopped speaking for a moment. *That must be John Taylor*, I thought as I pushed on.

I made it to the front office without a hiccup, and the receptionist smiled at me. "You sure you got that?"

"I'm good, thanks," I said, approaching the elevator. I had second thoughts and was about to abort my seven-box mission when the elevator opened and sealed my fate. I smoothly wheeled my tower into the elevator and was impressed by the handling of the truck. The stack was heavy, and the weight needed to be balanced evenly to avoid tipping too much. I exited the elevator and walked toward the front door. The door automatically opened, and I smoothly rolled out into the city.

Davis Street was on a hill, so I needed to account for the angle going down. I leaned the cart back. The seventh box rested against the side of my face as I literally felt the weight of my decision. The heft of the boxes fell on my arms, and I struggled to navigate the grade of the sidewalk. A couple of businessmen laughed as they passed me. I scowled at them as I continued to struggle, my arms burning from the weight. I was going downhill and needed to commit to the descent. If I tried to tilt the boxes upright to rest my arms, the tower would surely fall. My face was scrunched against the seventh box, my neck holding it in place, my arms continued to ache under the pressure. I slowly eased the boxes closer and closer to the busy street below. *I can do this, I'm so close*, I thought, seeing the light at the end of the tunnel. But fate argued as one of the wobbly wheels wobbled right off the cart and rolled away. The cart jerked, causing it to sway dangerously to the left. I tried with all my might to keep it from happening, but it was out of my hands as gravity took over. In one motion, the cart fell to the left and abruptly stopped when the axle hit the ground. The forward momentum pushed the cart from my grip and catapulted the boxes of John Taylor, Attorney at Law, into the busy street.

All I could do was watch in slow motion as the boxes hit the ground, spilling their contents evenly out into the road. With both hands cupping the top of my head, I stared in utter terror. I hurried over to the last box and managed to save it from upheaval, but all the other papers were everywhere. Thousands of papers were strewn across the sidewalk and into the street. As if it were an oil spill, I did my best to surround my disaster in some sort of cleanup relief, but a city bus had different plans. On schedule and on target, the bus passed with force, sending the entire contents of the other six boxes soaring into the air like a kite festival. Following suit, the cars behind the bus ensured another gust of wind, engulfing the entire block with legal documents. Papers stuck to the front of parked and moving cars, and a few managed to lodge themselves in the spokes of a passing bike.

I stood in awe of what I'd just done. My heart sank, and my fear of repercussion skyrocketed. I gave up the salvage effort, which was clearly a losing battle. A couple of Good Samaritans silently handed me handfuls of papers before walking on. My face was beet red as the city's eyes stared upon the sight I'd orchestrated. A driver passing by honked his horn and mockingly yelled out, "Nice shirt, asshole!"

Is this really happening? I thought. I wanted to cry and disappear, but all I could do was stand and watch the papers fly about, hovering and swaying left and right, covering more and more ground by the moment. Shaking myself out of it, I ran down the street to a pay phone and nervously dialed Steve. Almost crying, I proceeded to tell him what had happened. Before I could finish, he hung up on me, and soon I saw Josh running up the street toward the cyclone of papers.

"Dude! What the hell happened?" Josh asked, in shock of the display in front of him.

"The fucking wheel came off! That's what happened." My only saving grace was to use the crappy hand truck to direct the fault away from me.

Josh stood speechless for a minute and then slowly started to laugh. His laughter roiled into a deep and out-of-control belly laugh. He placed one hand on his stomach and the other in the air. "Oh my God, this is fucking awesome!"

I couldn't help it. A smile came to my face, and thanks to Josh, I could see the humor in what had just happened. My laughter was brief though, as the reality of the circumstances became real. "What do we do?" I asked.

"Man, you're screwed. Steve is going to kill you! He's back at the office talking with John Taylor. They're freaking out." As soon as Josh finished, I saw a small army of people from John Taylor's office, most of whom I saw in the mailroom. They were on the scene trying to salvage the papers. I could see on their faces that they were pissed off. Josh and I offered to help, but as we did, the guy who I'd given the boxes to in the mailroom stopped us and told us that Steve wanted us back at the office.

Josh looked at me with pity. It was still windy out, and we watched the papers fill the sky. It was beautiful in a way, like something you would see in an art film. As we walked back to the dungeon to face the dragon, Josh kept laughing and apologizing for laughing. He couldn't help himself, and I couldn't blame him.

The smell of copy dust filled my lungs again, though probably for the last time. "Good luck," Josh said as he peeled away from our side-by-side formation, leaving me to go it alone.

I didn't respond and continued walking past the machines. *Dead man walking*, I thought. The operators, who hadn't paid much attention to me when I'd first arrived, were now watching my walk of shame. Some looked on with pity, and others just shook their heads disapprovingly. I heard one of them whisper to the other, "Yeah, seven boxes."

How do they know I had seven boxes? I thought. I could hear Steve talking softly and apologetically to someone on the phone. I assumed it was John Taylor, Attorney at Law. When Steve saw me, he snapped his fingers and pointed at a chair in front of his desk, indicating for me to sit. I felt horrible, but in my defense, I blamed the wobbly wheel. *Where is Perry Mason to save me now?* I thought.

Steve finished his call and then sat, taking a deep breath. He looked at me without speaking for a moment, and I could tell he was doing his best to contain his rage. He took another deep breath. "Why would you transport seven boxes when the rule clearly states no more than five?"

I knew the rule, and I'd seen the sign, but I panicked and decided to lie about knowing the rule. After all, no one had informed me of said rule. I'd simply noticed the sign when Josh was breaking the rule. "I didn't know the rule."

"Josh didn't tell you not to carry more than five boxes at a time?"

"Well, no, he didn't."

"You didn't see the sign in the box room that screams, 'FIVE BOX MAX!!!'?" I had seen the sign, but I stood firm in my lie. Steve stood, walked to the door, and shouted for Josh.

Josh arrived only moments later and nodded at me. "What's up, boss?"

"'What's up?' Really, Josh?"

Josh shrugged, unfazed.

"Why did you not tell Jason about the five-box rule?"

"No one told me about the five-box rule," Josh simply replied.

"That is not the point!" Steve shouted, pointing his finger at Josh. "You were supposed to train him properly, and you dropped the ball, Josh!"

"You know what, Steve? You can go fuck yourself! I'm out of here!" Josh shouted.

"Oh really?"

"Yeah, really," Josh said, taking off his apron in true *You Can Take this Job and Shove It* fashion. He threw his apron across the room, turned, and left.

"That's just great," Steve said as he walked over and slammed the door. I realized at this point that one of two things was about to happen. I was going to get the job I applied for as a machine operator, or I was going to get kicked to the curb. I waited for Steve to speak. "You realize we just lost that client and it's your fault." He needed someone to blame, and now that Josh had just told him off, I was all he had.

Pleading my case, I said, "Wait a minute. I wasn't trained, and that cart is a piece of junk. The wheel literally *fell off.*"

Steve stood up and yelled in my face, "If you hadn't tried to carry seven fucking boxes on the damn cart, maybe it wouldn't have broken off!" At that moment, Steve canceled any options for me at this job. I simply stood up and walked out. I didn't look at the machine operators, even though I could feel their eyes on me. I passed through the towering boxes, and with a kick, the double doors opened to the sun and fresh air. I growled and squeezed my fists, releasing all the tension I'd just endured.

As I walked away from the Financial District, I felt bad for the people chasing after and picking up the papers, and I hoped the mess didn't cause too much trouble. I thought about walking over there to offer my help or at least apologize, but I walked away, putting it behind me. I headed back to Koji's, but instead of taking the subway, I decided to walk and blow off some steam.

I walked up Market Street all the way to the Castro and then to Koji's flat. I climbed the stairs and used my key. My silky purple shirt was soaked with sweat and stuck to me like glue. I couldn't wait to take it off. I walked in and passed Koji, who was busy on his computer. I went straight to the fridge, opened a beer, and proceeded to down it in one chug.

Koji came in. "Dude, what's up? How did it go?"

"You're never going to believe what just happened to me," I said, followed by a loud burp. I proceeded to tell Koji the story while he rolled around on the floor laughing, clutching his stomach, and begging for me to stop. I finished my tale, and Koji composed himself.

"The best part," Koji said, pointing at me, "is the purple shirt!"

"Yeah, super funny," I said, taking the shirt off and throwing it at him.

"Dude, I can't believe that happened."

"Yeah, hired and fired all within three hours."

"That has to be some kind of record," Koji said, cracking open his own beer. "Don't let it get you down. That Steve guy sounds like an asshole, anyway."

"Yes, you can say that again."

For the remainder of the day, Koji enjoyed messing with me. "You should call and ask for a letter of recommendation," he said. "Maybe you can get a job with a moving company now that you have experience." His comments were funny and well received. Koji always looked at life with humor, and he always seemed to be happy, never bogged down by the stresses of work. I remembered the day Koji confessed that his dad committed suicide. I didn't press him for details, nor did he give any. He just mentioned it and that was it. I envied his strength, though. We continued our party into the night, ordering and eating pizza and drinking way too much. It was exactly what I needed after the day I'd had.

Chapter Fourteen

The next morning, I went out for a fresh paper and found a couple of jobs that looked promising. One was for a sales position at the Gap clothing store. I had some retail experience, and at this point, until I could acquire some graphic design clients, I would do just about anything, including selling denim. I called and scheduled an interview for the next evening at six. I was excited to have a second possible job in such a short time.

Koji had left the house earlier to go mountain biking with a friend, and I was looking forward to exploring more of the city. But I also desperately needed to do laundry. Randomly, Ashley popped into my mind, and for some reason, I decided to call her. I hadn't planned on it, but knowing I was over her, I felt a wave of endorphins and decided we might be able to just be friends. I dialed her number and hoped the male voice wouldn't answer.

"Hello?"

Relieved to hear her voice, I said, "Hey, Ashley, it's me."

"What's up?" she asked excitedly. "Are you here?"

"Yep."

"You're in the Castro?"

"Yes, ma'am."

"Do you want to come over?"

"Uh, yeah, I guess," I said apprehensively.

"You don't have to if you don't want to…"

"No, I want to, but I need to do laundry. Is there a place by your apartment?"

"There's one across the street. Come over, bring your laundry." She gave me her address.

I collected my bag of dirty clothes and got into my car. I followed her directions and was surprised to find she lived only a short distance from Koji's. Even though there was a spot right in front of her apartment, I decided to park around the corner. I wasn't sure why I did it, as I sat in the car for a little while, convincing myself not to drive away. My mind was racing, so I sat and breathed deeply until my mind calmed. Looking in the rearview mirror, I ran fingers through my hair and checked my breath. *All clear, ready for takeoff*, I thought as I got out of my car and headed to her door. Just as I was about to knock, the door swung open.

"Hey!" She smiled. It was a smile I knew well and reminded me of better times when we had met years before. "How are you?"

"Good." I was good but seeing her so cheery pissed me off. I was surprised by my sudden anger. At this point, we had talked on the phone, and I felt good about seeing her and was excited about moving on in my life's journey. But although Ashley's stinger was removed, her poison still flowed through my veins. It was a cancerous poison, and the only remedy would be time. I wasn't sure how this would play out, but I was happy she'd kept her boundaries. She stood aside and invited me in. I smiled and gave her a compliment as I passed. "You look good."

"I try," she said, knowing she looked good. Already I could tell this was going to be a game. I wasn't sure why I decided to play, but I did want her to see that I was happy, and well, I wanted to throw it in her face, for it seemed that she was glad knowing I'd been destroyed and could only think of her. Seeing her now and feeling her love for attention, both bad and good, I felt compelled to take back whatever power I could that she had taken from me.

"So, this is it?" I said, browsing the apartment that we were supposed to share.

"Yep, this is it."

"It's not as nice as the photos," I said, even though it was.

"It's okay. I like it," she chirped.

"That's great. I'm glad you like it," I said, but I wasn't.

"So, how is staying at Koji's?"

"It's awesome. He said I could stay until I got a job."

"Oh. So, you are staying?" Her tone had changed.

"Maybe, I'm not sure." I was sure, but I wanted to keep her guessing. "If the right opportunity comes along, I might stay. After all, I uprooted my entire life for this move, and it just feels like I need to see it through, even if it's not with you."

"Yeah, totally," she said, not admitting or caring that she had screwed me over. She offered me a beer, and we sat across from each other in the living room. I hadn't really looked at her yet, but I could no longer avoid it. Our eyes met. There she was, the one for me, or so I had thought. As I looked at her, I noticed something was missing. It wasn't physical; it was emotional. Her magic spell that had enveloped all my senses was broken. She was beautiful, and I still had feelings for her, but my connection to her was gone, and I sensed she could feel it. We were both at a loss for words, and the moment became awkwardly tense.

"So, how long have you been in town?" she asked, trying to break the tension with small talk.

"A few days."

"Really?" She sounded surprised that I hadn't called her.

"Yeah, why so surprised?"

"I'm not. It's just I wasn't sure if you were coming and, well, never mind," she said, backpedaling. "Have you looked for a job yet?"

Though she would have thought it hilarious, I refrained from telling her about my adventure as a copy runner. I didn't want to look stupid. "Yeah, I have an interview tomorrow with the Gap."

"The Gap? You, at the Gap?" She laughed.

"What's so funny about working at the Gap? It's a job," I said in an attempt to defend my interim career direction.

"Wow! Okay." She smirked. "It's just…I don't see you working with those people. They are just so…Gap."

I knew what she meant. I was an alternative kind of guy and had always been somewhat of a rebel. The Gap represented the opposite of what I did. "Yeah, I know, but I need a job, and well, the Gap wants me." I shrugged.

"Yeah, I bet they are beating down your door!" She laughed.

I missed that laugh. It was such an ugly laugh, and she sounded like a dying hyena, but I loved it. "I see you still have the worst laugh ever."

"You love my laugh." She threw a decorative pillow at me.

"It's all right." The ice was melting, and things were warming up between us. I could finally breathe as we fell effortlessly into our old selves for a moment. "What about you? How is school and whatever else you're doing here?" I hadn't a clue about what she'd been doing for the past four months.

"School is hard but good, and well, everything else is pretty good."

"Pretty good? I am sure you have tons of friends by now."

"I do have quite a few friends. What about you? Have you made any friends in the last few days?"

I knew she was expecting me to say no. "As a matter of fact, I have. Or at least, I think we are friends." I told her about Star and the photo she took of me. I mentioned the great time we had at the Toronado and how much we had in common. I omitted the freakish panic attack, of course.

"Is she pretty?"

"Well, if you must know, she's really pretty." *Yes!* I thought, *I have taken my power back.* "Why do you care what she looks like?" I said, teasing her for a moment of jealousy.

"I don't care."

"Whatever, she's just a friend, anyway."

"Well, I'm glad you're making friends."

"Yeah, me too. So where is this laundromat you spoke of?"

"It's across the street. Let me get my laundry and we can go."

"Sounds good." I stood and finished the last of my beer. As I walked into the kitchen to set my bottle on the counter, I noticed a group photo on the fridge. It was of a few people all huddled together for a photo op. Ashley had her arms around a guy with her cheek pressed hard against his. She looked happy, and so did he. My heart raced, and it took all I had to contain my composure. *So, this is her new guy, probably the guy who answered the phone the other day*, I thought. I wondered why she didn't put the photo away before asking me over. Maybe Matt was right; she was so self-absorbed she didn't even know when she was hurting someone.

"Ready to go?" she said from her room.

I quickly jumped and moved back to the couch. I didn't want her to know I'd seen the photo. I knew if we got on that subject, it wouldn't go well. "Yeah, let's do laundry!" I said cheerfully.

We left her apartment, and I grabbed my bag of dirty clothes from my car.

"How's the Bug doing?" she asked.

"It's good." I patted the hood appreciatively. We crossed the street to a little neighborhood laundromat called the Missing Sock. There was a single sock hand-painted on the floor in red with white polka dots. The laundromat was clean and quaint, definitely not what one would expect. We loaded the machines with our wears. She handed me some laundry detergent.

"Thanks." I smiled in gratitude. I thought it strange how happy and disappointed I felt at the same time. I wished I hadn't seen that photo on the fridge. *Who is that jackass?* I thought.

"I'll be right back," Ashley said, disappearing out the door and down the street. I found a seat at a table with magazines on it and picked up an *SF Weekly*. I flipped through the paper but couldn't get the guy's stupid face out of my head. I threw the paper down on the table.

Ashley returned with two paper cups of coffee. "This is the best coffee you'll ever taste," she said, handing me a cup. She stood there waiting for me to take a sip and to see my response. She was like that. She was passionate about the simplest things. She had a favorite everything. I guessed this was her new favorite coffee. I remembered loving this enthusiasm before, but now that I was no longer under her spell, I found it kind of annoying.

I tasted the coffee. Yep, it was good, but it wasn't the best ever on Planet Earth, just a decent cup of coffee.

"So…?" she said enthusiastically, as if I were going to have some kind of coffee epiphany that would change my life.

"Oh wow! Yeah, it's the best," I said. My sarcasm landed me a punch on my right arm. "Ouch! What the heck was that for?"

"It *is* the best!" she said.

"All right, it's good." I rubbed my shoulder and laughed. I struggled with my emotions toward her. She could seem so sweet, but I knew it was a façade, and I couldn't let myself forget what she'd done.

"It is really good," she said in her baby voice.

That voice, I thought. *Ugh!* I hated her baby voice. If anything fluffy with four legs was in sight, she automatically turned on the cutesy baby voice. Man was I seeing clearly now.

Our machines smoothly transitioned to spin cycle, and the clock of my remaining time with her was ticking away. Suddenly the words came out before I could stop my mouth: "So who's the snuggle buddy in the photo on the fridge?"

She didn't respond right away. "Oh, that's Gary."

I didn't want to come across as angry or jealous, so I decided to lead with a joke. "So, Gary is your new gay friend who loves show tunes?" I laughed.

She laughed and said, "Yeah, you wish. No, he was a close friend, but now he's just a friend."

Even though it sounded like they had a thing but no longer did, my heart hurt and I wanted to kill Gary. I couldn't help it. I was jealous. Ashley could be lying to me. For all I knew, she was still seeing him, and this Gary guy was banging her. I thought about her having sex with the guy, and I began to panic, but I didn't want to show my true colors. I needed to get a grip.

I took a deep breath and composed myself. "I guess some things work and some things don't." I pretended that her and Gary being in a relationship didn't faze me one bit.

I could see out of the corner of my eye she was looking at me curiously. She seemed to be confused that I wasn't furiously freaking out and saying something like, "Did you enjoy fucking Gary?" I easily could have, but I didn't want to give her the satisfaction. I was beginning to realize she was just about the drama, and all she wanted from me was a reaction. She had purposely left the photo on the fridge *knowing* I would see it. As much as I wanted to, I wouldn't give it up. I waited silently, knowing she expected me to lose it.

A few more minutes of silence passed until I finally said, "Yeah, I guess you and I would know about that."

"I guess so." She sighed and looked out the window. "I wish it had been different with us."

I didn't say anything, but I wanted to say, "Then why the fuck did you leave me? It could have been different. It could have been like we had planned." I bit my tongue and said nothing.

"I just couldn't do it. I couldn't move in with you. I panicked and couldn't do it. I hate that I hurt you, but I had no choice." She got up and walked over to me, grabbed my hand. I looked at her. She was crying, and the game was over.

"You could've talked to me," I said, holding both her hands. "We could've worked it out. We didn't need to move in together."

"I know, but I just needed to do this alone, and I felt like you included yourself in my plans."

"Wow! I *included* myself…in *your* plans? We were in a committed relationship. We talked about marriage. What was I supposed to do? I wasn't aware you had plans that didn't include me. You should've mentioned that part to me." I was pissed at her comment about me including myself in her life.

"No, that came out wrong," she said, attempting to stop me from freaking out. "I just felt trapped, and for some reason, I felt like I needed to be on my own. You were so excited and took over all the planning. You never really asked me what I wanted or if I was even ready." There was a long pause as I thought about what she'd said. She was right. When she told me she wanted to go to school in San Francisco, I just assumed we would go together. I had fast-tracked all the details, but how could I not assume we would live together?

"I wish you would've said something. I thought you loved me." I looked away.

"I did, I do. I never stopped loving you," she said. I wiped the tears from her flush face. She grabbed my hand, and in one motion, she kissed me. I felt her lips shake against mine. I held her tight, not letting her go. Our soft, tender kiss quickly turned into a stronger, passionate one.

She pulled away, smiled, and led me by my hand out the door of the Missing Sock. I knew where this was going…it was obvious. I thought to stop her lead and pull my hand away, but I didn't. We continued across the street and upstairs to her apartment. She stopped to kiss me through the door of her bedroom. Without thinking, we made love, but it was different. She was different. I was there in what should've been *our* apartment. Holding her naked body close to mine, I felt renewed and alive. It was a feeling I'd longed for. When we finished, we lay there quietly. At that moment, I decided it would be the last time I would ever make love to her. The old, unjaded me wanted to cuddle and renew our love for each other, but the new me didn't. I was jaded, and there was no turning back. I knew the real Ashley, and soon enough, she would return. I was wounded, and I couldn't hide this scar, no matter how hard I tried. Even if I could salvage our relationship, I wouldn't. In this moment of clarity, seeing who she really was and how so many of her attributes really bothered me, I was done.

"That was fun," I said, kissing her on the forehead.

"Yeah, I needed that! We should get back to our laundry before someone steals it."

"People do that?"

"Yeah, it happened to me my first week here." She jumped up, pulled her cotton panties back on, and searched for her shirt. As we dressed, I heard the front door open and laughs echo through the apartment.

"Oh shit!" she said, closing her door.

"Who is that?" I asked. She pressed her ear to the door and listened.

"It's just my roommate and his girlfriend. Wait here, I'll be right back." Ashley quickly slid out the door, shutting it behind her.

I finished dressing and waited for her to return. I listened at the door. I heard a girl laughing and Ashley telling her to stop, as if they were teasing her. I wondered if she told them I was here. I was sure they knew who I was. She seemed embarrassed, like she was ashamed of me. Then I heard it, a second man's voice. *Could it be?* I thought. *Could it be her buddy Gary?* I had waited long enough, and this guy was not going to be a dirty little secret, nor was I. I was a free man. Filled with confidence, I swung open the door and strutted into the living room. Ashley had her back to me, talking with a guy and a girl sitting on the couch.

"Hey!" I said, walking over. I laid my arm across Ashley's waist. *Why is she hiding me?* I thought. *What kind of monster did she portray me as?* All my late-night calls when she first left me probably didn't help my rep, but hey, the heart wants what the heart wants. "I'm Jason," I said, smiling at her friends.

"Robert, Stacy…this is Jason," Ashley said. I noted a tremble in her voice.

"Hi, nice to meet you." Stacy smiled.

Robert looked uncomfortable with my presence, but I didn't care. I recognized both from the photo. I assumed they were friends with good ol' Gary. I wondered where the third voice was. I swore I'd heard three voices. I heard a door shut, and by the looks on Robert's and Stacy's faces, I knew I was about to meet Gary. I composed myself and looked over at Ashley. She looked scared. She'd seen me fight a guy at a bar once and knew how far I could go. Little did she know I had no intention of doing any such thing. In fact, what right did I have to beat the snot out of a guy who simply fell for the same girl I had years before? It wasn't his fault. The hammer fell as it dawned on me that Ashley was doing to Gary what she'd done to me so many times. Needing a drama fix, she'd orchestrated this entire scenario just to make Gary crazy and jealous, like she loved to do to me. *Two for one*, I thought. *If she wants a reaction, here it comes!*

At that point, seeing their worried faces anticipating the worst, I did the best thing ever--I turned and saw Gary stop in his tracks, looking at me. He must have gone to the bathroom after they arrived and was just coming out, out to his worst nightmare. What he didn't know was I no longer held any ill will toward him. In fact, I felt sorry for him, knowing what his relationship with Ashley was like. I was over it, and I just wanted to leave. Ashley did her best to buffer the interaction, and as I walked toward him, I could see his fear. He knew it was me.

"Hey! You must be Gary," I said, extending my hand.

"Uh, yes. Hi?" he said, flinching, probably expecting me to punch him or something. He accepted my hand, and I shook his hard, breaking my dad's rule. I squeezed his hand and held it tight. I could feel his fear pulsing through his hand.

Ashley looked at me half smiling, almost pleading for me not to make a scene, but I knew the truth. I looked at her and smiled, then still smiling, I looked into Gary's eyes and said, "Good luck, man. She's all yours." I released his hand.

He looked a little confused and walked over to join his friends sitting on the couch.

"Well, I really better get going. This was fun!" I turned to hug Ashley. She was dumfounded, and I held her tightly before breaking away to look into her eyes. "It was really great seeing you, and our romp was fun." With a loud and wet smooch, I slapped her ass, then turned and walked down the hallway toward the front door. I put my hand into the air, waved, and shouted, "It was nice meeting you all. Have a great night!"

"You too," Stacy awkwardly shouted back.

I left the apartment with the biggest grin plastered on my face and thought, *Shit! That was right out of a movie. It couldn't have been more perfect.* I felt a little bad, but really, it was a small victory and some just desserts for Ashley. I wasn't violent, I didn't yell at Gary, and everyone in that room knew Ashley and I had fucked. *That was awesome!* I wished I felt bad for her, but I didn't. She'd held a tight leash on me for so many years, and I broke it with a kiss and a pat on the ass. I couldn't help but feel a little sorry for Gary, considering what his future looked like with Ashley. *Oh well,* I thought as I went back to the laundromat to retrieve my clothes. I loaded my washed but still damp clothes into my laundry bag and hurried off to my car. I didn't want to wait around for Ashley, and I couldn't wait to tell Koji the good news. I had no doubt Ashley thought I would be waiting for her at the laundromat like an obedient dog. The old me might have, but I wasn't the old me, not anymore. I was done, and that was okay. In fact, it was great.

I drove to Koji's feeling more confident that I was on the right path. I stopped at a red light and looked up to the sky, thanking the universe for helping me stay strong. I found another laundromat a few streets away, so I pulled over to dry my clothes. I sat on an orange plastic chair and watched my clothes tumble. In my head, I revisited everything that had just happened. I was filled with the excitement and anticipation of telling Koji the details. I had closure and a little payback to boot. The memories of Ashley and I, which I had thought were good, began to fall like water off a duck's back, one at a time, leaving my mind and freeing up space to be filled with new and exciting experiences. Even though I truly didn't want to hurt Ashley, I knew in some way that I needed this simply for self-respect. *She's going to be just fine*, I thought. With or without Gary, she would find another guy to chase her. I sat staring at my clothes spinning round and round, hypnotizing me into a continuous daydream of the day's events. *Ding!* I was startled awake by the dryer's alarm. I shook off the daze and jumped back into reality. I folded my clothes and then headed home.

When I arrived at Koji's, I noticed he was tending to an almost stiches-worthy gash on his leg. "Dude. What happened?"

"Uh, my bike decided to attack me." Koji laughed.

"Sure, that's exactly what happened. Are you okay?"

"Yeah, just a flesh wound."

"Your flesh wound looks pretty nasty."

"I'm good. How was your day?"

"Hold that thought." I walked to the kitchen and grabbed a couple of medicinal beers. Medicinal for Koji, but celebratory for me. "Here ya go."

"Thanks, man." He must have noticed the Cheshire cat grin on my face. "Dude, what's up with you? Did you get stoned or something?"

"No, not stoned…"

"Then what?"

"Okay. So, remember when I said I wasn't going to call Ashley—"

"You didn't! You asshole. You called her. Why? If you're back together with her, I swear to God!"

"No, no, relax. I'm not back together with her."

"You swear?"

"I swear. I'm not back, nor will I ever get back with her, *especially* after what I did today."

"What'd you do?" Koji was all bandaged up, so we retired to the living room. I spared no detail of my adventures in laundry land and my sweet, sweet revenge. "Dude, you did not smack her ass on the way out!"

"I swear I did."

"You're my hero. That story is amazing, and I am proud to call you my friend." We burst into laughter, and for what must've been the tenth time, we clinked our beers. This was a celebration of my liberation from Ashley. Though I felt a little bad for doing that to her, I was happy Koji was there to remind me of what she'd put me through. Tomorrow I was going to get a job at the Gap and continue my path.

That night I slept hard. All the emotions and anxiety had finally caught up with me, and my body needed a deep sleep. I dreamt that I flew around the city, just like the astral projection trips I took when I was at my mom's cabin. Aside from the park, I hadn't really meditated since I'd arrived, and it reminded me how great it felt to explore these adventures in my mind.

I woke up early and made myself some cereal and coffee. Koji soon joined me. "Morning, gimpy," I said, laughing at his gait.

"Man, my leg is sore," he said as he gently pressed the tender, swollen flesh around his bandage.

"I still think you need stitches." I walked over and handed him a cup of coffee.

"Just what I need, thanks. So, what time is your interview?"

"It's at six p.m."

"What? Why so late?"

"Not sure, but that's what time the lady said. I figured I would explore the city a bit today and get my bearings."

"Sounds good. I would join you, but I think I am couching it today," he said, rubbing his leg.

"No worries. Take it easy, Danger Dan."

"Dude, you should wear the purple shirt for your interview!"

"Yeah, it seems to be my good luck charm. Maybe I should wear a matching scarf and beret."

"They will totally hire you!" he said, laughing.

"Well, I'm out of here, and thanks for reminding me that I need to buy a shirt. Good luck with your leg." I walked to the front door.

"Later, loser!" Koji yelled from the couch.

Chapter Fifteen

The wind was alive and blowing hard, battling the gel that held my freshly coiffed 'do. I headed toward my car, and with the turn of my key, I warmed her up. I needed to get a new shirt and decided what better than a Gap shirt for a Gap interview. There were several Gap stores in the city, but I didn't want to buy a shirt at the same store I was interviewing at. I found one only a few miles from Koji's. After circling and finding a parking spot down the street, I headed in. I figured I could pick up a shirt and check out the store to familiarize myself with the Gap. I'd been in one back in Orange County, and it looked almost identical to this one. It was huge and screamed corporate. Ashley was right; I didn't belong in a place like this. It wasn't that the clothes were all bad; it was just I was more on the fringe of society and not a fan of big corporate styles. The reality, however, was I needed a job, and I could put on a smile with the best of 'em.

I browsed the store, watching the employees and studying what they were doing. I noticed a lot of folding. There were various employees refolding the shirts that people had messed up while looking for their size. The employees were using little square boards that inserted into the bottom of the shirts. With a few turns, it created a perfectly folded shirt. I was impressed, and the mystery was solved as to how they got perfectly stacked T-shirts.

"Can I help you?" a voice asked from behind me, interrupting my spying.

"Uh, yeah. I need a shirt," I said, turning to face a potential coworker. I was pleasantly surprised to find myself face-to-face with Nicki, according to her name tag. She was super cute and totally my type. "Hi!" I said as if to start over with more enthusiasm.

"Hi." She smiled big to match mine. She reminded me of a hotter and younger Joan Jett. Not to say that Joan Jett wasn't hot, she just had a tomboyish thing going on that I wasn't into. I always had a thing for rocker chicks, and growing up in the eighties, they were everywhere. The all wore tight jeans and tight T-shirts that said Ozzy or Iron Maiden. I never dated them because back in the eighties, the rocker girls only dated rocker dudes. I was definitely not a rocker dude. Her hair was straight and had a bit of a rocker cut. She was pale and wore bright red lipstick. I could tell she hated what they made her wear. I could see her in leather pants or something besides the khakis and V-neck T-shirt she was in.

"So, what kind of shirt are you looking for?" she asked.

I just stared into her eyes, and for a moment, I was lost.

"You need a shirt?" she prompted.

"Oh, uh, yeah. I do need a shirt," I said.

She giggled at my nervousness.

"What's so funny? It's your fault," I said playfully.

"What did I do?"

"You hijacked my brain with that face of yours."

She quickly looked down as her cheeks reddened. "I see, well, I'm sorry, sir, for hijacking your brain." She quickly looked left then right to see if any manager had noticed our flirting.

"That's okay, I'll let it go."

She gave me a flirtatious grin and said, "Please don't tell my manager about it."

"Not this time."

"Thanks. I would hate to lose this great job," she said sarcastically.

"I'm Jason." I extended my hand.

She accepted my handshake. "I'm Nicki. It's nice to meet you."

"My pleasure."

"So, do you really need a shirt? Or do you just go into Gap stores and flirt with girls?"

"Honestly, I have a thing for girls who can fold shirts into perfect little squares." I chuckled.

"Oh really. Well, I suck at folding." She smiled.

"I'll let you in on a little secret. I need a shirt for a job interview with this here fine corporation."

"Are you serious?"

"Yep." I explained how I'd just moved to town and needed temporary survival money.

"Well, since you are interviewing with this fine company, I know just the shirt!" She walked me over to a stack of staple golf-style polo shirts and handed me a size medium in black.

"Why black?"

"It's your funeral." She laughed.

"I'm so not looking forward to this interview now." I grabbed the shirt from her pretty hands. "I guess this is the part where I ask you for your number," I said confidently.

"Oh, I think I can do that," she said. Which location are you interviewing for?

"Um, I think the Embarcadero?"

I followed her to the counter and paid for the shirt, minus Nicki's employee discount. She wrote her number on the receipt, smiled at me, and wished me luck. Another girl walked behind the counter. Her name tag read "Manager" below her name.

"Nicki, thank you for your wonderful help. I will definitely be back," I said loud enough for the manager to take notice. I took one more lingering look at Nicki's pretty eyes, turned, and left.

She was superhot, and we definitely had a connection. I was enjoying my adventure in San Francisco so far. I'd met Star, became a part of an art installation, got some sweet revenge on Ashley, and now, met a pretty girl named Nicki. Things were looking up for this kid in the big city.

I spent the rest of the day soaking up the city sights. The city was alive, and the energy was vibrating like a giant beast. The streets and the subways were the beast's veins, and the people were its life-giving force, each one of its millions of inhabitants helping to keep it going by pulling levers and twisting knobs. I would soon become a cog in this big, well-oiled machine. I was a part of its ever-growing soul. My gate, my forest, and my beach would become distant memories. My special places were still there, but I'd become a busy person again. I was full of words, ideas, and opinions that didn't lend much time to closing my eyes and meditating. I was, however, okay, and I would be okay because the city was a good distraction for me. I vowed to visit my special places soon, but for now, my senses were on overload, and for once in a long time, I didn't want to escape my situation. I took comfort knowing that I could escape at any time just by closing my eyes. I was thankful for my experiences and self-discovery I'd had at my mom's. I was thankful for meeting Old Man Dave, and with some luck, someday I would find a love like his and Jenny's.

I was early, as usual, for my interview. The Gap was located in the Embarcadero, adjacent to the Financial District. The area seemed dedicated to shops and restaurants catering to the people who worked downtown. I found a parking spot and fed the meter a hefty sum. I did a quick recon mission to see where the store was located. It was next to a Subway sandwich shop. I decided to eat dinner before my six-p.m. meeting because I wasn't sure how long it would take, and I was a bit hungry. I sat in my car and ate my sandwich. My mind drifted to thoughts of Nicki, commanding my full attention. She was so hot and super nice. I thought about the many astral flights I'd taken to the city and wondered if she was part of my path. As I ate, a nervous and nauseous feeling came over me. *Oh no! Please not now.* My social anxiety had just informed me that I was about to go into an interview, and let's just say my bowels decided to say hello. With about twenty minutes until my meeting, I had a minor emergency.

I trashed the rest of my sandwich and hurried into the shopping center. Thankfully, I saw a sign for a public restroom. I rushed inside, happy to find it empty. I hurried into the stall and quickly applied a double barrier of toilet seat covers upon the public throne. I downed my pants and sat. My cramping stomach made quick business. The cramping continued, and I winced in pain with each spasm. "Why now?" I said out loud. "Why me?" The last thing I needed was a turd alert. I sat for a few minutes, and soon the nauseous feeling faded. I was starting to feel better. I decided to stay a bit longer in case my stomach lurched again. Just then, the door opened, and someone came into the bathroom. I sat quietly and hoped they didn't need the toilet, as I occupied the only one. I heard the door open again and another person came in. *Great. Rush hour*, I thought. They both seemed to just need the urinal. I relaxed and waited for them to finish peeing and leave before I exited the stall. I waited for what seemed like an unusual amount of time for someone to pee. Then I heard it…something I never in my life thought I would hear in a public restroom. The two guys who came in were making noises. Not pee noises or a little gas. No, these noises were much more intimate. *Oh my God*, I thought. They were busy moaning and groaning. I panicked, and my mind raced with thoughts of what to do. *Do they know I'm here?* I thought. *They must know.* I shuffled my feet, hoping they would hear me and stop whatever they were doing. I shuffled my feet again and coughed, but that didn't stop them. All I could hear was sounds of heavy breathing. *What the hell!* I thought. I was trapped in a public restroom with two guys going at it. All I could do was sit there and wait. I looked at my watch. I had about ten minutes until I was supposed to be at the Gap. I didn't want to miss my interview.

I became pissed off and shouted, "Do you think you can do that somewhere else?"

The two men became silent, and then I heard them whisper. To my relief, the door opened, and without saying anything, they left. I peeked through the crack of the stall door to make sure they were indeed gone and hurried out of the stall and quickly washed my hands.

Once outside, I looked around but didn't see anyone who looked guilty. *That was weird*, I thought as I made my way downstairs to my interview. *Man, Koji's gonna love this one*, I laughed to myself. I did my best to put the restroom incident behind me so I could focus on the interview. I took a couple of deep breaths as I entered the store.

This Gap looked exactly like the one where I'd met Nicki. I walked up to the front counter, and a cute girl with way too much glitter makeup asked if she could help me.

"Hi, yes. My name is Jason, and I am here for an interview."

"Oh great! Nice to meet you, Jason. My name is Patty. I'm the manager at this store." She extended her hand, causing her twenty plus bracelets to jingle loudly.

I shook her hand, and as I did, I couldn't help but notice a scent. Nothing fowl, just incredibly familiar. As I released her hand, I asked, "Is that Teen Spirit perfume?"

Her eyes got big. "Yes! Yes, it is! It's my favorite! How did you know?" she asked.

"I'll never forget it. My girlfriend in junior high wore it." Her smile faded a fraction, and I noticed her embarrassment. I realized that my answer had reminded her that she was wearing perfume marketed toward teenage girls and not someone like herself in her twenties. So, I immediately said, "I love that smell!"

Her eyes widened again. "Me too! I've never stopped loving it. My sister makes fun of me because I still wear it, but I don't care."

"Hey, if it smells good, it smells good."

"Exactly, Jason, exactly." Everything about Patty seemed kind of manic. She moved and talked quickly and was probably a great multitasker. "Okay, we are almost ready to start. Why don't you go over there and wait with the others."

"Others?" I asked.

She pointed to the far end of the store where there were about ten other people, who I assumed were all there for the same job. *Oh shit*, I thought. *A group interview. What have I gotten myself into?* I walked over to the waiting group. I almost left, but I needed to see this through, and I really needed money. The group acknowledged me with a few smiles and a couple of nods. Most of them looked as nervous as I felt. I took a spot against the wall among the waiting.

A short while later and after the last customer was helped, Patty locked the doors, and with the aid of another employee, she arranged some chairs in a circle on the sales floor. Like cattle, our group assumed the chairs were for us and shuffled over, waiting for direction.

"Okay, if you guys could take a seat, we can get started," Patty announced before disappearing in a back room. It looked like we were about to play a game of Duck, Duck, Goose, and I kind of wished we would. I sat down, sealing my fate, locked in a Gap group interview. I tried not to feel like a trapped rat, and I assured myself it would be over soon. Everyone else sat down and quickly looked at one another, sizing up the competition as if we were all auditioning for the same part in a movie. The group was a mixed bunch. I took a deep breath and looked out the window, wishing I were on the other side of it.

A few moments later, Patty appeared from the back room with another girl. "Okay, everyone. As you already know, I am Patty, the manager here. I would like to introduce you to my assistant manager, Kara."

"Kara with a K!" Kara interjected, insisting that everyone know she spelled her name with a K, not a C.

"Yes, that's right," Patty said, "Kara with a K." Both laughed together as if they were excited about the special spelling of her name.

"Nice to meet y'all," Kara said, revealing her Southern drawl. "I am really excited for today's meeting, and I look forward to getting to know a little bit about each and every one of you."

I could see Patty silently mouthing Kara's words along with her as she spoke. I could hardly help but laugh. *Wow. Did they write this down and memorize it?* I thought. *This is actually entertaining.* When Kara with a K finished her little script, she looked over at Patty and they both grinned at each other as if to say, *Nailed it!*

"Don't you just love her accent?" Patty said. "It's so fun." The group sat awkwardly silent, not knowing whether they should comment on Kara with a K's accent. "Okay! So, let's learn about you," Patty said, breaking the silence.

Oh no! I thought. *This is the part when everyone says their name and talks about themselves.* I hated doing this, and for some reason, I always got extremely nervous. My heart started pounding, and I gripped my knees. My mind was blank as I tried to quickly plan what I would say. The only thing I could think of was *Hi, my name is Jason, and before I came here, I was trapped in a bathroom stall while two guys were getting it on.* I gritted my teeth and tried to force the thought from my brain. *You can do this*, I thought, giving myself a pep talk. I looked up, and yep, Patty was already staring at me.

"Jason, right?" Patty prompted.

"Yeah. Hi," I gave a half-hearted wave.

"Jason, why don't you tell the group a little bit about yourself?"

I felt my face flush as well as everyone's eyes on me. There were only about ten people in the room, but it might as well have been ten thousand. I quickly looked around, and mustering a smile, I responded to Patty's request. "Hi, I'm Jason, and I'm originally from Laguna Beach, California." That was it, that's all I had.

"Wow, Laguna Beach! I *love* Laguna Beach," Patty said. "You are so lucky to have grown up in such a beautiful place. You must have gone to the beach a lot." She was right. I was lucky. I wasn't a rich kid, but I was lucky enough to be raised in a wealthy town on the coast of Southern California. But for now, I was here at a group interview and I needed this job.

I quickly got myself together, and matching Patty's enthusiasm, I said, "Yes, Patty! I did spend a lot of time at the beach, and yes, I was *really lucky* to live in such a great town! And I feel equally lucky to begin a new adventure in this great, exciting city. And even better, the chance to work for a great company like the Gap! I'm excited and grateful for this amazing opportunity." End scene. The words came out of my mouth, and even though I heard a couple of scoffs from the group, I didn't care. This job was now mine to lose, and my dad didn't raise a loser. I focused on Patty and Kara with a K. If I looked around the group, I knew I would see rolling eyes or shaking heads disapproving my fake enthusiasm, but Patty, Kara, and I were connected. In their eyes at that moment, I was transformed into a model Gap employee. I joined the cult and drank the Kool-Aid. I knew exactly what they wanted to hear. To everyone else, I was mocking the process, but not to Patty and Kara. To them, I was right on track, and they could relate to my enthusiasm. They got it. I was halfway there.

"Thank you, Jason!" Patty said. "Thank you for being so candid and passionate about your hopes. I think we all should feel lucky for all the opportunities that come our way. I know I feel honored to be a manager at the Gap, and I'm sure Kara feels the same way."

Kara with a K nodded vigorously. I just stared at the two of them, smiling and focused on the task at hand. Get this job and a paycheck. The rest of the group told their names and the places they were from.

"Okay, now that we know a little bit about all of you, let's have some fun," Patty chirped.

Kara with a K walked over to a dressed-up mannequin and rolled it over to the group. "Okay, y'all," Kara said. "This is called Sell That Sweater Set!" Patty and Kara with a K both laughed. They probably came up with the name together.

Patty continued, "The sweater set is our best seller here at the Gap. We want you to be familiar with it, and we want you to get a chance to show off your selling skills to us." My heart pounded, knowing what they wanted us to do. "Who wants to start?" The room fell silent, and I knew I needed to jump at the opportunity.

"I'll do it," I said, standing up.

Both Patty and Kara were ecstatic with my enthusiasm. "Wow, Jason. That's just great!" Patty said.

I stood next to the mannequin dressed in a skirt and a light blue Gap sweater set. I didn't know what a sweater set was, but looking at the mannequin, I assumed it was a plain sweater with another buttoned sweater over it. Not rocket science. "Okay, Jason. Please pretend that Kara came into the Gap looking for a gift for her sister. How would you sell her this sweater set?"

I waited for more direction, but the room fell silent, awaiting my performance. I dared not to look over at the group by focusing on the mannequin. I felt my heart race as I glanced at Kara with a K. She was smiling, excited to play the fake customer. I took a breath, and without thinking, I began to speak in a rushed and slightly higher than usual voice. "This is a great sweater set. It's warm, it's fuzzy, and it's a nice blue color. And what's super cool is if you get hot, you can take the top sweater off and put it back on if you get cold again!"

The room echoed with laughter. Patty and Kara looked at me kindly, but I knew they desperately wished I'd nailed it, being their model interviewee. I quickly apologized and confessed I was nervous.

"That's all right, Jason. Good try. You did great!" Patty assured me.

"Yeah, right," I said, laughing at myself.

"No, really. It's not easy, but you will learn. Kara? Why don't you show the others how it's done!"

"I would love to, Patty! Hi, I'm Kara, and welcome to the Gap today. How can I help you?" she said to Patty. And yes, Patty was mouthing Kara's words.

"Thanks, Kara. It's nice to be here. I am looking for a gift for my sister. She is coming to visit, and I wanted to get her something cute."

"That is so nice. I have just the perfect thing for your sister. Have you seen our adorable sweater sets?"

"No, I haven't."

"Why, our sweater sets are great gifts and come in a rainbow of different colors to suit everyone's taste. This is the periwinkle set," Kara said, now pointing to the mannequin. "I love this color, and I love how it feels. I have owned a lot of sweaters, and this is by far the softest one I have ever felt."

"Wow, that is soft," Patty said, touching the sweater.

"What is your sister's favorite color?"

"She loves black."

"I love black too," Kara oozed. "Let me show you this same sweater set in black, and if you like, we can gift wrap it for you today."

"And that's how it's done, people!" Patty said, high-fiving Kara with a K.

"That's what I meant to say," I said out loud. Kara and Patty and the rest of the group laughed at my witty remark.

Everyone took a turn trying to sell a sweater set, and then Patty thanked us for coming in and told us she would notify the lucky person who would be invited to join the Gap family in a few days. I left the meeting feeling defeated and thinking that I'd lost the job, but I was also proud of challenging myself and facing my fears. *The Gap family, what a joke*, I thought as I left with the others.

When I got home, Koji was lying on the couch. I could tell from the multiple chip bags and beer bottles left on the coffee table that he hadn't moved much all day. "How'd it go?" he asked, stretching like a cat after a long nap in the sun.

"It was a disaster."

"No go, huh?"

"I'm not sure. I think I did all right. It's hard to tell." Ending Koji's interest in the interview part of my day, I said, "Dude. You will *never* guess what happened to me before my interview." I proceeded to tell Koji about meeting Nicki and then being trapped in the restroom by two horny guys. Koji rolled with laughter as I told him the details.

"Why?" he cried. "Why do these things always happen to you?"

"Dude, I have no idea, but it's like every day something weird happens to me."

My life had always been that way. For some reason, I often found myself in strange circumstances. Luckily, most of the time they were just funny things like witnessing two guys hooking up in a public restroom or dropping boxes of papers into the city streets. Koji was buzzed, and I wanted to catch up with him. I grabbed more beers from the fridge.

"When do you find out if you got the job, and more importantly, when are you going to call the hot Gap chick?" As soon as I was about to answer, the phone rang. "Got it," Koji said, jumping up and hobbling over to the phone. "Hello, Koji speaking." There was a pause, and then he said, "Yeah, he's right here." Koji looked at me with wide eyes. "It's Patty from the Gap," he whispered, handing me the receiver.

"Really?" I quickly put down my beer and grabbed the phone from Koji. "Hello, this is Jason."

"Hi, Jason! This is Patty! From the Gap!"

"Hi, Patty. How are you?" I said, even though I knew she was *just great!*

"I'm just great! And you?" she asked.

"I'm good. I just got home."

"Well, I am glad I reached you. It was such a pleasure meeting you today, and we were impressed with your enthusiasm at the interview."

"Thanks! I thought I blew it when I tried to sell the sweater set."

"No, no, you did great. We incorporate that exercise to see who in the group shows initiative. Trust me when I say your failed attempt was one of the better ones I've seen over the years."

"Really? Wow." I chuckled.

"We will train you on our selling techniques. You will learn the ins and outs of everything Gap."

"Are you saying I got the job?"

"Jason, it is my pleasure to tell you that you have been invited to join the Gap family! How does that sound?" she asked as if I'd just won a trip to Hawaii.

"Thank you. I'd love to join the Gap family." I looked at Koji by mistake. He was purposely biting his hand to prevent himself from laughing out loud. I quickly looked away, knowing I would burst out laughing too.

"Great, Jason. Is tomorrow too soon for you to come in for training?"

"Tomorrow's perfect."

"Wonderful! Come in at nine and check in with me or Kara. One of us will get you going."

"Thanks, Patty, for the opportunity."

"No problem, Jason. We will see you tomorrow."

I hung up the phone, and Koji unleashed his built-up laughter. "Dude, are you a part of the great Gap family?"

"Come on, dude. It's a job."

"I know, I know, but you have to admit it's pretty funny, right?"

"It's pretty funny," I admitted. "Shit! I just realized I only have one shirt and no money."

"No worries, I'll lend you a few bucks for a couple of shirts."

"Really? Are you sure?"

"Totally. You gotta be dressed right for your new family." He winked, pulling a long draw of his beer. "Besides, the way I see it, it's an investment in getting you off my couch!"

"Yeah, thanks." I picked up my beer and resumed drinking.

"So, are you going to call that chick?"

"No, not now."

"Why not?"

"I just met her, dude. It's way too soon. Besides, I'm definitely not calling her while you're in the room," I said.

"Whatever. If you're not going to call her, I'm gonna order a pizza."

"Now that's an amazing idea, the best you've had all day."

"Nope. Earlier, I jerked off."

"Oh! Way too much information."

"I'm just saying…it's better than pizza."

"Uh, I still think pizza is a better decision." I laughed.

We spent the rest of the evening eating pizza and drinking beers. I was stoked and relieved to have a job, even if it was only a retail position for the Gap. At least I was no longer a loser sleeping on a couch. Now I was an employed loser sleeping on a couch. It was a much higher caliber of loser.

Chapter Sixteen

I woke up early to Koji making coffee.

"Smells good, dude."

"I made extra. Grab a cup," he said, leaning against the kitchen counter. "I'm out of here for a few days. I have to go to Mendo and get a few things from my storage unit, and Star wants to visit her boyfriend."

"Say hi to Star for me. Oh, and can you ask her when the art show is?"

"You mean the one that has your huge face in it?" Koji laughed.

"Yeah, that one, asshole! The one your huge face should be in as well."

Koji waved a dismissive hand. "Will do, bro. Have a great first day at the Gap." He rinsed his cup and grabbed his car keys.

"Oh yeah, you can count on it!" I called after him. As I poured myself a cup of coffee, I noticed that Koji had left forty bucks under my car keys sitting on the counter. *Thanks, bro*, I thought as I pocketed the cash. *Now I can get a couple of shirts.*

I decided to take the Muni train instead of driving so I wouldn't have to worry about finding a place to park. I headed to the train and made my way downtown by eight thirty. I hesitated a moment before walking into the Gap. I wasn't nervous; I just felt more like, *here I go! Working at the Gap.* Don't get me wrong, I was grateful for the work even though it was minimum wage. I just wasn't excited about working at a clothing store and having to fold T-shirts and act overly cheerful about it.

Patty saw me come into the store. "There he is!" she said.

"Hey, Patty! How are you?"

She didn't answer my question about her well-being. Instead, she just rambled off a few instructions about what she wanted me to do and then said, "Okay, thanksss," lisping her *s* and quickly walking off.

My first task was to find Kara in the back office and fill out some paperwork. I followed Patty's directions to the back office and found Kara with a K sitting in what looked like a small broom closet converted into an office. "Hi, Kara," I said.

"Jason, right?" she asked, automatically turning her enthusiasm dial to level ten. "How are you this fine morning?" Before I could answer her question, she handed me a stack of papers and began blurting instructions on how to fill them out. When she finished rambling, she stood up and said, "Okay, sounds good? Okay, thanksss," lisping just like Patty had. Kara motioned for me to take her seat at the desk then left the office. I sat down and started filling out the paperwork. It was a lot of "initial here" and "sign here." I noticed some legal papers and tried to skim them. But honestly, when you're young and someone tells you to sign something, you pretty much just sign it. I worked for about fifteen minutes on the papers and was almost done when Kara with a K came back in. "So how are we doing! Did you finish?" she said in her Southern drawl.

"Yes, I'm just about done."

"Okay, great, Jason. Why that's just great! What I need you to do is shadow Marcus. He is one of our best folders. He'll show you the ropes for the first part of today. So, I'm going to need you to finish up on this here paperwork and head on out to the floor. Okay, thanksss!"

There it is again. How weird, I thought. It seemed that both Patty and Kara with a K were very manic. One second they would ask how you were doing, then cut you off by rambling on about something they needed you to do for them, then walk off saying, "Okay, thanksss!" with an overly excited emphasis on the *s*. I hadn't experienced anything like this before. It was as if corporate had a meeting about talking and directing with efficiency. I wondered if they taught a seminar called, *Pretending to Care and Getting It Done*. It seemed that once you became a part of the Gap family, it was all business. The Patty I'd spoken with on the phone and at the interview was now a swift-moving robot who barked orders. I didn't know how to handle this way of conversing, but I was in and only a week away from a paycheck.

I finished the paperwork and headed out to find Kara. She was standing with Patty, talking about displays and all things Gap. I handed Kara the paperwork. "Jason. That's Marcus over there," she said, pointing to the other side of the store at a tall black guy wearing a Gap women's sweater set in red. "He is going to teach you the art of the fold!"

"He's really good," Patty blurted out.

"Yes! He sure is. Marcus is one of our best, if not the best folder we have."

"Oh wow! Lucky me. I get to learn from the best!" I said with a chipper voice. They looked at me suspiciously. *Oh shit*, I thought. *They know I'm just making fun, but come on, they are way too impressed with someone's fucking T-shirt-folding skills*. Wanting to deflect, I quickly said, "I just want to thank both of you again for hiring me. I'm a little nervous and excited." This seemed to placate the suspicious thoughts I could see bouncing around in their heads.

"Oh. Well, it is our pleasure, Jason," Patty said. "We hope you will do great things here with us." They both turned to each other and, without skipping a beat, continued their dialogue about displays and mannequins and such.

I took that as my cue to head over to Marcus, Folder Extraordinaire. *Yup*, I confirmed. He was wearing a woman's sweater set, a pegged pair of khakis, and polished black penny loafers. His face shimmered with makeup, and diamond earrings pierced both ears. "Hi, are you Marcus?" I asked as I approached him.

He smiled. "Hi, yes, I'm Marcus," he said, flamboyantly placing his hand on his chest.

"I'm Jason," I said, extending my hand. He shook my hand with a dainty grip. I shook firmly, awkwardly crushing his limp fingers.

"Wow, you is strong. It is nice to meet you, Jason." He pursed his lips and examined me up and down. With a wave and a snap of his fingers, he said, "Congratulations on the job. I think you'll really like working here."

"Oh good. I am eager to get started. Patty and Kara said you could show me the ropes on folding?"

"Yes, I can, I sure can," he said in his soft voice. "Here, I got you something." He handed me one of the squares used for folding. It was just like the one I saw at the other Gap where I'd met Nicki the day before.

"Thanks," I said, taking the folding board from him.

"Don't say I never gave you nothing." Marcus smiled.

"Yeah, I guess I can't now," I said.

Marcus proceeded to teach me the art of folding T-shirts. It wasn't rocket science, but there was a technique to it. I was surprised how efficiently and quickly Marcus folded a large stack of T-shirts.

After a while, I was folding about five shirts to his ten. "Don't you worry, you'll get the hang of it soon enough," Marcus reassured me.

"I hope," I said as I fumbled with another shirt. I glanced at the clock on the wall and sighed. I'd only been at the store for about an hour. I was already feeling trapped in a dead-end job. *It's only the first hour, and I already want to quit*, I said to myself. I wasn't a quitter and had a great work ethic, but this was truly painful for a creative, right-brain thinker like myself. Folding T-shirts was pure torture. My day instantly got better when I looked over and saw Nicki watching me from across the store. I felt my face flush as I gave her a big smile. She walked over to Marcus and me folding away.

"Hey, girl!" Marcus said. "What are you doing over here?"

"I stopped by to see if my new friend got the job," she said, looking at me. "The shirt looks good." She pulled at my sleeve.

"Thanks," I said, still grinning.

"How do you two know each other?" Marcus asked. He looked back and forth at us, pursing his lips again.

"We met yesterday at my store."

"Oh, you is new friends, then. Darn girl, you always get the cute ones! I hoped he was on my team." Marcus pouted.

"Yeah, sorry, Marcus. I am on Nicki's team," I said. We all laughed.

"That's okay, boo. I still like you."

"Gee, thanks, Marcus," I said. "So, Nicki. What are you doing later?"

"Not sure. I thought I might wash my hair."

"Oh really?"

"Yeah, it's a hair-washing day," she said, stroking the side of her head.

"Well, I guess you don't want to go get a beer with me, then. You know because you need to wash your hair."

"I guess I could put it off 'til tomorrow, but I don't drink beer."

"Okay then, you don't get one. I get off at five. Where should we meet?"

"Why don't you just come by my place when you get off work?"

"Girl! You hardly know this boy. How you know he's not a murderer or something?" Marcus said.

"Yeah. How do you know I'm not a murderer?"

"I'll just have to take my chances." Nicki took out a dry-cleaning slip from her purse and wrote down her address. She told me it was close to the Gap she worked at. "You guys have fun today!" she said, faking an excited voice.

"Yeah, we'll have a blast." I scowled at her and laughed.

"Bye, Marcus," she said, hugging him. "Bye, Jason."

"What, no hug for me?" I held my arms apart, waiting for my hug.

"Nope, not for you." She laughed and turned to leave the store.

"You be nice to that girl." Marcus stared down at me.

"I hadn't planned on being anything but nice to her," I said. "She seems really nice." That was all it took for Marcus to open his book of gossip.

"Yeah, she's cool. She moved here from Colorado, and she plays the bass in a band. I used to date her roommate, Brian. That's how I met her. I won't go into detail but promise me you won't let her drink." I didn't think much about the warning because I had plenty of friends who liked to drink. Some of them could get pretty ugly when they'd had too much. I myself had had my fair share of regretful moments after drinking too many beers.

The rest of the day was filled with folding and folding and more folding. I noticed that after getting into the rhythm of folding, it made the time fly. I ate lunch with Marcus at Subway and discovered that he was hilarious. I liked when he snapped his fingers and started sentences with "Girl!" or "Child, please!" He was super funny and entertaining. He talked about growing up in Virginia and how his momma thought it was strange that he wanted to enter beauty pageants. He also talked about how his daddy hated him for being the way he was and that he hadn't talked to him in five years. I listened to his sad story of being a gay man in the South, and I didn't envy him.

"Well, at least you are a champion folder now," I said, trying to lighten the mood.

He dropped his chin to his chest and looked at me squarely before breaking out in laughter. "Honey, maybe I should call up my daddy and tell him all about my folding abilities! You is funny, Jason. I'm glad you came to work here."

"Me too, Marcus. You're all right in my book."

"Why, thank you, Jason. We is now friends."

"Deal."

"Well, I guess we better get back to folding. I'm sure the store is tore up by now!"

I couldn't wait until five. I was bored with folding and excited to go over to Nicki's for who knows what. Soon the clock struck five, and Patty and Kara with a K asked me to meet with them in the office. They asked how I liked the job and gave me a schedule. I asked about benefits, and they said that I would need to work forty hours a week to qualify. I told them that would be great and to schedule me for forty hours. They informed me that I was only scheduled for thirty-eight hours and that there were no other hours available. *Some family*, I thought.

With my first day done, I headed over to Nicki's. She had said it was easier to get to her place by taking the bus instead of the train. I was pleasantly surprised that the Muni bus was very efficient and only took about ten minutes to arrive. I was at Nicki's Gap in no time. I remembered I needed a couple more shirts, so I went inside and made a quick purchase. I noticed a guy dressing a mannequin in the window and thought that it looked a lot better than folding shirts. I decided that I would ask Patty about that job on Monday.

It was easy to find Nicki's place. I walked up to the door and pressed the buzzer, but no one answered. I waited for several seconds and buzzed again. Nothing. No one seemed to be home. As I was about to leave, a guy with long red hair walked up to the building. Marcus had described Nicki's roommate, his ex, as being a ginger with long hair. *Well, this must be him*, I thought. "Hi, are you Brian?" I asked.

"Who are you?" he asked.

"I'm a friend of Nicki's. I was supposed to meet her here."

"Nicki's in the hospital."

"What? What happened?"

"You obviously don't know Nicki very well," he said, passing me and searching for his keys to go inside.

"No, I just met her. We work together."

He looked at me with suspicion. "So, you know Marcus as well?"

"Yeah, I do. He mentioned you."

"Well, you can tell him to leave me alone, and as far as Nicki is concerned, she can find a new roommate."

I put my hand on his shoulder to prevent him from opening the door. "What happened?"

"Take your hands off me," he insisted.

I dropped my hand. "Sorry, I just want to know what happened to her."

He paused and then looked at me, obviously frustrated. "She's a drunk!"

"Drunk? She said she didn't drink."

Brian began laughing. "Oh my, that's a good one!" he said. "She's an alcoholic. Today, she was supposed to meet me at our landlord's office to try and stop them from evicting us for her continual belligerent tantrums. Instead, she decided to go to a bar. She showed up inebriated and proceeded to pass out after puking on his office floor. We couldn't wake her up, so the landlord called 911."

"Wow, that was quick," I said in disbelief. *How could that sweet girl I had just met be a total nightmare? Huh, and to think I was worried she might think I was trouble.*

Slamming the door shut, Brian disappeared inside. I almost went to the hospital but decided against it, and instead, I headed home to Koji's.

Koji was out of town, so I got a burrito from the taqueria across the street and grabbed a sixer from the liquor store. The taqueria was a new discovery for me, and there seemed to be one on every corner. It was basically a burrito bar, and for five bucks, you could get a burrito the size of your head, chock-full of whatever ingredients you desired. It was perfect for this couch-surfing Renaissance man.

I thought about Nicki and wondered why and how someone could become a total, fall-down drunk. My day had started with her telling me she didn't drink beer and ended with her in the hospital from alcohol poisoning. It was a shame. I really thought we'd had a connection, but I didn't want to get involved with someone who had such a big problem with booze. I liked to drink, but I never got like that…well, maybe a few times. But alcohol never ruled my life.

After ingesting half of my huge burrito and drinking a couple of beers, I decided to call Matt with an update on my life. I hadn't talked with him for a while and thought it would be good to hear his voice. Not to mention, I knew he would get a kick out of my adventures in the city thus far. I rang him up.

"Hello-my-name-is-Matt." He always answered the phone this way.

"Hello, this is Jason."

"Dude, what the hell? I tried calling you at your mom's, but she answered, so I hung up. She gives me the heebie-jeebies."

"Uh, sorry about that. I'm in SF touring Koji's couch." Before Matt could give me shit about Ashley, I told him everything, and by the end, we were both laughing, and he was genuinely happy for my little conquest. I told him about Nicki and her drunken behavior. He chuckled and said it sounded like she would make a perfect wife. That was Matt, always offering up great advice.

"I've been trying to get a hold of you. Maddison moved to SF," he said.

Maddison was a good friend of ours from Laguna who had dated our friend Brad. Maddison was cute, smart, and cultured. We never understood why she went out with Brad. He was the furthest thing from cute, smart, and cultured. Love is blind, I guess. Maddison had majored in art history and shared my love for art and anything vintage. We used to frequent museums and vintage clothing stores together looking for treasures that nobody else wanted. Even though she was attractive, and we were close, I only saw her in a sisterly way and not as a love interest.

"Really? That's great news."

"Yeah, she broke up with Brad and moved to the city. She asked me if you were there, but I didn't know. You want her number?"

"Yeah, of course. I'd love to see her." Matt gave me her new number, and I gave him Koji's number. "So, she finally ditched Brad, huh?"

"Yep, he's pretty broken up over it and is on a strict diet of vodka and OJ."

"Oh, brother, that sounds rough."

"It's pretty ugly." Matt chuckled.

Matt made fun of my new job as a T-shirt folder at the Gap, then reminded me of his friend Amy and her big-breasted roommates. Before hanging up the phone, I promised him I would call her and update him on their breasts.

I'd forgotten that he'd given me her number. I checked my wallet and found the note card that read *Amy, Matt's friend in SF.* I tucked it back in and decided to call Maddison. I was excited to talk to her and hopefully go to the Museum of Modern Art with her now that she was in the city. I dialed her number, but no one answered. The voice on the answering machine didn't match Maddison's, so I hung up without leaving a message. A half hour later, the phone rang. I answered, thinking it might be Matt calling back. "Hello, Koji's house."

"Jason!" a woman's voice said.

"Maddy!"

"Hey, mister, how are you?"

"Wow, I'm great. I just called you, but no one answered. I got your number from Matt."

"Yeah, me too. I just got off the phone with him. So, where are you?" she asked.

"I'm in the Castro staying with my friend Koji." Maddison didn't know Koji, but she was well aware of my situation with Ashley and had witnessed a lot of our drama. I didn't tell her about my sweet revenge. For some reason, I thought only a guy would appreciate that kind of story.

"Oh, so you are down there with all the boys," she said jokingly. We talked about Ashley and Brad and how we were both now single and how we should be each other's wingman. We laughed a lot, and it felt great to have another friend in the city. "So, what are you doing tonight?" she asked.

"I planned on digesting this huge burrito I just ate. I think I might die."

"Yeah, I think I had the same burrito problem yesterday. Well, if you are up to it, I'd like to go to this cool little bar in North Beach."

"Sure, why not? Sounds great." I was kind of broke and really didn't have money to go drinking, but I wanted to see her and catch up, so I grabbed the few dollars I had left. She gave me directions to her place. She lived in an upscale neighborhood called Russian Hill, which was across town from me.

After a train and a bus ride, I knocked on her door. She answered with a cheerful smile. Her blonde hair was cut short and suited her petite head. She reminded me of an old-fashioned movie star with a classic face; she looked like she could be in a movie with Clark Gable or someone like that. She was always impeccably dressed in vintage clothing. "Hey, you," she said. I hugged her, and she pulled away and looked me up and down. Her smile faded, looking concerned. "Are you okay?"

"Yeah, I'm fine."

"You're so skinny!"

"Yeah, I guess I lost a little weight."

"Geez! I'll say. You are skin and bones. As long as you're not sick." Her smile returned. She grabbed my hand and led me upstairs. I could hear people laughing in the apartment. "Hey, guys, this is Jason, my friend from Laguna Beach." Two girls and a guy were sitting in the small living room. The room was furnished with midcentury furniture. Maddison loved retro furniture, and she'd managed to live in the style of the 1940s and 1950s the best she could. She even had vintage magazines on the coffee table instead of new ones. I sometimes thought she'd lived during that time in a past life. She just had a look about her that was from that era.

"Hi," I said, giving a wave.

"Hello, I'm Audrey." She was pretty, and her smile was instantly infectious. Her short dark brown hair brushed over one eye. She wisped it to the side, showing her full face, as she stood to shake my hand. "I've heard a lot about you."

"Oh really?"

"Maddison said you are a great artist."

"Well, I wouldn't go that far," I said. "If I was a great artist, I wouldn't be folding T-shirts at the Gap." We both laughed.

"The Gap?" the guy said.

"Yes, I just started today."

"I work for the Gap as well," he said, pointing to himself.

"Well, that makes two of us, I guess."

"I'm Patrick." He stood up and shook my hand way too hard.

"Nice to meet you."

"Which store do you work at?" Patrick asked me.

"Embarcadero."

"Then you know Patty and Kara."

"You mean Kara with a K?" I said.

"Ha, yeah. Those girls are definitely high energy."

"That's an understatement." I chuckled. "Which store do you work at?"

"I don't. I work in corporate."

"Oh, I see. So, you don't fold T-shirts like me." Everyone laughed.

"No, my folding days are over. I'm now in charge of display."

My ears perked up when he said display. "You mean, like window displays?"

"Yes. Windows, kiosks, and shelves. Pretty much anything that is displayed, I have a hand in."

"Wow, that's cool." I noticed Maddison looking at me strangely, probably wondering why I was so interested in window displays.

"Hi, I'm Chloe," the girl sitting next to Patrick interrupted. By her body language, I could tell they were a couple.

"Oh, I'm sorry," Patrick said. "This is my fiancée, Chloe. We just got engaged."

"Cool, congratulations."

"Thanks," Chloe said, grabbing and interlocking her fingers with

Patrick's. They seemed really in love, and suddenly I missed that feeling they shared.

Chloe was dressed like Maddison in vintage clothing, and Patrick wore a fedora and what appeared to be a vintage suit. He looked straight out of an old gangster movie. I was wearing a pair of 501 Levi's and an old 1950s Pendleton shirt that had belonged to my dad. I'd discovered the Pendletons in his closet back in high school and liked them. You could always tell a Pendleton from a regular plaid shirt. There was something about the pattern or the colors they used that really set them apart. They had become the holy grail of shirts for vintage-clothing collectors.

"I like your shirt," Patrick said.

"Thanks. It used to be my dad's. He wore it when he was in high school."

"That's cool. He actually wore that in the fifties?" he asked, excited.

"Yeah, I have a few of them, but this is by far my favorite."

"It's a great shirt."

"Too bad I can't wear this at work," I said.

"Me too."

"We're heading over to Mr. Bings," Maddison said. "You guys want to join us?"

Patrick and Chloe declined. They were going to his place to plan wedding stuff. Audrey said that she might meet us there.

"It was nice meeting you all," I said as we turned to head back downstairs.

"You too," they all said.

"Oh wait! Jason," Patrick said as he hurried down the stairs after us. "Here's my card. We should have lunch sometime. I'm always down at the Embarcadero store checking on displays."

"Sounds great, thanks, I will."

"Okay, you kids, have a good time."

I slipped the card into my pocket. Maddison and I headed down a steep street to Mr. Bings, which I assumed was a popular dive bar. "God, I can't stand him!" Maddison said once we were out of earshot from her apartment.

"Patrick?"

"Yes, ugh. He's a total ass."

"Wow, you really don't like him. He seemed okay to me. Why don't you like him?"

"At first, he seems nice, but then his pompous, male chauvinistic side creeps out. He came around about a month ago and has been pretty much living at our place. All they do is hump ALL DAY. Seriously, *all day*."

I laughed hard at her frustration. "Wow. They've only known each other for a month?"

"Yes, and now they're getting married!"

"That's fast."

"You think? Don't get me wrong, I'm all for love at first sight, but this guy's an asshole. He is super controlling and belittles Chloe. The poor girl just takes it. Anyway, sorry. I'm just frustrated."

"No worries… So, is she moving out with him?"

"Yes. Next week they're moving to the East Bay to his amazing flat that has a bay view," she said sarcastically, mocking him. We both laughed.

"I've missed you, Mad."

"You as well. You sure you aren't sick?" she asked, referring to my thin build.

"I promise, well, at least not my body. My brain, however, I can't speak for." I laughed.

"All right. I just haven't seen you so skinny."

I guess I hadn't noticed my weight loss. I'd been way too consumed with my broken heart. "Don't worry, after a few more burritos, I will be fat as hell."

"That makes two of us." She patted her belly. We both laughed. "Well, here we are," she said as we rounded the corner. A large, illuminated sign blinked "Mr. Bings." It was a small corner bar that was a short walk from her apartment. We entered, and there were various guys yelling at a soccer game on TV. A few of them looked over and did a double take when they saw Maddison. She was a beacon of light in this kitschy dive bar. We found a small table in the back and ordered a couple pints of beer.

"Cheers," I said, lifting my glass.

"Cheers and welcome to SF," she said.

"You, too." We clinked glasses.

"Yeah, I guess you're right," she said. "Here's to new beginnings." We clinked our glasses a second time. "So, the Gap! Really! Why aren't you doing your art?"

"Trust me, I want to. I just don't have any leads here yet. I will, though," I said determinedly.

"So, how is the Gap?" She said this as if it were the worst job in the world.

"Well, if you like to be ordered around by overly fake and smiling cheerleaders and you like pretending that folding T-shirts is the best thing you've ever done, then it's pretty good."

"So, basically it sucks."

"Yeah, pretty much," I said, laughing. "I've had worse jobs, and well, it's a start." I told her about the copy delivery job, which triggered her to spit out her beer a few times from laughter.

"I can totally see you there just gawking at the billowing papers in the street!"

"It was poetic from an artistic point of view. Too bad nobody got it on film."

"You could call it *Lost Memo*," she said, laughing.

"Ha-ha, it was my accidental attempt at performance art. Hey, do you guys have another roommate lined up for Chloe's room?"

"No, we don't. Do you want to move in?" she asked enthusiastically.

"Totally! I'm literally sleeping on a couch right now, and I'm sure Koji doesn't want me to be a permanent fixture."

"I bet. I'll ask Audrey if she is okay with a boy rooming with us, but I don't see why she wouldn't be cool with it."

"How much is the rent?"

"Three hundred."

"Sounds good to me." I raised my glass.

"Roommates!" She lifted her glass.

"Roommates!"

Maddison told me that she'd gotten a job at the Circle Gallery selling art downtown. She invited me to see the installation and have lunch with her tomorrow. After a couple more beers and a lot of plan making, we headed back to her place. I hugged her goodbye on her front step and made my way to the bus stop.

I unlatched the door to Koji's apartment and heard his telephone ringing. I rushed in and answered it just in time. "Hello, Koji's house."

"Jason, it's Maddy. I talked with Audrey, and you're in."

"Awesome!"

"Can you move in next weekend?"

"Yeah, perfect. I'll have a paycheck by then for rent."

"Cool. I'm super excited," she said.

"Me too."

"I see museums in our near future."

"Totally."

"Well, good night."

"Night."

Chapter Seventeen

The next day was Saturday, and I had the day off from work. Maddison told me to stop by the Circle Gallery and check out the art. When I saw the gallery, I realized why they called it the Circle Gallery. The building had a huge semicircle built into the façade. It was interesting for sure, and I was excited to see some art. When I entered, I immediately saw Maddison talking with some prospective buyers. She winked and gave me a little wave with her hand low at her side.

Peter Max was on collection. I'd never heard of him, but by the prices, I assumed he was well known. His style was brightly colored pop art that looked like it would sell in a big New York gallery. I liked some of the pieces, but it wasn't really my cup of tea.

Soon, Maddison found me. "Hey! I can't get lunch, but I was wondering if you could help me set up my email?"

"Your what?"

"My dad bought me a computer and I need to set up my email."

"What's an email?" I asked.

"I don't know!" she said, laughing. "My dad said it's like a phone but on the computer. I figured since you use a computer for your graphics, you might know how to set it up."

"I can *try.*"

"Great! I get off at three. You want to meet me here or at my place?"

"I'll meet you here."

"Okay, I gotta go. I think I just sold a painting."

"Good luck."

"Thanks!" She hurried back to her customers.

I left the gallery, thinking about Nicki and hoping she was all right. I decided to stop by her work to see if she was there. When I entered the store, I saw her right away. She was, of course, folding T-shirts. She had her back to me.

"Hey, you," I said as I approached her.

She turned, and her eyes met mine. She looked dead tired. "Hey. I'm so sorry about yesterday."

"Are you okay?" I asked her.

"Um, yeah. I feel like crap, but I can't miss another day of work. I'll be fine. Brian told me some guy was waiting for me outside. I assumed it was you."

"Yep, I was that some guy. He was pretty mad at you."

"He still is." Her spark was gone, and I could tell she was embarrassed by her actions.

"So, you still want to hang out?" I asked. I wasn't sure if I wanted to hang out with her, but I felt bad and didn't want to just kick her to the curb.

"You still want to hang out?" She smiled and punched my arm.

"Oh. So, now you're beating me? What's next?" I said, and we both laughed.

Nicki told me the story about her getting too drunk and passing out at her landlord's office. I already knew the entire story, and I pretended I was hearing it for the first time, but I appreciated her honesty. I asked her how she was back at work after having alcohol poisoning, but she laughed it off and said that Brian was exaggerating. I wasn't so sure.

"Thanks for not hating me."

"Hate you for getting too drunk? You're going to need to do a lot more than that to scare me off," I lied. I didn't hate her, but I thought she was fragile, and I didn't want to make her feel worse by expressing how I really felt. I didn't want to lead her on, but I didn't know what else to say.

Her eyes brightened. "I better get back to work. I was totally late today, and they're watching me like a hawk."

"Sure, no worries. I'll just call you later."

She went back to folding, and I turned to leave the store.

On my way out, I saw Patrick talking with two employees by the front window. I walked over, and not wanting to interrupt, I stood a few steps away, waiting to make myself known. Patrick finally saw me standing there. He smiled and put one finger up, gesturing for me to wait. He finished talking to the other employees and walked over. "Hey, Jason."

"What's up, Patrick?" I said, shaking his hand.

"Are you working here today?"

"No. I just left Maddison's gallery and decided to stop by to see my friend Nicki."

"Cool. I'm here working on an installation for Gap's new fragrance, Lavender."

"Awesome. Can I see what you're working on?"

"Totally." He showed me the window and how he wanted to display the bottles. He said he was having a problem getting the attention of the street traffic. I looked at the bottle of perfume. It said, "LAVENDER by the GAP." I remembered visiting a lavender farm by my mom's place with Ashley. They sold bundles of lavender tied up with twine.

"Why don't you line the bottom of the window with bunches of lavender? Then hang a blown-up picture of the bottle with the word *lavender* on the wall."

"Hmm, bunches of lavender." Patrick's face lit up. I told him about the lavender farm and that it was only a couple of hours away. He asked me if I could help him source the farm. Creativity came easily to me, and a window display needed a creative person. I followed Patrick over to the other two employees who were trying to plan out the window. "Hey, guys, this is Jason. He works down at the Embarcadero store and has a great idea for the Lavender campaign." Patrick told them about the farm, and they seemed to like the idea. Either that or they just went along with whatever Patrick said. That seemed to be the Gap corporate family way.

"Well, I better get going," I said to Patrick.

"Let me walk you out." Patrick followed me outside. "At Maddison's, you mentioned you're an artist."

"I am."

"What kind of art do you do?"

"Well, back home I was a graphic designer for a few different surf and ski companies. Now that I am here, I don't have the same connections, hence the T-shirt-folding job."

"I can tell you are creative, and I really like your idea about the lavender bundles for the window display."

"Thanks. I think it'll look great."

"Have you thought about working in display for the Gap?" Those words were music to my ears. I was trying to find a way to bring it up, and I didn't know if it was even possible to get a job like that without experience.

"Actually, yes, I have."

"Well, this might just work out. We've decided to add another display person at our flagship store on Market Street. You would work alongside Chris. He handles all the displays there, which is a tremendous amount of work for one person."

"Really? That sounds terrific!"

"No promises," Patrick said. "I will arrange for you to shadow the display person at Embarcadero and see where it goes. If it works out, then you will need to interview for the position."

"Sounds great to me. Thank you so much!"

"No problem. Thank you for the lavender idea. Let me know what you find out about the farm." He handed me another card just in case I lost the first one.

"Will do," I said. I could kind of see what Maddison was talking about. Patrick was very fast-paced and, in a way, kind of pushy. I guessed you needed to be that way if you wanted to make it in the corporate world. Whether he was an asshole or not, he was the guy who was going to get me on the display team and off the T-shirt team.

On my way back to the Circle Gallery to help Maddison with her email account, I noticed a little, secluded courtyard park. An ivy-colored wall enclosed the courtyard, and the iron gate leading inside was open. I was reminded of my gate and the ivy-covered wall that guarded my special place. I entered the courtyard, and to my surprise, it was empty of people. It was almost as if it was private property and I wasn't supposed to be there, but I decided to take advantage of the solitude regardless. It was a simple square courtyard with one large tree in the center surrounded by four benches.

I sat on a bench, tilted my head back, and looked straight up. I could see spots of sun filtering through the large branches. The light glinted and caused my eyes to squint and blink. I closed them and took a deep breath. It seemed like months since I'd really breathed deeply. With my eyes closed, I thought about how the universe was guiding me and how many coincidences had occurred since arriving in the city. I'd only been here a short time, but I'd already experienced so much, and I felt really connected to the universe. It felt amazing. I realized that all the meditation and focused energy practice I'd done at my mom's cabin was already having an effect on my life.

I tried meditating to reach my special place, but the sounds of the city and my overloaded mind wouldn't allow it. It had been so easy before, but now it felt like the first time I'd tried to do it at my mom's cabin. I felt a little sad, like I'd lost something, and I hoped I would find somewhere in the city where I could find my special place again. I needed to remain grounded, and the only way I could achieve that was to visit beyond my gate.

I opened my eyes and sat still for a few minutes. I noticed a homeless man rolling his overfilled shopping cart into the courtyard. He didn't notice me at first, but as soon as he did, he said, "Hey, man, you got a dollar?" He was wearing military fatigues and guessing his age to be about the same as my dad's, I thought he might be a Vietnam vet. I'd seen a few homeless vets in the city, and like them, he looked broken and at the bottom. I felt bad for him, as I felt for all soldiers who had to kill and be killed for nothing. I searched my pocket and pulled out a one-dollar bill. I extended my hand.

He limped over and took the money. "Thanks, man. God bless you."

I didn't know where my life was leading or what would happen to me, but I knew that I never wanted to be homeless or without love. I retreated from the park as two other homeless people entered. I must have found just a brief moment in time that the park was vacant. I was grateful for that tiny moment and moved on.

I waited on a bench outside the Circle Gallery for Maddison. She must've noticed me and came out to wave me in. She said the gallery was empty and her boss had left for the day. We sat among the pop art and talked. I told her about Nicki and that I had run into Patrick.

"Ugh! I really dislike him, but if he gets you that job, I will rethink," she said.

I told her briefly about my mom's house and astral projecting to the city.

She laughed and said, "Maybe Nicki is your soul mate and the universe decided to send you a drunk girl!"

"Yeah, thanks. That's just what I need. Besides, I don't think Nicki's the one. She doesn't have long, spirally hair."

"Wait, what?"

I told her about my mom's predictions.

Maddison laughed. "Wow! She got it all down to the fluffy black-and-white pet."

"I know, it sounds weird, but when you come from a planet far away like my mom, it makes perfect sense!" I smiled.

"Well, I hope it comes true." She patted me on the shoulder.

"Wouldn't that be something…"

"Okay, we're out of here."

"Don't you need to stay until three?"

"Nope. I think the art buyers are done for the day, and I'm over it." Maddison was funny that way. She didn't take things too seriously, and she appeared to be a young soul. She was kind of flighty, unlike me; I was constantly worried and frightened about every little thing. I wished I didn't care as much, like Maddison. Maybe one day.

Maddison interrupted my thoughts when she came from the back office with her purse slung over her shoulder, keys jangling from her hand. We closed the gallery and walked up the hill to Maddison's place.

"I am never going to get used to these hills," she said, out of breath.

"Yeah, you're telling me," I said, also out of breath. We walked up the small flight of stairs to her apartment.

"I'm home!" Maddison yelled as we opened the door.

"Hey!" Audrey yelled from the kitchen. "Are you hungry?"

"Starving! I have Jason with me."

"Oh, hey!" she shouted as we started up the stairs.

"Hello!" We went into the kitchen, where Audrey was stirring a large pot.

"Good thing I made a lot," she said, smiling at us.

"It smells great," Maddison said as she just about stuck her entire head into the pot to see what was bubbling inside.

"I got a bunch of free pasta and sauces from work," Audrey said. "They only keep it for two days before they throw it out."

"Mm, it really smells good! Audrey works at a super fancy restaurant down the street," Maddison said.

"Are you a cook?" I asked.

"No, not yet. I'm a waitress."

"She should be a cook," Maddison said.

"Aw, thanks!"

"Seriously! This girl is the best chef...I am telling you." Maddison grabbed a bottle of wine and poured three glasses.

"Oh, thanks," I said as she handed me one.

"So, I hear you're our new roommate," Audrey said, happily accepting a glass of wine.

"Yes, only if you're okay with it," I said.

"Since you're Maddison's friend and she trusts you, then so do I," Audrey said.

"Then, yes. I am your new roommate. Cheers!" I lifted my glass. Maddison and Audrey touched their glasses to mine, and we all took a sip.

Audrey went back to stirring her sauce. I couldn't help but check her out. She was wearing a tiny top and cotton short shorts that were, well, *short*. She was super tan and had a nice figure. She was obviously comfortable with her body, and she didn't seem to mind that I saw her in skimpy clothing.

Maddison noticed me looking at Audrey's lower half and made a joke by slapping her butt. "Look at that ass!"

Audrey jumped when she felt the slap but didn't seem to mind.

"I wish I had your ass," Maddison said. I said nothing. "It's okay, Audrey doesn't like boys."

"Maddison!" Audrey scolded.

"What? He's gonna find out sooner or later. Plus, it's not like you're in the closet."

"True," Audrey said.

"It's probably better that he knows he has zero chance." Maddison laughed.

"I wasn't even checking out her ass," I said, obviously lying.

"Oh, you were too! How could you not? It's amazing!"

"Okay, that's enough about my ass." Audrey left the kitchen and quickly came back wearing a pair of sweats.

"Oh, now that's no fun," Maddison said.

"Wow, Maddy, you are really fascinated by her ass," I said.

"Yeah, I wonder about you sometimes." Audrey smiled.

"Well, all I can say is I don't have any plans to change sides. But if I did, your ass would be the first one I'd grab."

"Wait," I said. "Does this mean I can check out your ass and it's not creepy?" I asked Audrey.

"No," she replied.

"The boy's got a point, Audrey."

"I promise I won't look," I said. We all laughed.

"Food's ready, so grab a bowl," Audrey announced.

I took a bite. "This is delicious." I steadily shoveled spoonful after spoonful into my mouth. "Thank you so much."

"No problem, enjoy. I need to take a shower," Audrey said.

"You're not going to eat with us?" Maddison asked.

"No, I already ate at work. I have a date, so I'll leave you guys to it."

"Oh, a date? Which one is it tonight?" Maddison asked.

"God!" Audrey said. "You make me sound like a whore."

"Hey, if the shoe fits…" Maddison teased.

Audrey grabbed the hand towel hanging on the stove and threw it at Maddison, missing her head. "I'm not a whore," Audrey said, walking away. "I just have a lot of friends."

"Yeah, right. Friends!" Maddison said sarcastically. Then she turned to me and said, "Lots and lots of friends."

"I heard that!" Audrey yelled from the hallway. We heard the bathroom door close and the water turn on.

"Well, that was weird," I said.

"Yeah, Audrey's ass is always good for a laugh."

"I must say I'm a bit relieved she's gay," I said with my mouth full of pasta.

"I bet. Imagine your frustration seeing her every day and thinking you might have a chance."

I choked on a little bit of pasta at Maddison's comment. "Yeah, this is way better."

"Speaking of ass, are you going to call drunk girl?" Maddison had a funny way of giving people nicknames that were literal to their looks or actions. Poor Nicki was now forever the "drunk girl" to Maddison.

"Not sure. I like her, but honestly, I'm a bit scared of her drinking abilities."

"Yeah, I can see why you might shy away from that. Not to mention, she wouldn't be a cheap date."

"No, I suspect not."

"Just tell her you can't afford her drinking habit." Maddison chuckled.

"Yeah, that's nice."

"It's the truth."

"I wouldn't even bother, but she seemed so damn cool and cute."

"What about this Star girl...the one with the photos? I really want to go to her show and see your big face."

"Not a chance! I'm doing my best to forget that ever happened."

"C'mon, it's not like you're naked. It's just your face."

"Yeah, my huge fucking face bigger than life on the wall. I think I prefer a naked photo of myself."

"I can see if we have a space large enough at the gallery for your giant head."

"Yeah, that's just what I want. I don't think Star and I will be a thing. She's more like a sister. Besides, I think I scared her away with my laughing fit at the Toronado."

"I'm bummed I missed that one!"

"Well, I think if I was with you, it might not have happened. I think it was the combination of culture shock and being nervous about being on a date with someone other than Ashley. I like her though, and she's a good photographer. We'll definitely be friends."

"You never know..."

"This is true," I said. "Enough about me and my female conquests, or lack thereof. How about you?"

"No, not this lady. I'm taking a break from boys."

"Let me guess, Brad tarnished the male species for you." I teased.

"Not exactly. I just need a man, and Brad is still such a boy."

"Oh man, I wish I could record that!"

"Don't you dare tell Matt I said that."

"I won't. I don't really like Brad anyway. Brad never liked me because he was jealous of my close friendship with Matt. Guys can get jealous over their friends. Not sure why, but it happens."

"I can see that."

"I have to say though, you are a bit older than Brad," I said.

"What?" Maddison threw the dish towel at me. "I am, like, two years older! It's not like I robbed the cradle. Oh wait, that's what you did with Ashley."

"Ashley was eighteen, and I was twenty-one. We were only three years apart."

"Yeah, that's still a big difference at that age, Mr. Man!"

"Yeah, I guess so."

"No wonder she left you. She was way too young to settle down. Not to mention, so are you."

"Well, I guess," I said, looking down.

"Aw, I'm sorry. I didn't mean to get you all sad about it."

"It's all good. I get more mad than sad these days."

"Perhaps you should call her for some more revenge sex!"

"That actually sounds pretty good right now," I joked. "Well, let's see this computer you speak of." I rinsed my pasta dish in the sink.

"Okay. It's in my room, follow me." We went down the hall and into her room. It was nice, and as expected, it was furnished with vintage items. "Sorry, it's messy."

"Like I give a shit." I turned her computer on, and she handed me a small box with what looked like a phone line connected to it. "What is this?" I asked, examining the box.

"I think that's a modem."

"What's a modem?" I'd been using computers for a few years, but I had never used email. It was new technology.

"I think it plugs into the wall and then into the computer."

"So, it's a computer phone?" I said, confused.

"If I knew that, I would be able to hook it up myself."

"Let's see if we can make it work." I tried to hook it up several different ways, but I ended up frustrated and defeated an hour later.

"That's okay," Maddison said assuredly. "I'll call my dad and maybe he can walk me through it."

"Sorry. If Koji was in town, he might be able to help, but he won't be back until tomorrow night."

"Whatever, it's not like I need to email someone right away."

"All right, I'm gonna head home. I need to take a shower."

"Oh okay. I was thinking of going to the MOMA tomorrow if you—"

"Yes!" I said, cutting her off.

She laughed. "I knew you couldn't resist a museum. I'll meet you there, say, eleven?"

"Sounds good. Where is it located?" I waited while she wrote down the directions. "Cool. Can't wait," I said after she handed them to me.

"Me too. I haven't been, and I hear it's supposed to be really good."

"Well, I'll see you tomorrow," I said.

"Oh wait, let me show you the room before you leave."

"Right on."

"It's right across from mine."

I walked out of her room, and Maddison passed me. She opened the door to Chloe's room. She reached in, and with a lift and a shove of something, the door opened all the way.

"What was that?" I asked.

"Oh, that's just the bed."

"What?"

"Yeah, you have to lift the corner of the bed to get the door all the way open." Maddison laughed. I walked in and saw the smallest bedroom I'd ever seen.

"Wow! That is small."

"We prefer the word *petite*," Maddison said.

The room appeared to be more like a tiny walk-in closet than a bedroom. It was maybe six by eight feet. "It's better than a couch any day."

"It's cozy." Maddison smiled at me.

"Yeah, *that's* the word I would use. Well, I'm off, so see you mañana."

"Ciao," Maddison said. "I'll tell Audrey's ass you said goodnight."

"Oh, please do, by all means," I said, descending the stairs.

Chapter Eighteen

I headed back to Koji's and jumped in the shower. I heard the phone ring and rushed to dry off before sprinting down the hallway. "Koji's house," I answered.

"Jason," a man's deep voice said. To my surprise, it was my dad.

"Hey, Pops. What's up?"

"Well, I was going to ask you that same thing," he said sternly. I could always tell when my dad was mad or annoyed with me. It was the way he talked to me like I was still twelve and in trouble for something.

"I'm in San Francisco," I said, trying to convey excitement.

"Yeah, I know."

"Oh right, you just called me," I said, laughing. "How did you know I was here?"

"I saw your friend Matt at the beach. He told me you were in San Francisco. I thought you were at your mom's?"

"I was, but now I'm here."

"I see." There were a few seconds of silence. I could tell he was annoyed that I hadn't told him about my plans. I just wanted to show him I could make it on my own. For me, that wasn't possible if I talked to him. His idea of doing things always seemed to clash with mine.

"So, how's it going?" I said, making small talk.

"Well, Jason. I'm just trying to figure out what you are doing with yourself and why you didn't let me know where you are. I'd like to know what's happening with my son."

"Sorry, Pop. Right now I'm staying at Koji's, but next weekend, I'm moving in with Maddison. You remember Maddison from Laguna?"

"Is that something you can afford?" My dad meant well, but sometimes his caring was overwhelming.

"Yeah, it's just a room I'm renting from her and her roommate. I just got a job, so I will be fine."

"I see. Are they okay living with a guy?"

"No. I forced my way in and said I'm living here."

"Jason, I am just trying to figure out what you are doing."

"Then just ask me like a normal person and not like a private investigator."

"Well, I'm not trying to sound like a private investigator."

"Well, sometimes you do."

"Excuse me if I'm interested in what my son is up to."

"Honestly, Pop, I'm fine. I'm hanging out with some old friends, and I'm making new ones. I have a job, and I'm happier than I've been in a long time."

My dad's tone changed after I told him I was happy. He saw how Ashley's games had destroyed me and was worried about me. I thought about telling him about the copy delivery job, but as soon as I was about to, I stopped. I figured he would just tell me that I should have done a better job or something like that. I loved that story and didn't want him to take the joy of it away. I loved my dad, but we saw the world differently. I was, however, more grateful than I could ever show him. He had taught me to be courageous and to never give up. He was always a great inspiration to me when times got hard. We talked for a while about random things and then said goodbye. It was good to hear from my dad, but there was a reason I was keeping my distance and not calling him. I was trying to make it on my own, and I wanted him to respect me as a man.

As soon as we hung up, the phone rang again. I almost didn't answer it, thinking it might be my dad forgetting something. "Koji's house," I said.

"Hello-my-name-is-Matt," he said, announcing himself.

"Hey, what's up?"

"Someone wants to talk to you." I heard him handing over the phone.

"Hey, man," a voice said. I knew instantly it was Brad, Maddison's ex.

"What's up, Brad?" I said.

"Not much, man. How's the city?"

Knowing why he wanted to talk to me, I got straight to it. "You mean, how's Maddison doing in the big city?" I laughed.

"Oh, is she up there?"

"He's on his fifth vodka and OJ," Matt yelled in the background.

"Dude! You need to slow your roll," I said.

"So, how is she?" Brad asked.

Brad and I weren't great friends, and he was asking a favor as if we were close. I was Maddison's friend and was definitely on her side if there were going to be sides. But I could hear the despair in his voice, and having just gone through the same thing myself, I bowed to his plea. "She's okay, I guess."

"What do you mean by that?"

"Well, she's working at a gallery, and honestly, if you must know, she has zero interest in dating anyone. I think you broke her." I chuckled.

The line went silent, then Matt picked it back up. "What was that all about? He's a mess and just wants to see if she's dating anyone."

"Yeah, no problem, glad to help," I said sarcastically.

"Don't take it personally," Matt said.

"Whatever. If he wants to find out about her, he should call her, not me, and not be such a dick."

"So, what's up with you?" Matt asked, trying to change the subject.

"Not much, just doing my thing."

"How's folding T-shirts?"

"Great, and it's going to change into window display if I play my cards right."

"Well, I guess that's better," Matt said. "By the way, I ran into your dad at the beach."

"Yeah, I just talked to him. Thanks." I laughed.

"He was taking photos of Lori by the water."

"Oh no, really?"

"Yeah, it was pretty awesome. She had a tiny bikini on."

My dad had fallen in love with Lori, a young aerobics instructor. After knowing each other for about three months, they were engaged. She was pretty, and all my friends teased me about it. They would say, "How's your stepmom?" or "How are those titties?" My dad, being a photographer, had taken a series of artistic nudes of her. Let's just say they were all over the house like a shrine. It was annoying. My friends, on the other hand, loved coming over and seeing half-naked Lori on the walls.

"Your stepmom's hot," Matt teased.

"Uh, nope."

"I pretty much just want to talk about your stepmom's tits," Matt said, laughing. I hung up on him, hoping he wouldn't call back. He didn't.

I thought of Nicki and decided to call and see how she was doing. The phone rang a few times before her answering machine picked up. I hung up without leaving a message. I was really attracted to her, but I wished she didn't have such a problem with booze.

Chapter Nineteen

The next day, Maddison and I had a great time at the San Francisco Museum of Modern Art. The museum was showing a special exhibit of Ansel Adams's photography. I loved his work and lost myself in his dark landscapes for a while. Maddison loved modern art, so we would usually split up for a bit when we went to museums and then walk through the Impressionists section together. It was amazing to see such great works of art, especially works that were painted so many years ago by the masters.

My favorite painting of all time is Van Gogh's *Irises*. I first saw it on display at the Getty Museum in Los Angeles, and it stopped me in my tracks. I stared at it for at least an hour. Sometimes I would drive two hours in traffic from Laguna Beach to L.A. just to see it.

We spent a few hours studying the art and then headed back to Maddison's and ordered a pizza. She said the best pizza in SF was at Escape from New York. She'd called and ordered a large pie for us to share.

"So, are you folding shirts tomorrow?" Maddison asked.

"Yep. I'm the shirt folder tomorrow, but at some point, I'm supposed to shadow the person who handles visual display. Patrick was supposed to talk with my manager and set it up."

"You should be doing art."

"Yeah, you and I both know this," I said. "The problem is no one else does."

About twenty minutes went by before the doorbell rang. Maddison went downstairs and answered the door.

"That will be fifteen twenty-five," I heard the pizza guy say to Maddison.

"Jason, can you spot me a five?" Maddison yelled from downstairs.

"Yeah, just a sec." I jumped up and started digging through the wadded-up dollars in my pocket. I found a five-dollar bill and headed downstairs. As I got to the door, I stepped around Maddison to hand the pizza guy my five dollars. I immediately recognized his pale skin, jet-black hair, and lanky frame. "What the hell?" I said as I saw the one and only Damien Kirk standing in Maddison's doorway, holding our pizza. He was a friend from Orange County.

"Dude!" Damien said, looking up as my words broke his money-counting concentration.

"What are you doing here?" I said, still holding out the five dollars.

"Wow, this is fucking weird," Damien said.

"Yeah, you think? Maddison, this is Damien Kirk from Laguna. He worked at Mark's record store."

"Oh yeah, I remember you. Wow, so everyone is moving up here!"

"No, now that I moved here, they're all staying back there." He grinned.

"Yeah, I guess we should probably move back, then," I said. "It's been a long time. How are you?"

"I'm good. As you can see, I'm a big success," he said. We all laughed. "Do you live here?" He looked up at the building.

"No, well, yeah—I mean, not yet. I move in next weekend. I'm staying at my friend Koji's for now."

"Jason is a professional T-shirt folder," Maddison said, laughing.

"Fuck you, Maddison." I laughed back.

"What? You mean we're both a success?" Damien said.

"Uh, yeah, that's it. I got a job at the Gap."

"The Gap! You?" Damien asked.

"Yeah, I know, and trust me, it's temporary."

"That's fucking awesome!" Damien laughed.

"Oh, tell him about the mannequins!" Maddison said

"Oh yeah. I may be dressing mannequins soon."

"Dude! Can you get me one?"

"How did I know you would ask me that? I really don't think they're giving them away." I remembered Damien had a couple of mannequins back home. He'd kept one in the back of his Cadillac hearse he'd bought from a mortuary. The other one had resided in his bathroom, holding the toilet paper. He was crude but creative.

"I gotta go. I have more deliveries, but here's my number," Damien said as he scratched his number on our receipt. I gave him Koji and Maddison's number. "How random seeing you here."

"I know," I said. "I'll call you this week for sure."

"Right on," he said. "Well, you guys have a good night."

"That was so weird," I said to Maddison as we climbed up the stairs.

"What are the odds?" She shook her head.

"Weird things are happening for sure! I gotta call Matt. Can I use your phone?"

"Yeah, but don't tell him you're here."

"Oh right. Brad."

"Yeah, Brad."

"I'll wait until I get home. I'm starving. Let's try this super yummy pizza you've been talking about."

We ate what was, yes, one of the best pizzas I'd ever had. I was happy and excited about hanging out with Damien soon. We had been pretty good friends back home, and I had hung out with him whenever I wanted to tie one on. Let's just say whenever I hung out with Damien, I ended up with a major hangover.

After a while of talking, eating pizza, and drinking some beers, I felt my eyes getting heavy. "I'm super tired. I think I will head home."

"You can stay in Chloe's room. She's staying at Patrick's now."

"Thanks, but I need to wear my Gap clothes for tomorrow."

"I think I have a sweater set you can borrow." She giggled.

"Well, I wouldn't be the first guy at the Gap to wear that," I said, referring to Marcus.

"What? A guy was wearing a sweater set?"

"Yeah, his name is Marcus, and he's actually really cool. You would love him. He was dating the drunk girl's, I mean, Nicki's roommate."

"I definitely want to meet this Marcus."

"On that note, I'm out of here," I said, grabbing my jacket. "I'll catch up with you in the next day or so."

"Sounds good, mister."

The bus was pretty empty, and I made it home quickly. I was happy to be learning my way around this busy city. I was starting to get my city legs. I called Matt, who was drunk, as usual, on a Sunday. I wondered why a lot of my friends were drunks. I tried to tell him about the coincidence of seeing Damien, but he just kept rambling about boobs and some girl he'd met at a strip club. He accidently hung up on me, and I didn't call him back.

A few hours later, Koji came home from Mendocino. "Hey, man, how goes it?" Koji said as he walked into the living room. He dropped his backpack on the floor with a thud. Raising his hands above his head, he yawned and stretched like a lion.

"What's up, traveling man?" I said back. "Beer's in the fridge."

"You read my mind." He grabbed a beer from the fridge and popped the top. He drank about half the beer in one swig, burped, and said, "I hate that drive."

"How was Mendo?" I asked.

Koji plopped down on the couch. "Mendo was Mendo, but it was good to see my mom. I just really hate that town now, and there's nothing there for me anymore. Not to mention, I had to watch Star and her ex rekindle whatever they have going on."

"Oh really, it was a cuddle fest?"

"I'll say. I mean, the guy's all right, but I think it's more lust for him and love for her."

"Why don't you say something?"

"I have, but Star does what Star wants."

"Yeah, I can see that about her. Well, I guess I'm officially in the friend zone with her."

"Yeah, I think you were always in the friend zone with her." Koji laughed.

"Why do you say that?"

"Dude, you and Star aren't a good match, anyway. She's way too mellow, and you are, well, you are you," Koji said.

"Thanks, I think. Jackass."

"No problem," Koji said, getting up and walking toward his room. "I'm down for the count."

"Right on. I work tomorrow, so I'll see you when I get home. Oh, and I'm moving out next week."

"Really?"

"Yeah, Maddison's."

"Man, you work quick."

"Well, I don't want to be on this couch for much longer."

"You know you're always welcome to dirty my couch anytime."

"Thanks, I think, again."

"No worries. Let's catch up tomorrow. I want to hear all about it."

"Will do."

"Night," Koji said, and he disappeared into his room.

Chapter Twenty

I needed to be at work by seven. Something about it being a delivery day. I headed out into the misty morning gloom of San Francisco. It was chilly, and I could smell the salt in the air from the ocean. I hurried to the Muni station and ran down the stairs to catch the arriving train. *Just in time*, I thought. I made it downtown thirty minutes early. Patty was inside, and I waved, getting her attention. She smiled and waved back really hard as if she was extremely excited to see me, but I was pretty sure it was just her normal wave.

"Hi, Jason. How are you, early birdy?" Patty said.

"I'm good, Patty, and you?"

"I am a nine and quickly moving toward a ten!"

"Oh, I see. That's a good number."

"Yes! It's always good to get started on a high number to carry you throughout the day."

"I'll remember that," I said. "So, Patty, did Patrick from corporate talk with you at all about me?"

"He did indeed, but first we need you to do the job you were hired for before we can entertain any other options. Does that sound good? Okay! So, why don't you start sprucing up the T-shirt section, then we will get started unboxing the new merchandise, *okay, thanksss.*" There it was again, that damn "Okay, thanks" line. It was like a corporate slap in the face. They list a bunch of stuff, say "okay, thanks," and walk away. What if I said, "No, it's not okay, thanks." Well, I would most likely get fired, but I really wanted to say it.

With sails deflated, I walked over to the sea of messed-up T-shirt stacks and started refolding them one by one. *Here goes the start of a very long day*, I said to myself. I looked across the store of disheveled shirts. As I folded, the employees filtered in one by one like sheep and soon fell in line folding and primping. Marcus came in and I was excited to see him. If I had to fold T-shirts all day, at least I could listen to the hilarious rants of Marcus. He saw me and waved like he was both on a model runway and a parade float at the same time. I smiled and waved back. I thought he would come over and start folding shirts with me, but he didn't. Instead, he rolled out two contraptions that looked like vacuum cleaners.

Patty gestured for me to come over. "Okay, Jason, you've met Marcus, correct?"

I smiled and acknowledged Marcus.

"Good to see you, Jason," Marcus said in a very professional way. He was holding back his full persona at work. I liked the over-the-top Marcus I'd had lunch with, but I knew why he wasn't being his "fabulous" self.

"Marcus is our resident visual-display person here," Patty said.

"Oh, I thought you folded shirts like me," I said to Marcus.

Patty explained that our store was one of the smallest in the city and that Marcus helped wherever he could when he was done with his displays. "Marcus, Jason will be shadowing you for a few days. Patrick just called me, and apparently, he wants to fast-track Jason into visuals." I noticed that Patty looked a little pissed about it, but I didn't care.

"Oh my, you know Patrick?" Marcus said to me.

"Yeah, uh, yes, I do." I spared them the details on how I knew Patrick and just left it at that.

"Patrick wants you to show Jason how display works at the Gap," Patty instructed.

"I can certainly do that," Marcus said.

"Jason, I want you to spend the first half of the day with Marcus, and then after lunch, you can go back to the folding team."

"No problem, sounds great!" My sails were full once again.

"Well, let's you and I get this started," Marcus said. Patty left us standing next to a stack of about fifteen boxes and the two vacuum-looking contraptions.

"What are these?" I asked Marcus.

"Those are steamers. We is going to unpack and steam the new clothes before we dress the mannequins."

"Steamers, huh?"

"Mm-hmm. So, you must know Patrick *real* good."

"Why is that?"

"Well, you just got here and are already training for visuals."

"His fiancée and one of my best friends are roommates, and that's how we know each other."

"Oh, I see," Marcus said in an almost pouty tone.

"You don't think I am after your job, do you?"

"I hope not, as we just became friends and I worked really hard to get this job."

"Marcus don't worry. Between you and me, my Gap career is

definitely temporary. Plus, if I get the job, I will be working with Chris at the Market Street store."

Marcus's mood instantly improved. "Oh, Chris, I love that little man!"

"Yeah, Patrick said he's really cool."

Marcus and I steamed the clothes and hung them on a rolling garment rack. I was a little nervous about the whole display thing, but as soon as Marcus showed me the Gap corporate display guide folder, I knew it would be a breeze. "All we do is follow the diagrams in this folder?" I asked.

"Pretty much."

"How is that even creative?"

"Honey, it's not. The creative process starts way before us."

I was relieved that I wasn't responsible for creating window display designs, but at the same time, I felt a little unchallenged creatively. "Do you ever try to do your own thing?" I asked.

"That dream doesn't exist in the Gap world. Once I tried to mix it up and add my own flare without asking."

"What happened?"

"Let's just say there is a reason I work at the smallest store in the city," Marcus said, sounding defeated.

"Ouch, that sucks."

"You're telling me."

"What about the bigger stores?" I told Marcus about the window idea I had suggested to Patrick and that he had asked me to get the lavender from the farm I knew about.

"That was corporate. If Patrick was in an actual store working on a display, that means it's for a new item launch or something big."

"Yeah, it's for the new Lavender scents."

"Hate it!" Marcus said with attitude.

"What do you hate about it?"

"It's just cheap-ass spray from China. I think you can find the same spray at a drugstore!" Marcus laughed.

"You mean, like Patty's Teen Spirit spray?"

Marcus about fell over, and his eyes teared up. His hand covered his mouth, holding back his laughter. Knowing he knew what I was talking about, I started to laugh myself. I couldn't help it. With a burst, Marcus let it go all at once. His full and colorful laugh filled the room. His laugh reminded me of James Earl Jones's. It was deep and loud and just made you smile, if not laugh along. Now I knew why he'd been trying to hold it back. I looked over, and sure enough, Patty was staring at us, not impressed by our behavior.

"Oh shit, she's coming. Shh, Marcus, Marcus!" I said in a loud whisper. Marcus contained his laughter by biting his lip.

Patty approached us. "Hey, you guys. Are we having fun over here?"

"Ms. Patty, I am sorry for my outburst. Jason told me this funny joke, and well, nature took its course." At this point, both of us could smell Patty's overuse of Teen Spirit. I avoided eye contact with Marcus, knowing it would surely cause another outburst.

"Okay, guys. Let's keep focused. Don't make me separate you two," she said, trying to make a joke.

"Don't worry, Ms. Patty. We'll be good boys from now on." Marcus smiled. Patty walked away, and as she did, Marcus looked at me. His eyes were still tearing and wide open. I looked away, feeling another bout of uncontrollable laughter building. I walked away and went to the bathroom.

When I returned, Marcus was calm and dressing a mannequin to the specs of the corporate guidebook. "Where did you run off to?" Marcus asked.

"I had to leave before I exploded."

"Did you smell it?" he said, asking if I could smell Patty's perfume.

"How could I not?"

"That stuff is nasty. How do you know what Teen Spirit is?"

I told him the story about my girlfriend in junior high who wore it. I also told him about my interview and how I had asked Patty if she was wearing Teen Spirit.

Marcus looked as if he was dying inside. "Don't tell me anymore, save it for lunch. I am going to split a rib if you keep going."

I stopped talking about Patty's perfume and refocused on steaming. Although I was making meager wages, I was having a lot of fun. Working with Marcus was more like hanging out with a friend who always made you laugh.

Marcus and I ended up eating lunch at Subway. We joked and laughed about Patty and Kara with a K. I told Marcus about Maddison, and well, I told him a little bit about everything. Marcus had the best quality all friends should have: he was a good listener.

After lunch, Marcus taught me how to decipher the corporate manual and dress the mannequins depicted in the photo diagrams. After a couple of hours of mannequin dressing 101, I ended the day folding T-shirts and watching pretty girls walk by. *This job's not so bad*, I thought. Before I knew it, I was off work and heading home.

On the Muni ride home, I fell into a daydream. I thought about fishing and Old Man Dave. I thought about my gate and my special place. I closed my eyes and tried to breathe deeply and meditate. It didn't work. I wasn't sure why I tried while riding in a bus.

When I got home, Star was sitting at the kitchen table, and Koji was making burgers.

"Hey! What's up, Star?" I walked over and gave her a hug.

"What, no hug for me?" Koji held his arms out.

"I'll give you a hug," I said, holding up a fist.

"Real nice." Koji laughed. "Sometimes a guy needs a hug too."

"Well, someday that might happen for ya," I said, and we all laughed.

"Aw, I'll give you a hug," Star said, throwing her arms around Koji's neck.

"Yay! I got a hug," Koji said. He headed toward the back door. "Hey, man, you want a burger? I've already grilled some up."

"Why, yes, sir."

"Koji tells me you've been a busy guy," Star said.

"Yeah, I guess."

"Where did you find a place to rent?" she asked.

"My friend Maddison has a place in Russian Hill."

"Oh, fancy town!" Star winked at me.

"I wouldn't exactly say fancy. My room is smaller than most closets," I said. Koji walked in from the backyard and plopped down a plate with a burnt burger on it for me. "Nice," I said. "Thanks."

"No problemo, amigo," Koji said.

"Oh, I forgot!" I said, jumping up. "I need to call my mom."

"What for?" Koji asked.

"I need to find out about a lavender farm."

"A what?"

"Never mind," I said as I abandoned my charred burger. I dialed my mom's number. As it began ringing, I took a deep breath. I never knew what I was getting into when I called her, but I always needed to take a few deep breaths. She answered, and I asked her about the lavender farm. She was able to give me the information and the phone number. Apparently, she knew the lady who owned the farm. My mom had sold her some pottery for her gift shop. I thanked her and got off the phone quickly. "Wow!" I said, hanging up.

"What?" Koji asked.

"That was about the easiest, unemotional phone call I've ever had with my mom."

"She's that bad?" Star asked.

"Well, let's just say, I pity the girl who marries me," I said.

"Oh. I'll keep that in mind." Star laughed.

"Oh, I forgot," Koji shouted from the grill. "You got a message."

I perked up, thinking it might be Nicki. I had planned on calling her.

"Some guy named Damien called about an hour ago," Koji said.

"Oh cool."

"Who's Damien?" Star asked.

"He's a friend from SoCal who lives here now. He delivers pizza for

Escape from New York."

"I love that pizza," she said.

"Yeah, me too," I agreed.

"He said something about you meeting him at Club Deluxe in the Upper Haight," Koji said.

"Club Deluxe?" I asked.

"Yeah. It's a cool-people bar," Koji said.

"What does that mean?"

"You know, the cool rockabilly guys who dress like they're from the fifties and hang out in a greaser gang. Kinda like you," Koji said, laughing.

"Whatever," I said, dismissing his dig on my style.

"I think they swing dance there," Star said.

"Swing dance?" I asked.

"Yeah. I went there with my friend. Her boyfriend is a swing dance teacher. They drink cocktails, play music from the forties, and dance."

I dialed Damien's number, and he picked up quickly.

"What." Damien rudely answered the phone.

"Hey, Damien."

"Hay is for asshole horses."

"Okay, well, I will remember that," I said, confused by his meaningless statement. "It's Jason, by the way."

"Oh, hey, man. I called you."

"Yeah, I just got the message."

"You want to go out?"

"I'm not sure. I work tomorrow, and I don't want to be all hungover."

"I'm only going for a couple of hours. This band I want to see is playing there. It should be good."

"Cool, yeah, I'm in. Should I meet you there?"

"No, come over here and we can walk there together."

"Right on." Damien gave me his address, and with Koji's help, I figured out where he lived. "You guys want to go?" I asked him and Star.

"No, I'm not in a swinging mood," Koji said.

"I would, but I need to get home and work on my project," Star said.

"Oh yeah, when is that, by the way?"

"Early next month," she said. "They had to push it back because the current artist at the gallery is staying longer."

"Thank God!" I said, laughing.

"Hey!"

"I'm totally kidding. I can't wait to see my huge head on the wall of an art gallery." I laughed.

"It's going to be fine," she said. I wasn't so sure.

Chapter Twenty-One

With the little map Koji drew for me, I navigated the city streets. Damien lived on the way to Haight Street, which ended up being just a short walk up a really, really steep hill to his apartment. After about ten minutes of huffing and puffing, I found his building and rang number seven. I waited. Nothing. I rang again. The second time, the door buzzed loudly with electricity as it unlocked. I was still getting used to the electric locks. I quickly opened the door and headed inside. I found my way to the elevator and pressed the button for the second floor. Based on the postmodern architecture and décor, I could tell the building was designed in the 1960s, and it hadn't been renovated. The elevator struggled upward, and I worried for a moment until the door opened.

I found Damien's apartment by simply following the loud punk rock music. I knocked on number seven, and Damien yelled, "It's open!" I opened the door and was greeted by wafts of cigarette smoke and dirty clothes. Damien's apartment looked exactly like I thought it would. The walls were covered with vintage records and posters of bands he liked. Stacked against the walls on the floor were hundreds of vinyl records. Rows and rows of records. Damien was sitting, flipping through them when I came in.

"Hey," I said.

"Hey back. I'm looking for Gary Numan."

"Noooo!" I pleaded. Gary Numan was Damien's favorite artist from the eighties, and he loved to play the same song over and over while staring at a static station on his TV. It was incredibly annoying, and for some reason, he picked right now to do it. "Dude! *Please* not the Gary Numan torture," I said, laughing.

"But you like Gary Numan."

"I do, but not the way you do."

"All right, how about some Threads?"

"Yes! Great idea." It had been a while since I'd heard my friend Mark's band. Damien quickly found the LP record and put it on. The room filled with a fast-yelling punk rock pop tune, and my head bobbed along with the beat. "So, what's this bar like?" I asked.

"It's pretty lame, but it's pretty cool."

"What does that even mean?" I shook my head. Damien was a very confusing friend to have. He often said things that really made no sense to anyone but himself. He was rude to most people, but if he called you his friend, he was true blue.

"The place is cool. It's just that there are some douchebags who hang out there. I mean, they wear fucking zoot suits. Zoot suits."

"Zoot suits?"

"Yeah, you know, like the forties zoot suits, bright yellow and a way too long jacket with a dangling chain pocket watch."

"Yeah, I think I know what you are talking about. Jim Carrey in *The Mask*?"

"Exactly. They wear their garb and swing dance."

"What's wrong with that?" The whole swing dancing thing sounded kind of cool.

"Don't get me wrong. The swing dancing is totally cool. The swing kids of the forties were like the punk rock kids of the seventies and eighties. It's just the zoot suit riot guys think they're too cool for school. Anyway, they're just annoying, but the chicks are hot."

"Oh yeah?" I said, perking up to this news flash.

"Yeah. They dress in vintage clothes and are just super-hot."

"Well, let's get there and check it out."

"Okay, I just need to get ready. There's beer in the fridge." Damien disappeared into the bathroom and closed the door.

I grabbed a beer from the fridge and browsed through Damien's weird collection of posters and records. He had funny vintage record covers on the wall. My favorite cover was of a sassy guy with a trumpet and a bolero outfit. Next to him was a lady caressing him. The album was called *What Now My Love. Wow, he must slay the ladies with his crazy trumpet skills*, I thought, sitting on the couch and swigging my beer. The phone rang on the coffee table in front of me. "Should I get that?" I shouted to Damien.

"Yeah," he shouted back.

I picked up the receiver. "Hello, Damien's house."

"Hello-my-name-is-Matt."

"Hey, man! It's Jason, what's up?"

"I see you found Damien."

"Yup." I swallowed the last of my beer. "He delivered a pizza to Maddison's house the other night. It was weird seeing him appear at the door with a pizza, out of the blue."

"That's spooky. Sometimes I think Damien is not of this earth," Matt said.

"I'll say. So, what's up with you?"

"Well, I just found out from Mark that Damien moved there. That's how I got the number, so I thought I'd give him a call to let him know you were there as well."

"Cool. We are actually listening to a Threads album as we speak."

"That's the other reason why I'm calling. Mark's band is playing up there at the Purple Onion."

"Right on. When are they playing?"

"In a few weeks. I'm hoping I can crash at Damien's."

"It would be awesome to see you, man."

"Yeah, for sure. What are you two up to for the night?"

"We're going to a club in the Haight."

"Which one?"

"I think it's called Deluxe?"

"That place is pretty swanky."

"So I hear. I'm gonna get me a swing dance girl." I laughed.

"Dude, Amy hangs out there with her roommates. You should call her."

"Maybe another time. I want to catch up with Damien."

"Aw, how romantic." Matt laughed.

"Fuck off." I laughed back.

"So, when do you move into Maddison's?"

"Next weekend. I'm super excited to finally have a room of my own."

"It might be a good idea with all that jerking off you do!"

"Hey, a guy's got to do what a guy's got to do." I said, jokingly.

Damien came out of the bathroom with his freshly coiffed hairdo. "Nice hairdo," I said.

"Thanks, it is nice," Damien said.

"What's that stuff you put in your hair?" I asked him.

"Brylcreem. It's what the guys wore back in the day."

"Can I try some?" I felt the top of my head and decided it needed some slicking back before we hit the town.

"Yeah, go for it."

"Here, Matt's on the phone. Later, Matt." I handed the phone over to Damien and headed to the bathroom to fix myself up a bit. I closed the door and looked in the mirror to assess my hair. As I looked, I caught myself in a moment. It was very strange. I had obviously looked at myself in the mirror thousands of times in my life, but this time, something was different. Something had shifted or changed, as if I'd seen myself instantly age, but not literally or physically. I felt different, and somehow, I'd witnessed the change. This feeling scared me a bit. It was difficult to explain, but all I knew was I felt older and wiser, and I had changed in that tiny moment of time. *That was weird*, I thought, shaking my head.

I found Damien's hair cream lying on the counter among the used toothbrushes and gross brushes covered in hair. *Brylcreem, huh?* I read the tube of clear goo. I squeezed a dollop of goo into the palm of my hand and rubbed it together with my other hand. I dragged my fingers through my hair, creating a slick new do. I liked slicking back my hair into a 1950s-style pomp, but I'd never used this brand of gel before. It was thin and greasy, unlike the waxy pomade I usually used. I took a long look in the mirror. The feeling I'd had before was gone, but the vision still rattled me. I shrugged my shoulders and took one last look before I headed out.

Damien was sitting on the couch, shoveling a slice of leftover pizza into his mouth.

"Can I get a slice?"

"Yeah, over there." He pointed toward the kitchen counter, where several pizza boxes were stacked. I lifted the top one and found an assortment of pizza slices inside.

"How old is this pizza?" I said, looking over at Damien.

"Yesterday," he said as he struggled to swallow the huge mouthful of pizza. I chose a slice of cheese, avoiding day-old meat. Who knew how old it really was.

"Do you have a microwave?"

Damien shook his head, his mouth stuffed like a chipmunk's.

I laughed at his gluttonous pizza ambitions. "Maybe, you should slow down."

He swallowed hard and said, "I hate it. I'm so fucking sick of pizza. I eat it as fast as I can just so I can get full and be done with it."

"I can see how that would happen," I said, taking a bite of the cold slice. "Mm, still good to me!" I happily chewed away.

"I get all the leftovers from the restaurant."

"That's pretty cool, free food."

"Until you're sick of it. You ready to head out?"

"Yep, let's go."

We left the apartment and walked through the brisk air and darkened streets toward the famous Haight-Ashbury District. I thought about the feeling I got in the mirror and decided to ask Damien about it. Damien was a pretty "out there" person, but he did have some moments of sincerity and caring attributes. "So, have you ever felt yourself get older?"

"Whataya mean?" Damien said, obviously confused by my question, and rightly so.

"Well, I felt myself get older today when I was looking in your bathroom mirror. I felt myself instantly age."

"Dude, what are you smoking?" Damien laughed.

"Never mind."

"No, sorry, dude. It just sounds weird is all."

"I know. I had an epiphany, and I feel like I've hit the next major step in life. In fact, I am no longer Jason."

"What? Now you're starting to worry me."

"I'm serious. I no longer identify with Jason."

"*Okaaayy*," he said, still sounding uneasy and somewhat confused by my strange behavior. "So, if you're not Jason, who are you?"

"J," I said instantly. Just J."

"What does that even mean?"

"Not J-a-y, just the letter J."

"Ha-ha, dude, you've lost it!"

"I'm serious. I'm now known as J. Don't call me Jason." I demanded it so.

"Whatever, dude—I mean, *J*. You are now officially weirder than me!"

"I guess so," I said. I'd had this feeling a few times in my life. It was always a confirmation that I was on my path. When these epiphanies happened, I would get a huge endorphin rush and an overwhelming feeling of peace and comfort. It was as if the universe was giving me a big bear hug. I rarely told anyone about my experiences because they were too difficult to explain, and this was no different. I was excited and felt like I'd officially become a man and the universe was preparing me for growth and opportunity. It wasn't until this moment that I felt my soul grow another notch. I was no longer Jason. To me, Jason was a boy's name, and a simple, sharp J was a man's name. *From this day forward, I will be J.*

Soon, we arrived at Haight Street. It was filled with people of all kinds: hippies, punks, grunge, tourists, and homeless people panhandling. Each panhandler was trying to be more creative than the other, hoping to get you to let loose of some change. One sign stood out above all. It simply read, "BEER." *Winner!* I thought as I gave the holder of the sign a dollar.

"Dude! Don't give them money," Damien scolded me. He worked on the street and knew the dynamics and was jaded by the constant begging of the homeless in droves. A few blocks later, we stopped in front of Club Deluxe. The exterior was tiled with mint and black squares and had a large chrome door with a porthole window that asserted its 1940s vibe. It was a little intimidating, and I found myself becoming nervous as we approached the door. Even though I'd turned twenty-one two years ago, I always felt anxious walking into a bar. Usually, I would be asked to leave immediately because I looked too young. I always needed to convince the bouncer I was of age. It was embarrassing, and I always felt like everyone was staring at me, thinking I was just a kid. I sucked in my breath and thought about my dad. I remembered him saying to me, "If you are ever nervous about doing something, just pretend you own wherever you are, even if you're only walking into a place to order a sandwich. If you pretend to own the place, you'll get what you need." Resolved, I walked up and grabbed the door. I forcefully pulled it open, maybe too forcefully because groups of people sitting at tables all turned their heads in my direction. I smiled at them as I pretended to confidently stride in. They all looked for a moment and went back to mingling. *No bouncer, yay me, I'm a man!* I thought.

The club was packed, and I felt like I'd gone back in time. Big band musicians were playing swing music to my left, and people dressed in vintage clothing were dancing in pairs. I looked to my right and saw a nice bar constructed with mahogany. Bottles of top-shelf alcohol were illuminated behind bartenders who had slicked-back hair and wore white shirts with black ties. The whole place looked like the interior of a 1940s cruise ship. Matt had been dead-on when he said this place was swanky.

I noticed a guy at the bar ordering a drink. He looked familiar to me. I couldn't place where I knew him from, but I knew I'd seen him before. Probably at a party somewhere in Orange County. He turned around, drinks in hand, and did a slight double take when he saw me. I watched as he walked the drinks over to two girls sitting at a table. Both girls had dark hair and porcelain complexions. They were both attractive. I wasn't sure why, but I felt compelled to walk over to them. Matt had told me that his friend Amy hung out at this bar. At that moment, I was one hundred percent sure one of them was Amy. It was a strong gut feeling that I couldn't explain. I just knew. Everything in the city so far had been one huge string of coincidences, from Damien calling me to go to this club and Matt calling Damien's house just as we were listening to our friend Mark's band. The same Mark who had given Matt the phone number to call who then informed me that Amy hung out at the same club we were going to. I felt now that I was supposed to be friends with Amy.

For whatever reason, it was to be determined. Tonight, I could feel the universe pulling me toward the two girls sitting at the table. It was as if I already knew them without actually knowing them. I started having the same feeling I'd had back at Damien's house when I looked in the mirror, but it wasn't about me. It was more of a direction to go. Out of character, I headed straight over to them, and without skipping a beat I said, "Which one of you is Amy?" I looked back and forth at them as they looked at me, puzzled.

"Uh, I am," the girl on my left said cautiously. I was so sure I was supposed to meet her that it didn't surprise me when I was right. "Do I know you?" she asked.

"Hi, I'm Matt's friend."

"Wait! Are you Jason?" she asked, looking up at me. Her eyes sparkled green.

"Actually, it's J."

"Oh okay. Matt told me he had a friend who was moving here and that you were cool. It's nice to meet you, J." She stuck out her petite hand.

"You, too." I smiled and gently shook her hand. Amy was way prettier than I thought she would be. I didn't know why I'd thought this because Matt dated pretty girls. It was just that she was really put together. Matt's girls were pretty but tended to be a little rough around the edges. Amy was upper crust for sure and way out of my league, and Matt's.

"These are my friends, Sean and Angie. They're from Orange County as well."

"Hey, guys," I said.

"Hey, nice to meet you. You look familiar," Sean said.

"Yeah, so do you. I saw you at the bar and recognized you from Orange County. It's why I thought one of you might be Amy. I just told my friend Matt, uh, well, our friend"—I looked at Amy—"that I was going to Club Deluxe. He said you hung out here and that you might be here tonight."

"So, you asked the first two girls you saw, 'Which one of you is Amy?'" Angie asked.

"Uh, yeah, pretty much," I said, as if it wasn't a big deal.

"Wow, what are the chances of that?" Sean said.

"The way my life has been going, pretty good." I laughed. "And seeing you from Orange County, I thought maybe you knew Matt, and Amy."

"Still," Sean said, "that's pretty random."

"I agree," Amy said. "I guess we were meant to be friends." She smiled at me.

"Looks that way. I could always use more friends here."

"Well, a friend of Matt is a friend of mine," she said.

"You might want to rethink that. I know a lot of his friends, and well…" I teased.

"I'm trying to figure out where I know you from. You look super familiar," Sean said.

"I know I've seen you somewhere, but I can't place it. I grew up in Laguna Beach."

"I grew up in Huntington Beach," he said.

"Oh, well, I used to hang out there all the time."

"That must be it. We probably went to the same show or party," Sean said.

"Small world." I looked over and saw Damien at the bar trying to order a drink but failing among the crowds. "I'm going to get a drink. I'll be right back." I walked over to Damien, and patting him on the back, I told him I would get this round.

"Good luck," he said.

I stood there and waited for a moment and then I heard it. I heard a girl call the bartender by his name, Mike. I thought about my dad, *own the place.* I took a breath and shouted, "Hey, Mike!" As I did, Mike the bartender looked over at me. With a smile, I said, "Hey, what's up, Mike? Can I get two gin and tonics over here?" He looked puzzled, trying to figure out how I knew him or how he knew me. Strengthening the charade, I said, "How you been?"

His confusion was my gain. He didn't want to be embarrassed about not remembering someone. He walked over, and I extended my hand. He shook my hand, still trying to place my face. Assuming he must know me, he became cheerful. "How's it going?" he asked.

"I'm good. What's new?"

"Not much. Same ol' thing, different day."

"Tell me about it."

"You want gin and tonics?"

"Yeah. Thanks, man."

Mike the bartender made quick work of our drinks and then slid them over to me. I handed him my money, but he waved his hand and smiled. "I got it…it's on the house."

"Wow! Thanks, Mike." I grabbed the drinks and turned to a dumbfounded Damien, who stared at me in utter amazement.

"What the hell just happened? You don't even know that guy!"

"You and I know that, but he doesn't."

"Dude! That was pure genius."

I motioned for Damien to follow me as I headed back to the table where Amy, Angie, and Sean were sitting. "Hey, guys. This is my friend Damien. He's from Orange County too."

"Wait. I recognize you. You've delivered pizza to my place," Amy said.

"I remember you. Your roommates have big boobs." Damien grinned.

"Yep, they definitely do." Amy laughed.

"Are they here?" Damien asked, looking around.

I could see that Amy wasn't sure if he was being funny or creepy, but I knew it was the latter. "No, sorry, they're not here tonight," Amy said, dashing Damien's dream.

"Damien is also a friend of Matt," I said to Amy.

"Really? That's cool."

"You know Matt?" Damien asked.

"I do, we're friends," Amy said.

"What kind of friends?" Damien asked.

I softly swiped Damien across the shoulder for being too nosy. "Dude, c'mon."

"It's all right, I don't mind," Amy said gently. "We dated briefly, but now we're just friends."

I looked at Amy and remembered the day Matt received the package from her in the mail with toys from Chinatown and the San Francisco postcard with her lipstick kiss on it. I remembered reading the postcard and thinking she was a cool chick. I had told Matt he should stop chasing whores and be with someone better, like Amy. *What a dumbass*, I thought as I looked at Amy. She was pretty, really pretty. She had long, straight black hair with short bangs cut like Bettie Page, the pinup girl from the 1950s. She was wearing a red, form-fitting Mandarin collar dress and vintage high heels. I could see why Matt wanted to have a fling with her.

Sean had his arm around Angie. She was also very pretty and wore a 1940s-style dress. Sean's reddish hair was slicked back, and I could tell he was of Irish descent. He looked at me. "Hey, J. How did you get those drinks so fast?"

"It was amazing!" Damien blurted out.

I proceeded to tell them how I knew but didn't know the bartender and how I got the drinks for free.

"Nice! I will definitely try that one." Sean high-fived me.

"Thanks." I smiled.

"So, are you guys going to dance?" Amy looked at me then Damien.

"Uh…I don't exactly dance, per say," I said. "Do you swing dance?"

"I do, I love it." She smiled.

"Yeah, it sounds fun. I'd like to learn sometime—"

"Hey, Amy!" A deep voice rang out, interrupting our conversation.

"Carson! Hi, handsome," Amy said. "I was beginning to think you couldn't make it."

He casually kissed her on the cheek. *Hmm*, I thought. Carson looked like a stereotypical all-American star quarterback. He was tall, handsome, and way too charming. He had perfectly straight teeth and, of course, dimples. I hated guys like that. They had it way too easy. Carson was dressed in a nice vintage suit, and his light brown hair was slicked back.

I looked over at Damien, who rolled his eyes back at me. I frowned at him and quickly shook my head as if to say, *don't say anything stupid*. Damien could literally, at any moment, make everyone around him want to kill him with just a few strategically placed words.

"Carson. This is Angie and Sean, my friends from Orange County I told you about. And this is J. and Damien. They're from Orange County as well."

"Hey, nice to meet you guys." Carson grinned. "Are we dancing?" He extended his hand to Amy.

"Yes!" Amy took a sip of her drink before taking his hand. He escorted her to the dance floor. A new band had come onstage, all dressed in a similar style of vintage clothing. The four band members—a singer, a stand-up bass player, a drummer, and a guitarist—started to play a song that was familiar to me. I'd heard it from one of my dad's big band records he sometimes played.

As the music started to rumble and the rhythm roared, the lead crooned in a Frank Sinatra–sounding voice through a vintage microphone. Carson and Amy moved smoothly as if they had danced together many times. They were great. He spun and twisted her around, sometimes dropping her close to the floor and swinging her back up and over and around his shoulders, then back to the ground. He smiled, and she laughed. Everyone on the floor twisted and turned and kicked just like dancers from an old movie. I'd had no idea there was a resurgence of swing. It was amazing, and I couldn't wait to learn it myself. Amy was adorable, and I was envious of Carson.

When the song ended, Amy, now out of breath, headed back to our table.

"You were so cute!" Angie said.

"Yeah, that was awesome. You are really good," I said.

"Not even," Amy said. "You should see some of the other dancers here. They're remarkable." She took a sip from her drink and looked up at me. "You should try it, J."

"There's *no way* I'm dancing here tonight. I have no clue what to do or even how to begin."

"If you like, I can teach you what I know," Amy offered.

"Really?" I asked.

"Of course. Why not?" she said.

"That would be great." I smiled.

"Amy! Amy!" Carson shouted from across the bar. He was sitting with a group of swing dancers and was waving her over.

"Go ahead!" Angie said. "Our flight tomorrow is really early, so we're gonna head out."

"Are you sure?" Amy said. Angie and Sean nodded. "It was so great to see you guys. I'm happy you were able to come up for the weekend." Amy and Angie hugged.

"I'll miss you. When are you coming out for a visit?" Sean's chain wallet clinked as he hugged Amy.

"I'll miss you, too. Hopefully soon." Amy hugged Sean again. I got the feeling that Amy and Sean had been friends for a while.

"It was nice meeting you guys, have a safe trip," I said to Angie and Sean.

"Yeah, you too, man." Sean said. I shook Sean's hand, then he and Angie headed toward the exit.

"I wonder if you and Sean met before. It seems like it," Amy said to me.

"Yeah, it is weird. How do you know Angie and Sean?"

"I grew up with Sean…he's a dear friend of mine. We used to go to the same punk/goth shows and dance clubs back in the eighties. He dated my best friend Denise. I met Angie when they started dating last year, but I don't get to see them as much as I'd like to. Anyway, are you guys gonna hang out here?"

"Sure, for a bit."

"Oh good. I'll see you later then." She waved and turned, then headed over to Carson and his cool-kids group.

Damien and I replaced Amy and Angie at the table. We sat sipping our drinks.

"The girls in this bar are stuck up," Damien said.

"Yeah, maybe, but Amy seems really cool."

"You mean the Amy who's with Carson?" He laughed.

"Maybe they're just friends. She wasn't with him when we got here…"

"Dude, you are delusional. You see what Carson looks like, right? He looks like fucking *Chris Isaak*. Did you see them dancing? They're totally fucking."

"You're probably right, but I like her. There's something about that girl."

"Whoa! First, you tell me that you saw yourself age in the mirror, then you decide to change your name to J, and now, you have a short conversation with a girl and suddenly she is something special." Damien reached across the small cocktail table and put his hand on my shoulder. "Dude. You really need to get laid."

"Oh really? When's the last time you got laid?" I laughed.

"Last night!" Damien held up his hand and laughed.

"Yeah…not the same."

"Nobody does me like Rosey does!" He smirked. "By the way, how did you know that was Matt's Amy?"

"I didn't, but when I saw Sean with them, I just had this gut feeling.

And tonight, Matt told me that Amy hangs out here."

"Hmm, I have to admit, that's pretty strange."

"Yeah, no doubt."

I thought about how random it was. I walked into this bar, walked over to two strangers, and asked which one Amy was. Out of a packed club, Amy was one of those two girls. Sean was right. *What are the odds of that?* I thought.

I excused myself and waited in line to use the restroom. After relieving myself at one of the urinals, I walked over to the sink to wash my hands. I quickly glanced up at the mirror, but this time I didn't get a strange, aging epiphany. Oh no, this time I was met by the most horrific white-man, Jheri-curled, greasy ringlet hair I'd ever seen. *No!* I thought. *Nooooo! My hair has been like this the whole time?* I had wavy hair to begin with, but I could control it with a thick, waxy pomade. But when I added the thin, greasy Brylcreem and took a brisk walk in the San Francisco fog, my hair went *crazy*. It was so fucking curly and greasy looking. I was mortified. All I needed was some gold chains and Koji's purple silk shirt. *Why didn't Damien say anything?* I thought. *I look like fucking Richard Simmons!* I did my best to wipe my hair with paper towels. It was no use. The curly, greasy do was here to stay.

I headed back out and sat down. "Dude! Why didn't you tell me I have a fucking Afro?" I said, pointing to my hair.

Damien started laughing hysterically. He pointed at me with one hand and covered his mouth with the other.

"Nice. Thanks, Damien." I slouched in embarrassment.

"I didn't even notice, dude. Sorry." He tried to contain himself.

"How could you not notice?"

"What happened?"

"Your fucking Brylcreem. That's what happened!"

"Oh yeah, that stuff's pretty greasy. I didn't realize you had such pretty curly hair." He lost it again.

"Fuck you," I said.

"Hey! You should go ask some girls to dance!" he teased. I kicked him under the table. "Ouch! C'mon…no need to get violent. I think it looks pretty."

"Yeah, very funny. I finally meet a cool girl who seems normal, and I look like Richard Simmons!"

"Oh shit, dude! You totally do look like Richard Simmons!" He covered his mouth again.

"You're such an asshole."

"You should get out there and do some *sweatin' to the oldies*." Damien laughed even harder.

"Okay, I admit that's funny. Fuck it." I had no choice but to join in and make fun of myself. It was funny. I relaxed as we laughed at my humiliating hair-*don't* and talked about old times. I told him a little bit about my recent retreat at my mom's, and he told me that I was officially crazy.

Behind me, I heard Carson's booming voice saying goodbye to his friends. I looked over and saw Carson holding Amy's hand as they walked out the door.

"Does that answer your question?" Damien asked.

"Yeah, I guess you're right."

"I am right, so drinks are on you!"

"Wait, I don't remember making a bet," I said.

At that moment, the door swung open and Amy walked back in. She looked over at me and smiled and then rushed over to the bar. *What is she doing?* I thought. *She must've left her credit card with the bartender.* She walked over and handed me a napkin with her name and number. I held the napkin and looked up at her.

"Sorry, I forgot to give you my number. Give me a call if you want to learn how to swing dance." She smiled.

"Uh, cool. I do, yeah…thanks." I smiled back.

"I can show you around town if you like. I know what it's like being new here."

"Uh, yeah. That would be great."

"Matt said great things about you, and I thought you might want to meet some people here."

"Yeah, for sure. Thanks, that's cool of you."

"No problem."

"Can your roommates come?" Damien interjected.

"Damien, shut up!" I snapped.

Amy looked at Damien pointedly. "Oh, honey." She patted him on the shoulder. "If they did, trust me, you couldn't handle either one of them!" she teased. "Okay, you guys, have a good night…I gotta go." She waved at us both and disappeared out the door.

I folded the napkin and stuffed it safely into my shirt pocket, then looked over at Damien. "Drinks are on you, I presume?"

"That did not just happen," Damien said.

"Read it and weep." I pulled the napkin out and slapped it across Damien's smug face.

"Yeah, whatever. You're in the friend zone. Plus, Matt boned her. Not to mention, she saw you with a Richard Simmons Afro." I kicked him again and he yelled out, "Ouch!"

"Sounds like someone's jealous. Anyway, dude. She's cool, and I don't care if I am in the friend zone. She's nice, and I feel like I was supposed to meet to her. I can totally feel my path."

"Dude, you've seriously lost it." Damien shook his head and got up to use the restroom. I sat and thought about the night. I thought about Damien's mirror and the change I went through. *It's so strange. I totally feel different.* I wished I were out with Maddison instead of Damien. I loved the guy, but Maddison would've been a way better wingman. I was excited about my new friend Amy, and I was looking forward to experiencing my next "coincidence." I was progressing in this city, I had a new friend, and I was going to learn how to swing dance. I had a job and soon would share an apartment with my good friend Maddison and her lesbian roommate. Not to mention, my friend Damien could get unlimited, free pizza. Life in the city was awesome.

Chapter Twenty-Two

Koji was asleep when I got home, so I called Matt. "Hello-my-name-is-Matt," he answered.

"Hey, man."

"Hey, what's up?"

"I met Amy!" I was still excited.

"You called her?"

"No. I ran into her at Club Deluxe."

"How did you know it was her?"

"Well, that's the weird part. I didn't."

"Uh, okay?"

"Yeah, it was weird. I walked in the door and saw two girls sitting at a table. I remembered you told me that Amy hung out there. For some reason, I walked over to them and said, 'Which one of you is Amy?'"

"Wait. She was one of them?"

"Yes! That's why I'm telling you the story."

"Oh, right." Matt laughed. "So, what you are saying is that you are magic."

"Exactly! It was one of the weirdest nights I've ever had. When she said she was Amy, I told her I was your friend—"

"And then she screamed?" Matt laughed.

"Actually, I'm surprised that didn't happen! Anyway, I told her who I was, and she remembered that you told her I was moving up here."

"I can't believe you randomly asked two girls if one of them was her."

"It was pretty strange."

"What would you have done if neither one of them was Amy?"

"I have no idea! You're an idiot, by the way, for not pursuing her."

"Well, she does live about five hundred miles from me. Are you guys going to hang out?"

"Yeah. She said she would show me around."

"Wait till you see her roommates!"

"Yeah, Damien told me."

"What? How does Damien know Amy's roommates?"

"He delivers pizza to them, and Amy recognized him at the club. Damien, of course, remembered her roommates' big boobs!"

"Sounds like something Damien would say," Matt said. We both laughed.

"He was in rare form, for sure," I said.

"I don't doubt that, but you gotta love him."

"Or not! So, hey, can I ask you a question?"

"Dude, green light. You can go out with her. Why do you think I told you to call her?"

"I thought you just wanted me to meet some people."

"I do, but when I was hanging out with her, she reminded me of you. She gave her roommate a tarot reading, and I told her that she would love you."

"But I don't do tarot."

"I know, but you've always been into all that weird shit."

"Weird shit, huh." I dismissed his ignorance. Matt was right, though. I'd always been interested in esoteric things. When I was young, a psychic told me that I had psychic energy and that I should pursue it. I'd always felt a strong pull leading me through life. I just assumed I got it from my mom.

"Yeah, I think she's perfect for you."

"Even if that's so, I think she's seeing someone. But thanks for the green light."

"Oh really?"

"Yeah, some tall, handsome, captain-of-the-football-team kind of guy. They were swing dancing tonight and left the club together."

"That blows. Well, she's super fun, and there's nothing wrong with having a new friend."

"This is true, I guess. So, are you still coming up?"

"I'm trying to figure it out with work, and Damien said I could stay with him."

"I'll be at Maddison's, so you can stay with us if you want."

"Thanks, I thought about that, but I don't want Maddison to think I'm spying on her for Brad."

"Oh right, I didn't think about that. Is Brad coming to the show?"

"Nope. He's staying down here, which is probably for the best. I think he would go into stalker mode if he saw her."

"Yeah, that's not good, but It'll be cool to see you."

"Hell yeah."

"Well, I got a butt load of T-shirts to fold tomorrow, so I should hit the hay."

"Have fun at the Gap." Matt laughed.

"Thanks, asshole."

"Nighty-night."

"Later, jerk." I chuckled and hung up the phone.

Chapter Twenty-Three

I woke up the next day feeling great. I took a quick shower and got into my Gap outfit. Koji appeared from his bedroom, scratching his head and looking still half-asleep. "What up, bro?" he asked.

"Hey, morning."

"How was last night?"

"It was cool. You should've gone."

"Maybe in my next life." Koji rubbed his belly and yawned.

"Well, this guy met a girl," I said, pointing my thumb at my chest.

"Nice!" Koji high-fived me.

"She's a friend of Matt."

"Wait. She's a *Matt* friend?"

"Yes, but I know what you're thinking. She's not a slutty stripper."

"Did you hook up?" Koji wiggled his eyebrows and made an hourglass shape with his hands.

"I wish. She's just a friend, and I think she has a boyfriend."

"Perfect! That's just what you need, a girlfriend that you can't get attached to." Koji poured a cup of coffee and sat down at the kitchen table.

"Ah, very funny, but maybe you're right. I'm not in a hurry to get tied down anyway. I'm having fun meeting new people, and I think it would be good for me to be single for a while. Hey, by the way, if I asked you to call me J. instead of Jason, would that be weird?"

"I'll call you fuckhead if you want." Koji held up his coffee cup and grinned.

"That's what I thought you would say."

"Why J.?"

"I just feel like it's my name now, if that even makes sense."

"Not a bit, but what do I know?" Koji said.

"Well, I'm off to Gap hell."

"Right on, dude…oh, I mean, J."

"Later."

"Later."

On my way to work, I passed the Gap store where Nicki worked. Through the window I saw her folding T-shirts. I thought about stopping in, but for some reason, I kept going. It was hard to explain. I liked her, and just a few days ago, I was super stoked to have met her and felt we'd had a good connection. But for some reason, the spark with Nicki had fizzled. It wasn't in the stars for me to take on another drama queen. From what I had witnessed, Nicki was just that. Though Amy seemed to be with Carson and not a prospect for me, I just felt it was time to hang out with girls who had less baggage. After my night out with Damien and my mirror epiphany, I felt different, and my needs had changed. My life was finally on track; it didn't involve drama, and I wanted to keep it that way.

When I got to work, I was surprised to see Patrick talking with Patty and Kara with a K. "Hey, you guys!" I said.

"Jason! What's up, my man?" Patrick said. "Did you get a chance to get that info for me about the lavender farm?"

"I did," I said, pulling it out of my pocket. "I planned on calling you today on my break."

"Awesome, thanks!" he said, looking at the slip of paper I handed him.

Patty and Kara with a K stood there, both looking annoyed that Patrick and I were chummy. I got the impression that they didn't like their new employee becoming friends with their boss. *A litter power hungry, I guess. Oh well, ladies, sorry*, I thought.

"Hey, what time are you and Chloe moving out on Friday?" I asked.

"Oh right. You're moving in—that's great. We will be out on Thursday, so any time after that."

"Awesome, thanks. Well, I better get to my T-shirts."

"Okay, Jason. I'll see you later."

"Oh wait. I forgot to mention," I said. "I went to Club Deluxe last night and saw some swing dancing."

"Cool. We almost went there last night as well. Did you dance?"

"No. I don't know how, but I'm going to learn from a friend."

"We can show you some moves if you like."

"That sounds cool, thanks."

"Patty, Kara, I'll see you later," Patrick said.

"Thanks, Patrick!" Patty and Kara said in unison like the corporate robots they were.

"All right, Jason. See ya, my man." He shook my hand.

"See ya," I replied. Patrick left the three of us standing there. I looked at Patty and Kara with a K, and for some reason, they didn't seem as warm toward me. "Well, I'll get to it," I said.

"Okay Jason," Patty said.

I happily went about my folding. I thought about Amy, Star, and Nicki. I'd met three cute girls already. The sting from Ashley was fading, and her spell over me was almost gone. I was super excited to learn how to swing dance and hang out with Amy some more. She seemed way out of my league, but that had never stopped me before. I had to keep reminding myself that I was in no hurry to find love. I just wanted to have fun, meet girls, and discover myself in the city, my new home.

Marcus called in sick, and I spent the entire day folding T-shirts and greeting people. I was glad when my shift was over. Even though I was on an upswing, folding T-shirts all day was incredibly boring. I was happy to punch out and head home.

I easily navigated the city streets to the bus stop just in time to jump on and grab an empty seat. The bus traveled up Market Street toward Koji's, and I watched as the city passed by and the faces of the masses flooded the streets. The people seemed to multiply in a never-ending stream. I'd only been here for a short time, but I felt like I belonged. My connection to the universe was stronger than it had ever been, and I experienced daily affirmations that confirmed I was on my path. I didn't need to look hard, as I'd always had this power or energy, but I'd just never harnessed it. I trusted it now. I gave myself fully to the universe and whatever guides I might have. Like a giant puzzle, my life had clicked into place and finally made sense to me. Everyone I knew was a part of my puzzle, just as I was a part of theirs. I couldn't wait to see where the next piece of my puzzle would be found.

I opened an *SF Weekly* newspaper and perused the music section. I noticed that Man or Astro-man? was playing on Friday. They were a band from Orange County. Matt was friends with the guitar player, and I'd gone with him to see them play. I remembered the show being super fun. They played a mix of what I could only describe as 1950s space music combined with modern punk rock. They were playing at a club called Bimbo's 365, and I knew Maddison would want to go with me.

I lost myself in the want ads and dance club section of the paper. After a while, I looked up and noticed that I'd missed my stop. I was all the way by Haight Street. "Damn it!" I hurriedly yanked on the cable above to inform the bus driver that I wanted to get off at the next stop.

"Panhandle," the driver shouted as he pulled over to let me and others out.

The Panhandle was a narrow greenway that seemed to stretch as far as I could see, ending right before Golden Gate Park. The Panhandle was lined with huge oak trees and a cement pathway on each side. It ran parallel with Haight Street. This was the park Damien and I had walked through on our way to Club Deluxe. In the daylight, I was able to see its beauty, and it reminded me of a smaller version of New York City's Central Park.

It had been a while since I'd been in the woods at my mom's, and after being thrown into this concrete city, the park was a sight I sorely needed. I walked through the park, drawn toward a pathway that seemed less traveled and led over a hill. Once over the hill, I was unable to see any surrounding buildings. I could still hear the hustle and bustle of cars and beeping horns, but it was slight. The hill had a filtering effect, muffling the noises of the city. On the other side, there was a clearing and a huge oak tree. The tree caught my attention right away as if it were calling to me.

I walked down the hill and over to the massive oak, perfectly centered in the grassy clearing. I looked left and right and was surprised to find myself alone. For the moment, this place was mine. I looked up at the huge oak tree and noticed the afternoon light leaving streaks of light through the leaves and the wind causing them to dance and flutter in the gentle breeze. The breeze was unusually warm and felt soothing. The limbs of the oak were massive, and the trunk was huge. I'd never seen such a colossal oak tree before.

I rested my hand on the tree and closed my eyes as the breeze surrounded me. I focused on the energy of the tree and could instantly feel it surging through its massive trunk. The energy seemed to run from the earth up through the tallest branch and into the universe above. It was invigorating. I opened my eyes and looked around. I was still alone. I sat at the base of the massive oak and again closed my eyes. In an instant, I was at my gate. I was amazed at how easily I was able to focus and go to my special place. *It must be the serenity and the energy of the tree helping me*, I thought. I'd assumed that the next time I wanted to go to my special place it would be harder because of the amount of time that had passed since I'd last meditated. Perhaps I was able to connect to the energy quicker after accepting that I was on my true path.

I closed my eyes and returned my focus to my mind's eye and my gate. I passed through, following the path through the grove of pepper trees and across the little bridge. I looked out at the pond, up the valley, and over the grassy dune to my beach. It was as I'd left it, calm, warm, and safe. I sat at the water's edge and watched the sun kiss the horizon. I stood and walked, absorbing the energy of my special place. I stayed a little while before turning and heading back to the gate. I thanked the universe as I lifted the latch and left. I stopped and stood, scanning the distant farms and taking in the beauty of the scenery. I breathed deeply in through my nose and out my mouth and opened my eyes to the Panhandle.

Not ten feet from me, a man stood staring at me. I startled and looked both left and right. No one else was around. I looked at the man. He was huge, like seven feet huge. He had a long beard curling down to his stomach, and by the looks of his tattered clothing, I assumed he was a homeless hippie. His eyes were a bright, glassy blue, and his skin was red from spending too many hours in the sun. He wore a beaded necklace, and at the end of it was a crystal that he held, twisting it back and forth with his fingers.

I tried to ignore him, but his unnerving gaze never faltered, making me nervous. *Why is this strange person staring at me?* Finding the courage to engage the giant, I asked, "Can I help you?"

No reaction. His face was frozen with a slight grin, and I felt his stare pierce through me.

"Can I help you with something?" I raised my voice, both annoyed and scared. I stood up, trying to square off with the urban giant who still stood motionless. "Are you deaf?" I shouted.

Suddenly, he jerked out of his dazed daydream. In an oddly soft voice, the giant said, "Hey, man. You found it." He smiled at me, instantly disarming my defenses. He chuckled as he slowly walked toward me. "Hey, I mean you no harm." His head cocked to the side, and he continued to smile. I took it as a sign that he was just a bit crazy but harmless.

The urban giant stopped a few steps away from me. He continued to grin like a child and twisted his crystal back and forth as if by compulsion. "You were saying…?" I prompted.

"Oh, yeah, man. You found it…you found *my* tree."

"This is *your* tree?" I asked.

"Yeah, man. I planted this tree."

I stepped away from the tree and turned to look up at it. "You planted *this* tree?" I said, pointing at the massive oak.

"Yeah, man. I planted all the trees." He waved his arms and pointed at the other large oak trees in the distance.

"This tree must be over a hundred years old, and you look, maybe, fifty at the most?"

"Oh no, not even close," the man chuckled as if I was being silly. "I planted these trees thirty years ago when I worked for the city."

I looked back at the tree and then back to the giant. "You're telling me this tree is only thirty years old?"

"Yes."

"And the others…you planted them at the same time?" The other trees looked about twenty to thirty years old, but this tree was at least three times the size of the others. "That can't be right. This one is enormous."

"Yes." He nodded in agreement. The giant approached the enormous oak tree, and with one fluid motion, he reached his arm out and caressed the side of the tree. He stroked it as if it were his horse. But it wasn't a horse. It was a tree. He was petting a tree. "She grew fast because I fed her a lot."

I was intrigued. "You fed her…What did you feed her?"

"Love, lots of love."

"I see. So why aren't any of the other trees as big?" I pointed at the several oak trees surrounding this one.

"I didn't feed those trees…only this one. Yeah, man. I fed this tree just like you did."

"What do you mean? How did I feed the tree?"

"I saw you. You gave it part of yourself." He grinned.

"I don't know about that."

"Sure, you do." He petted the tree, looking up at it like a proud father.

"Um, okay. That's pretty interesting. Uh, well, you have a nice day." I started to walk away. When I glanced back, the giant man was still standing there caressing the tree with one hand and twisting his crystal with the other. I continued on my way.

"Wait!" the giant called. I stopped and turned. "How did you find it?" he asked.

I didn't really know what to say. "Uh, I walked over the hill and saw it?" I held up my palms up as if to say, *I don't really know what you are asking me.*

"No, how did you find *it*," he asked again like I would understand his question the second time around.

"I'm not sure what you mean, dude. I was taking a walk and I just came across the tree and decided to sit down under it."

The man laughed and tilted his face to the sky. "So many!"

"So many?" I asked.

"Yes, so many I see at my tree. Everyone likes to feed my tree."

"I'm sorry, but I still don't know what you mean."

"No one ever knows how they find my tree…they're all lost."

"Well, I'm certainly not lost. I just sat under the big tree. Anyway, you have a nice day with your tree." I turned to walk away.

"Ha! They never know. They never know."

I walked away from the giant man and his giant tree. As I reached the top of the hill, I turned back and looked down to take another look at the man. He appeared to be talking and laughing with the tree. I wondered what he meant about so many people finding his tree but never knowing how they'd found it. It was a deep statement for sure, but after a second, I shook my head dismissively. He was obviously crazy, and there was no way that tree was only thirty years old—there was no fucking way.

Curious, I watched him sit down with his back to the tree just as I had done a few minutes earlier. When I had meditated by the tree, I could feel its energy radiating, and I had used the tree's energy to help get me to my special place. *I wonder if he's doing the same thing*, I thought. *I wonder if that's how he feeds the tree, by meditating. Could he and others make the tree grow bigger just by meditating under it?* I shook my head and shrugged the thought away. *There is no way that tree is the same age as the others. That's just silly.*

I found my way back to Koji's and called Maddison to see if she wanted to go to the Man or Astro-man? show with me.

"Yeah! Where are they playing?" she said.

"A place called Bimbo's 365."

"Cool, that place is awesome! It's a club from the thirties, and a mermaid swims in a tank behind the bar."

"Wait. Did you say *mermaid*?"

"Well, not an actual mermaid, but a topless girl wearing a mermaid tail."

"I like this place already."

"Why did I know you would say that?" Maddison laughed. "It's super close to my place—well, soon to be your place too. Is this weekend still good?"

"Yep. I saw Patrick today, and he said they would be out by Thursday, so I was thinking I could move my stuff in on Friday. Then we could go to the show?"

"Sounds good but let me check with Audrey first."

"Yeah, for sure."

"By the way, you sure made a good impression on Patrick."

"What do you mean?"

"He was over here this afternoon moving some things out, and he said you're a terrific guy for helping him with a project at work."

"Oh cool. I guess I am terrific!" I said. We both laughed.

"I think he has a man crush on you."

"Good, as long as I get that visual display job. I'm so sick of folding T-shirts. Why can't people just find their size without tearing up an entire stack of shirts?"

"Think of it as job security." Maddison teased.

I told Maddison about meeting Amy at Club Deluxe and the epiphany I'd had in Damien's bathroom. My name change and the whole "Mirror, Mirror, on the Wall" story was a bit strange to her, but I had to admit, it *was* strange. I couldn't blame her or anyone else for thinking it strange.

"You should invite Amy to the show," Maddison said, changing the subject.

"You think?" I was unsure if it was the right move. I was fairly sure Amy was dating Carson.

"Yeah, totally. That band is so fun, and I think she'll have a blast. Plus,

I can get a good look at this Amy girl and make sure she's worthy."

"Uh, I don't think that will be necessary. I'm fairly sure she's just a friend."

"Well, you never know."

"This is true. Maybe I'll call her."

"Yeah, just ask her as a friend. Either way, we will go and have an amazing time."

"Fuck yeah," I said. She laughed as I told her about the giant in the park, and then we hung up.

That night I built up the courage to call Amy and ask her if she wanted to see Man or Astro-man? with me. I got her machine and left a message about the show and gave her Maddison's number, since I would be moving in soon. The next couple of days I worked closely with Marcus, learning more about visuals. There wasn't much room for creativity, but it was way better than folding T-shirts, and thanks to Patrick, I also secured an interview with the visual manager who worked with him. My appointment was scheduled for Friday at the flagship store. I was excited and looked forward to the opportunity.

Part III

Chapter Twenty-Four

Friday came, and though I had been anticipating it all week, I didn't feel ready. I was nervous about my meeting. I arrived early and walked around the store. It was monstrous in size. The amount of stuff people consumed boggled my mind, and this was only one of many stores. I saw Patrick talking with two other people. I could tell they were Gap family for sure. I decided to walk over. Patrick's back was to me, so I tapped his shoulder.

Patrick spun around and smiled when he saw me. "Jason, my man! How are you?" He shook my hand.

"I'm good, thanks."

"Guys, this is Jason. He's the one who helped with the concept of the Lavender display."

"Oh great," one of them said with fake enthusiasm.

"Have you seen it?" Patrick asked me.

"No, no, I haven't been to the store yet." I didn't mention I was avoiding it because that was where Nicki worked.

"It's almost done," Patrick said. "You should stop by after you're finished here, and I can show you what we've done with your idea."

"Totally, sounds good."

"Great. I need to run, but you're in good hands with these two. Jason, this is Heather and Ron. They will be talking with you about the visual position. Is Chris around today?" Patrick asked Ron.

"He should be in the back," Ron said.

"Great. Make sure you introduce Jason to Chris. That is, if he gets the job." Patrick laughed.

"Let's hope," I said.

"All right, guys, I gotta go. Jason, I'll see you later today."

"Yeah, see you there." Patrick walked away, leaving me, Heather, and Ron to talk. *Well, here we go*, I thought. I extended my hand to whoever would take it first. Ron shook my hand and then Heather. "Nice to meet you guys," I said.

"You too," Heather said.

"Yes, you as well," Ron said in a deep smoker's voice. Ron was tall and bald and wore eyeliner and mascara. When he looked at you, he batted his eyelashes quickly, as if he were playing Snow White in a Disney movie. I fully expected both Ron and Heather to be fake and condescending like Patty and Kara with a K, but they were super nice and seemed genuine. To my surprise, they were cool and mellow, and being from corporate, they were definitely in charge of all things visual. I guessed the further up the ladder you went, the less pressure you had to prove yourself.

They walked me through the store, showing me the ins and outs of this mega Gap. They then asked me to dress a few mannequins to make sure I could put clothes on a life-size doll. It was pretty strange. They gave me a naked mannequin, skirt, shirt, belt, and purse and watched as I simply put the items on the mannequin. As I finished, I decided to fold the cuffs of the shirt and pulled the collar up.

"Oh, I love it!" Heather said.

"Mm-hmm, yes," Ron said. "You really gave her some flair, Jason. Nice job!"

"Oh, thanks." I was confused. All I did was dress a mannequin. I mean, how else do you dress one? They had even chosen the clothes.

"Love the collar, nice touch, and the cuffs are super-duper," Heather said.

"I thought it might look a little more, uh, fun?" I was searching for words that would sound like I was into it. I realized they just wanted me to follow the corporate rules but add a little flair to show creativity. Luckily, flipping up a collar and rolling the sleeves into cuffs was all they needed to see from me. I was happy that they were happy because I really wanted this promotion.

"I think we have seen enough," Ron said.

"Yes, I agree. Jason...welcome aboard!" Heather smiled.

I was elated. My shirt-folding days were behind me, and I wouldn't have to deal with Teen Spirit Patty and Kara with a K. I would miss Marcus, but I was sure I would see him again.

"Let me go find Chris," Ron said.

Heather shook my hand, excused herself, and quickly hurried to the back of the store and was soon out of sight.

"Jason, this is Chris," I heard from behind me. I turned around and saw Ron and another guy.

"Hi." I extended my hand, and Chris shook it with an intentionally limp wrist.

"Nice to meet you," he said evenly.

"Chris, why don't you show Jason around," Ron said.

"Sounds great! Thanks," I said.

"Okay, follow me." Chris turned around and flipped his bangs from his face in the same motion. Chris was about five feet tall and of Asian descent. I followed him as he sauntered across the store with one hand on his hip. Along the way, he stopped at a couple of mannequins, fixing collars and straightening sweaters. "Ugh! So much to do," he said in an overly dramatic way.

"Yeah, this store is huge," I said.

"You haven't seen anything yet." He waved his hand in the air somewhat dismissively and continued to walk in front of me. When we arrived at the back of the store, Chris produced a key and unlocked a door labeled "Visuals." I expected to see an enormous room with mannequins and display items. But to my surprise, it was the size of a walk-in closet crammed with way too much stuff.

"Oh wow," I said as we entered the visuals room.

"You can say *that* again," Chris replied. A small table and a couple of chairs had been squeezed into the back of the room. "Have a seat and we'll go over some things." Chris motioned to one of the chairs. I sat, and he joined me. Chris went right into the ins and outs of the day and what needed to be done. He explained how to use the steamer to remove wrinkles, and he emphasized to never ever leave a nude mannequin on the shop floor.

There seemed to be something amiss with Chris. He didn't appear happy to have me as a coworker. Sometimes I wished I didn't have the gift of reading people's energy. Chris's energy screamed that he didn't want me here. Not being afraid of confrontation, I decided it was time to break up the tension.

"So…what's the problem?" I asked him.

Chris stopped and looked at me, a little dumbfounded. "The problem?"

"Yes. Is there something wrong with me working here?"

Chris seemed uncomfortable with my question. "No. I just…no," he said.

"Look, I'm not sure why you're annoyed that I'm here. I just want to learn how to do my job so that I can get paid."

Chris sighed and closed his eyes. When he opened them, a tear fell down his cheek.

"Uh, are you crying?" I asked.

"I just work so hard."

"I'm not following. What does that have to do with me?"

"Well, I heard they were bringing in a new visual person and that you are friends with Patrick, so I figured you're my replacement."

"Oh. No, you got it all wrong."

"I do?" Chris wiped his tear.

"Yeah. I just met Patrick. He's a friend of a friend and is just helping me out. Between you and me, I have zero experience and will quit just as soon as I find a graphic design job. Graphic design is what I do. Besides, I was told that you needed help because this location is so large."

"Really?" His eyes were hopeful.

"Totally! You have nothing to worry about."

Chris took a big sigh and thanked me for being honest with him. "I like you already," he said, relieved.

"Well, I like you, too!" I laughed.

"I guess I could use the help," Chris said, regaining his swagger and flipping his hair again.

As we left the small visuals room, I joked, "Well, I guess it's time we step out of the closet."

"Child, I did that *years* ago." Chris said, and we both laughed. He looked at me, and I could tell he was curious to know if I was on his team.

"Nope, on the other team," I answered his look.

"Yeah, that's what I thought. You're way too butch."

Though Chris was a short guy, he walked across the room as if he were a supermodel. I could tell he was going to be fun to work with. His dramatics were already entertaining me.

I spent a couple of hours training with Chris, and then Ron gave me my new work schedule. My shift was over, and I left the store with a skip in my step. I was no longer folding T-shirts, at least not all day. *I'm an official mannequin dresser*, I thought, chuckling to myself.

I walked up Market Street toward Koji's and decided to stop at the little courtyard park I'd found last weekend. It was empty, so I went in, sat on the bench, and closed my eyes. My mind raced, and all I could see was static. I was detached from my inner self, and I couldn't focus on my gate or my special place. I was just way too excited, and my adrenaline was pumping. I was okay with it at the moment because I had too much to do and see. In fact, today was the day I'd be moving into Maddison's house and going to the show at Bimbo's. I hadn't heard back from Amy and figured she was busy, but I wasn't worried about it. Not today.

I left the park and walked past the Gap that Nicki worked at to see Patrick's window display. It looked great. The window was about twenty feet across, and the displayed lavender made it look like a field. In the center of the field was a mannequin flying a kite. I saw Patrick inside talking with someone. He noticed me outside and waved me in. I needed to get to Koji's to grab my stuff, so I pointed at my wrist, indicating that I didn't have time, but I pointed at the window and gave him a thumbs-up. Patrick smiled and returned the thumbs-up, waving me on. I was happy he didn't insist that I come in. I was having an amazing day, and I didn't want to see Nicki. Not that I expected anything bad to happen, but I just wanted to avoid any potential drama at all costs.

When I walked through the door at Koji's, I could hear him laughing with someone on the phone. I walked into the living room and began packing all my things into my large, army rucksack. Koji came in a few minutes later.

"Dude, you're out of here?" he asked.

"Yep. Today's the day."

"I'm gonna miss you, man, and all the weird things that happen to you every day." He grinned. "So, how stoked are you living with two hot chicks?"

"Maddison's more like a sister to me, and Audrey...let's just say she doesn't play on our team."

"What?" Koji seemed confused. I looked at him, waiting for him to get it. "Oh, she likes the ladies."

"Exactly." I laughed. "Besides, I've barley spoken to her."

"Maybe you'll convert her."

"Yeah, that's exactly what's going to happen. She's been gay her entire life, but now that I'm her roommate, she won't be able to control herself. My manly charms will woo her for sure." I said.

"Well, why not?"

"One can only wish..."

"Oh, by the way, you got some mail from Lance."

"Are you serious?" Lance was a friend of ours whom I used to do graphic design work for. He owed me for a job, and I hoped I was about to get paid. I grabbed the envelope from Koji and tore it open. "Yes! A thousand bucks!"

"Nice!"

"Dude, I'm so glad he paid me. I totally thought he was going to stiff me."

"I talked with him last week, and when he found out you were living here, he asked for my address."

"Nice work!" I slapped Koji's hand. "He probably didn't want me to tell you that he stiffed me."

Koji laughed. "He is a cheap bastard."

"Yeah, you think? I better go cash this before it bounces down the street. Thanks for letting me crash here. I really appreciate it."

Koji opened his arms wide, and we hugged and slapped each other's backs. I always thought it was weird that guys end a hug with a slap on the back. I grabbed my bag and promised to keep in touch.

Chapter Twenty-Five

I stuffed my army bag into my parked Bug. Thankfully, she started up on the first try. I stopped at the bank on the way to Maddison's and cashed the check. I was now one thousand dollars richer. I circled her building until I found a spot, parked, and headed for the door. I could hear girls laughing as I knocked.

Maddison answered the door with a huge smile and an equally huge hug. "Hey, mister!"

"Hey, Mad. How's it going?"

"Good! Come on up."

With my bag in tow, I headed up the stairs to the small apartment. Audrey was sitting in one of the chairs in the small, cozy living room.

"Hey, Jason," Audrey said. I smiled and waved.

"Do you need help with your stuff?" Maddison asked.

"Nope, this is it."

"What? That's just an army bag."

"Yeah. I have my clothes, my pillow, and a sleeping bag." I smiled.

"What, no teddy bear?" Audrey laughed.

"No, I left him back at home," I said. "I planned on getting a bed once I found a place, but the sleeping bag is fine for now."

"You can sleep on the love seat, but it's a little small," Maddison offered.

"I'm fine, really."

"You want to put your stuff in your room?" She motioned for me to follow her.

I remembered the room was a little smaller than the visuals room at the Gap. I laughed as we both walked in.

"It's still small," she said.

"I've always wanted to live in a closet." I smiled.

"It's *totally* a closet."

"It's perfect," I said.

"Hey, guys. I'm off to work," Audrey shouted from the hallway. We stepped out of my bedroom/closet and said goodbye to Audrey as she descended the stairs to her waitress job down the street.

"Bring home goodies!" Maddison called after her.

"I'll try," Audrey said. "Have fun at Bimbo's."

Maddison turned to me. "Oh! I forgot! She called," Maddison said, holding my arms and shaking me.

"Who called?"

"Amy! The swing dance girl!"

"What? No way."

"Yes way. She said she was already going and was excited to meet up with you."

For some reason, I totally did a happy dance and ran into the kitchen, spun around, did a jig, and ran back to the living room.

Maddison laughed at my happy dance. "I thought this girl had a boyfriend."

"I think she does."

"Anyway, she called and that's that!"

"I was thinking of asking Damien to come along hoping he'll bring a pizza."

"Ah, you are a genius."

I called Damien, but he wasn't around. We ate some of Audrey's leftover pasta and some wine. "This pasta's delicious," I said.

"Audrey is a good cook," Maddison said with a mouth full.

"Hey. Let me pay you my portion of the rent now so I don't blow all my money on booze and fast women."

I paid my first month's rent of three hundred dollars for a six-by-eight-foot room. It was a lot for the space, but I was happy to do it. The room was small, but it was mine. Maddison disappeared to get ready like girls do, and I explored the apartment, getting my bearings. There was a poster on the wall with weird drawings of long creatures. Then I read the caption below: "Penises of the Animal Kingdom."

"Nice poster!" I shouted to Maddison.

"What?"

"I said, nice poster."

"I can't hear you, what?"

"Never mind." I helped myself to more wine and stepped out onto the tiny back porch. It was just big enough for one person. I looked over the rooftops of the city and felt exhilarated for what was to come. So much had already happened. I felt blessed for having good friends whom I could count on. To me, having friends was always important, especially close ones. I looked up into the sky and thought about my astral travels to the city, circling the area with my light energy. I felt like I'd flown right above where I was standing now. I wondered if my astral travel to the city was having a direct impact on all the coincidences I had experienced since I arrived here.

"You ready to go, bro?" Maddison startled me.

"Oh. I didn't see you there."

"You were spacing out."

"I am kind of a space cadet."

"I know. It's what I like about you."

"Ditto," I said.

"Let's blow this peanut stand, spaceman."

We headed out into the chill of another San Francisco night. Arm in arm, we huddled together and marched in unison down the steep streets to North Beach, a neighborhood known for its amazing Italian restaurants, hip bars, and strip clubs. After a few blocks, we filtered into a line in front of Bimbo's. It looked like there was a good turnout for the band.

"This should be fun," Maddison said. As we walked in line, I let go of her arm. She looked at me in a funny way and then realized why I'd dropped her arm. "Oh yeah. You don't want her to see us arm in arm."

"Oh, c'mon. Don't make it a big deal, please."

"Maybe I should be all up on you...make her jealous."

"Hmm," I said, rubbing my chin. "Not a bad idea!" We waited a few minutes as the line continued to form down the street. Finally, the line began to move, and we made our way toward the club.

"Oh no. Look at the poor girl," Maddison said.

"Where?"

"Over there." She pointed to the sidewalk on our right. There was a girl lying on the edge of the sidewalk with her head hanging into the gutter. She was dry heaving into a puddle of vomit.

"Oh man." My jaw dropped when I realized I knew the girl. "Oh shit. That's Nicki."

"Whose Nicki?"

"Nicki from the Gap!"

"No! Drunk girl?"

"Yep."

"Should we help her?"

"Well, I guess we better." I was pissed. I wasn't even with Nicki, and I didn't want her drama in my life, but here I was, sucked into her world. I couldn't ignore her, I couldn't, but I debated if I should help her or leave her to her own devices. *Maybe this is meant be*, I thought. I was thinking too hard and decided to just help her because that was the type of guy I was. Just as

Maddison and I started to move toward her, another guy came out of Bimbo's who was also drunk. Maddison and I watched as he walked over to Nicki and helped her up. They both staggered down the street and into the night. "Dodged a bullet there!" I said.

"I'll say."

The line started moving again, and I refocused my attention to being excited. We got inside, and the place was amazing. Maddison had been right—behind the bar was a mermaid swimming. The club was draped in red and gold velvet. Chandeliers hung from the ceiling, and the floor was checkered. It looked like a speakeasy. I was stoked to be here, seeing the show instead of taking care of a drunk girl.

"Jason! Jason! *J.!*"

Maddison poked me. "I think that girl is trying to get your attention."

I turned to see Amy and Carson, the tall guy from Club Deluxe, standing by the bar. She smiled and waved at me. My heart skipped, and I was instantly nervous. She was more beautiful than I remembered. All I could see was her face, and everything else disappeared. I waved back and walked over. "Hey! How's it going?" I shook Amy's hand.

"I'm Carson!" Carson announced.

"Uh, yeah, I met you at Deluxe earlier this week," I said. Carson's face was blank, trying to place me but failing.

"You look different…your hair?" Amy asked me.

Maddison gave me a confused look. "I'll tell you later," I mumbled to her. "Different hair product." I smiled at Amy.

"You look good." She returned the smile, and my heart continued to race.

"And who is this?" Carson extended his hand to Maddison.

"This is my friend Maddison."

"Nice to meet you." Carson grinned like a shark. *That was weird*, I thought.

"Hi, Maddison. I'm Amy. It's nice to meet you."

"You too," Maddison said. "You guys look great!"

I looked at their stylish, vintage outfits. They did look good. Amy was wearing an emerald-green form-fitting dress. It looked like it was from the 1940s. She noticed me looking at her, and she blushed. Her eyes sparkled, matching the color of her dress. She was crazy good-looking. I was wearing one of my dad's vintage Pendletons.

"I like your shirt, buddy," Carson said to me. *Did he just call me buddy, like a dog?* I was really beginning to dislike this guy. "I'm going to get a drink…you guys want something?" Carson asked.

"I'd love a gin and tonic," Amy said.

"Me too," Maddison said.

I stopped Carson. I reached into my pocket and pulled out the seven hundred bucks I had left after paying rent and peeled off a hundred-dollar bill. "I'll get this round," I said, handing the crisp bill to Carson.

"My kind of guy." Carson smiled and headed to the bar.

"Big spender," Maddison teased and nudged me with her arm. I was showing off. I couldn't help it, and my ego got the better of me. Amy didn't seem like the type of girl who would like me more if I had money, but I was generous. So, I guess it wasn't exactly out of character for me.

"So, are you from Orange County or here?" Amy asked Maddison.

"I'm from Orange County and hang out with Jason's, I mean, *J.'s* crowd."

"We're roommates," I chimed in. "I actually just moved in today."

"That's cool," Amy said.

"It's way better than sleeping on my friend's couch," I said.

"Well, not really," Maddison said, looking at Amy. "He's sleeping in a room the size of a closet…in a sleeping bag." She laughed. I nudged her back, hard.

"Well, I haven't had a chance to get any furniture yet, but I hope to by the end of the week," I said.

"I know some great vintage stores I could show you, though I'm sure Maddison does as well," Amy said.

I realized that Amy didn't know if Maddison and I were a couple or just roommates. *Is she trying to figure it out?* I wondered. *Isn't she with Carson?*

"Maddison has amazing furniture," I said. "Her apartment is like a vintage shop."

"I do like my vintage things," Maddison said.

"Oh, sounds like you got it covered, then," Amy said.

"No, I would totally be into checking out some shops with you," I told Amy.

"Are you sure?" Amy said, looking at Maddison.

"Oh, we're not together." Maddison laughed.

"Oh good. I mean…I didn't want to cross any boundaries. Not that I was asking you out or anything." Amy blushed *again*.

I smiled. "Nope, we're just friends."

"Hey! Don't be talking to my man!" Maddison joked and put her arm around me.

"You wish," I said, peeling her arm off. I smiled. "Aren't you with Carson anyway?"

"Oh no. Carson's my neighbor and, well, dance partner. We just hang out a lot and dance all the time." *Yay me*, I thought. "Besides, I don't date men who are prettier than women." She laughed. "You should see the train of girls he brings home! I adore him, but he's a dog."

"I guess I just assumed," I said.

"Well, you assumed wrong." She smiled.

Wait. Did she just give me a smile, like, that kind of smile? I thought.

"Okay, drinks all around," Carson said in his loud, super-tall-man voice.

"Thanks, Jason," Maddison said.

"I thought it was J.," Carson said.

"Yeah, it is. Well, it's both, but I go by J."

"I keep forgetting about your weird mirror thing." Maddison sipped her drink and winked at me. I sighed.

"Anyway, thanks for the drink J. or Jason," Carson said, handing me my change.

"Yes, thanks, J." Amy smiled up at me and took a sip from her straw.

"My pleasure. Cheers!" I raised my glass.

"Cheers!" Carson clinked with our glasses, spilling a little of our drinks on the floor. He was like a big puppy, clumsy.

"Wow, all righty, then." Amy laughed a little. "Let's go watch the band."

The set was great, as I expected, but it seemed to go by too fast. After the show ended, we funneled outside, back into the crisp air.

"They were awesome," Amy said.

"I love this band," Maddison replied. "So, it was really nice to meet you, Amy."

"You too," Amy said. "I'd really like to see your place and all the cute things you must have."

"Yeah, of course," Maddison said, and she and Amy hugged.

Carson looked at me. "I'm not hugging you, man."

"No, that's totally fine with me."

"I'll hug you," Amy said. As she embraced me, I squeezed her hard, lifted her up, and spun her around. "Whoa!" She giggled.

"Well, I guess you could say we've danced," I said, laughing and setting her back down.

"I guess so." She fixed her dress and smiled at me. There was something about the way she looked at me. I couldn't explain it, just that there was a feeling in her eyes.

"So, Maddison. Maybe you want to get a drink sometime?" Carson asked. He'd been putting the moves on her all night. With a girl like Maddison, you had to be really, really good if you wanted to get her attention. She was a class act for sure. After Amy told us about his train of girls going in and out of his apartment, there was no chance for him.

"I'm seeing someone right now but thank you," Maddison said.

"Oh right. For sure," Carson said.

"Ooh, shot down!" Amy belly laughed and winked at Carson.

"Shut up," Carson said. That made Amy laugh more.

"Hey, don't be sad," I said. "She only dates ugly, nerdy guys. So, look at it this way, you're just too good-looking for her." We all laughed except for Carson.

"Hey, Matt told me that he's coming up with Mark and his band," Amy said, changing the subject. "They're playing at a place up the street from here called the Purple Onion."

"The Purple Onion. I love that place!" Maddison said.

"I do too," Amy said.

"Yeah, he told me about it, and I think I'm going with Damien. In fact, I think Matt is crashing with Damien," I said.

"Wait. You know Matt? Our Matt?" Maddison said, looking at me.

"She's not a Matt girl," I replied.

"What's a Matt girl?" Amy asked, looking at the two of us.

Maddison gestured to Carson, who was talking with two girls a few feet away from us. "You know, like him…a train of—"

"Oh God, no," Amy said quickly. "I mean, Matt is cute and charming and all. And we dated a little, but I quickly realized that he was a player, and well, I'm not. It's cool, though. We're just friends."

"Matt isn't a player. He's just really, really friendly." I laughed.

"Oh, is that what you call it?" Amy chuckled.

"Yeah, I *guess* you could call it that." Maddison rolled her eyes, joining in Amy's defense.

"Anyway, let's get off the subject of my best friend who isn't here to defend himself."

"Oh God! He would love knowing that we were talking about him," Maddison said.

"You're probably right. So, Amy. Maybe I'll see you at the Purple Onion?"

"Yeah. I'll be there, along with my roomies."

"Do they know that Damien is going to be there?" I asked.

"Nope, but I will definitely warn them."

"Hey now! How are we all doing?" Carson returned from his conquest.

"Not as good as you, apparently," Amy said.

"Just making some friends." Carson grinned and placed a folded napkin into his pocket. A phone number, no doubt.

"You are incorrigible!" Amy slapped his arm jokingly.

"Ah, c'mon. I'm just a nice guy." Carson shrugged.

"Yes, yes, you are, Carson." Amy winked.

"You kids coming our way for a drink?" Carson asked.

"Uh, I think we are staying around here for the night," I replied.

"Haight Street seems really far right now, and it's cold." Maddison placed her arm around mine.

"All right, guys. That was fun. I'm glad we got to hang out," Amy said.

"For sure. It was great seeing you again. Let me know if you still want to help me shop for furniture." I smiled.

"I will."

Maddison pulled my arm. "Okay, good night."

I took one last glance at Amy before I turned and followed Maddison's pull.

Maddison looked over at me and noticed my crocodile grin. "Oh God!"

"What?" I asked.

"You are totally smitten for that girl."

"Not even." I laughed.

"Just look at your face," she said.

"Uh, I can't. It's on my face."

"Well, trust me, you are into that girl."

"She's really nice."

"She's totally cute," Maddison said.

"You think so?" I said even though I knew it.

"Yeah, I'm straight and I would totally hump her." Maddison laughed.

"You think she liked me?" I asked.

"Well, all I can say is she was really curious if we were a couple, so I would say yes. Girls don't care about who a guy is dating if they are not interested in them."

"Yeah, I guess you're right." My smile grew. "You think I should call her to go shopping this week?"

"Ugh, do I need to even answer that?"

Chapter Twenty-Six

Monday arrived quickly, and I was glad when it came because I had spent the entire weekend struggling to keep myself from calling Amy. I was never good at playing it cool when it came to girls. If I liked a girl, I embraced it. I figured if they liked me, it was supposed to be, but something was different about this one. I really liked Amy. I liked her even though I really didn't know her. I liked her when she sent Matt that care package with the little toys from Chinatown. I remembered thinking Ashley would never do something like that. I was envious of him and mad at him that he didn't seem to notice how special that was. He really blew it with her. I wondered if I really had a chance with this girl. I was at least going to try. Even though I was intrigued by Amy, I struggled with not wanting to get into something so quickly. I needed to be single for a while and renew my soul. I needed a reboot for sure. I decided I owed it to myself to take it slow and keep it light. I would entertain the idea of Amy, but I wouldn't get serious. *It is time to have fun without strings*, I thought.

My first day on the Gap visual team was great. I basically followed Chris around and helped him dress and undress mannequins. This job was cake. I got to know Chris more, and he seemed cool. He told me about coming out to his Filipino family. Being gay was strictly forbidden, and his mother refused to believe him. His last resort was to bluntly tell his mother that he loved sucking dick. She listened. I felt bad for him. I couldn't imagine how hard it must have been for him. I told Chris about Ashley and how I ended up in the city. I felt comfortable with him right off the bat. I told him about Amy, and he said I should call her tonight. I was going to wait until tomorrow, but he changed my mind.

After work, I walked home through Chinatown. It was an amazing place, and it felt like I'd been transported to China. I'd never experienced a different culture like this. I explored the enormous shops full of imported goods and strange items made in China, no doubt. I wandered the streets and back alleys like a tourist in a far-off country. I found a marketplace where live turtles, armadillos, chickens, and strange meats I'd never heard of were sold. There was a box truck full of whole pigs that people were haggling over. I was blown away that this place existed. A lady in one of the many shops talked me into buying a toy Buddha. She said it would bring me good fortune. I parted with five dollars in hopes that she was right.

I headed home and was happy to find myself alone when I entered the empty apartment. *Maddison and Audrey must still be at work*, I thought. I saw the answering machine light blinking. The first message was from my mom telling me to call her. She had read in the news about a man who had a gun on the Golden Gate Bridge and wanted to make sure it wasn't me. The funny thing was, I wasn't surprised by her crazy message, so I ignored it. To my delight, the next message was from Amy: "Hi, this is Amy calling for Jason— I mean, J. I'm going to Southern California to visit my parents this week and may not be back in time for the show this weekend. I just wanted to let you know. Anyway, have a good time and see you when I get back. Bye." I was stoked she'd called, but also bummed she wasn't going to be there.

I'd left several messages for Damien over the weekend, but I still hadn't spoken to him about the show. I decided to call him, and to my surprise, he finally answered. "Hey, dude," I said.

"Hey, what's up?"

"I tried calling you all weekend."

"I just got back today. I was down south visiting Cassandra."

"Oh cool. How is she?"

"She's a girl." Cassandra was Damien's girlfriend. They kind of broke up when he moved up to the city. She wanted to move up here, but he didn't want her to.

"So, how'd it go?" I asked.

"I got laid…then it sucked."

"Well, that can happen. So, you missed Man or Astro-man?," I told him.

"Oh yeah, I saw that in the *Weekly*. Was it good?"

"It was awesome. Guess who I went with?"

"Yourself."

"C'mon, dude, just guess."

"Okay, yourself." He laughed.

"I went with Amy. The girl from Club Deluxe."

"No way, you asshole."

"Yep."

"You and her."

"Well, she brought Carson, and Maddison came with me."

"Oh. Oh, I see, so it was a double date. She went with her tall douchebag boyfriend, and you showed up with Maddison." He snickered.

"Actually, it wasn't like that. She's not with him at all, dude."

"She said that?"

"Yes, she did, and yes, he is a douchebag, but he's not her douchebag! He tried to pick up Maddison, not to mention several other girls at the show."

"Wow, he really works hard. I wonder if that's what I should do. Work harder to get the ladies."

"I don't really think it will work the same for you." I chuckled.

"Oh yeah? Why not?"

"Never mind. You're the best."

"You know it, suckah," Damien said. "Well, right on. I'm glad the Amy person from Club Deluxe likes you. Is she going to the show this weekend?"

"No, she said she was going to OC to visit her family."

"Oh, and maybe Matt?" Damien put the thought in my head.

"Well, she didn't mention it, but I really don't know. You think she is? I thought Matt was flying up to see the show?"

"I don't think he can make it. He said he may have to watch the shop for Mark while he's up here. Anyway, who knows what chicks do. They say one thing but mean and do another."

"You have a point, but I'm not going to worry about it. She's not my girlfriend, and whatever she does is her business."

"Yeah, good luck with that *all* week," Damien said.

"Anyway, are we going to the show this weekend?"

"Yep."

"Okay. I'll head over to your place on Friday and ride with you and the band to the show. I assume you're having a preshow party?"

"You know it."

"Sounds good, man. Well, I'm starving, so I'll let you go."

"All right, dude. Have a good one and don't jerk off too hard to your girlfriend who's not your girlfriend and is probably fucking Matt." Damien laughed.

"Has anyone ever told you you're an asshole?"

"Every day," Damien said proudly.

I hung up on Damien's cackling laughter. *I really don't know why I am friends with him*, I thought.

My thoughts wandered to Nicki and if she was okay. I'd always been the guy who helps people in bad situations, but if I had helped her, I wouldn't have seen Amy at the show. I also wouldn't have found out that Carson was just her friend. And the best part was realizing I wasn't in the friend zone, yet. I still had a chance. *I'm sure Nicki is fine, and if she's not, well, that's on her. I definitely do not need someone who passes out in gutters in my life,* I thought.

The week went by agonizingly slow. I was still adjusting to my new job, which I discovered was more challenging than I'd previously thought. Market Street Gap was a huge store, and it was a lot of work changing out the displays every day. I couldn't imagine doing it all alone like Chris had done for years. Not only was I settling into my new job, but I was settling into my new home as well. I acquired a bed from a thrift store, and I was now accustomed to lifting the corner of my bed every time I needed to get in and out of my room. My room was sparse, but it was cozy. After hanging a few pictures on the wall, it was home for me and my Buddha from Chinatown.

Chapter Twenty-Seven

I woke up on Friday with one plan: get drunk with Damien and go see my friend Mark's band, The Threads, play. It was going to be a good time that I would seriously pay for on Saturday morning. I was excited to hang out with my pals and hear some great music. It had been a week since I'd seen Amy, and I hoped to see her soon, but I needed to focus on me, stay grounded, and gain perspective. I was still interested in seeing her, but the last thing I needed was to fall in love. At least not now. *I have my entire life to do that*, I thought. I was only twenty-three, and I felt like I'd already been married and divorced. My heart was still healing, and I needed more time, for sure. I was determined to keep my options open for any and all opportunities.

As I expected, Damien was already drunk when I arrived at his house. "Dude, you're already fucked up."

"I am not," he slurred. He could never pace himself. He was always on fast-forward at warp speed. There was a big bottle of Kessler Whiskey on the counter. I grabbed the bottle and took a big swig.

"I better catch up," I said. I felt the burn of the bottom-shelf whiskey go down, not smoothly. "So, when are Mark and the boys getting here?"

"They should be here any minute." Damien reached for the bottle.

"This is going to be a good show, I can feel it."

"Fuck yeah!" He took a big chug from the bottle of swill.

"Take it easy on that shit, man."

"I'm fine. I'm a professional." He waved his hand dismissively.

"Yeah, right. I've heard that before."

"Whatever."

Soon I was feeling no pain, and from the looks of Damien, he was feeling nothing at all. I was super excited to go out. I hadn't been out with my drinking buddies since I'd lived in Orange County. I mean, Koji was good for a few beers, but sometimes I liked to hang out with my reckless party friends. It felt good to get a little crazy from time to time, and from past experiences, this night wouldn't be any different.

Mark and his band arrived, joining our Kessler party. The last time I saw Mark, I was at his shop selling my old punk rock records for money to move. He had tried to talk me out of it, but I really needed all the money I could get. We continued drinking while catching up. I'd almost forgotten that we were going to see them play until I heard Mark shout, "Hey! We're late!" Everyone slowly shuffled toward the door as if a zombie party had broken up.

We stumbled down the stairs and piled into Mark's cargo van filled with music equipment. There wasn't any room for Damien and me. We literally had to lay over the drum set in the back to fit in the van. We flew down the San Francisco streets as if we were being chased by cops. Mark was smiling and laughing at nothing. I could see his jagged front teeth broken by a fan's bottle years ago. He hadn't seen any reason to fix it. His laughing made me laugh.

Every time the van turned left or right, everyone yelled, "Whoa!" It was like Mr. Toad's Wild Ride at Disneyland. All of us were laughing, and it was a miracle we didn't get pulled over or crash. Soon, I felt the van come to a screeching halt. Damien and I slammed into the back of the front seats. We were tangled up with the drum set.

"We made it!" Mark yelled. Mark's drummer opened the sliding door that Damien and I were pinned against, and we ended up toppling out into the street. We lay there, laughing hysterically. It took a good minute or two before we could gather ourselves from our pile. When I finally made it to my feet, I found myself face-to-face with Amy. She had been standing outside the club with her roommates waiting for the doors to open.

"Hey, darlin'." I gave her a big hug and kiss on the cheek. I was a bit buzzed, and thankfully, I hadn't seen her standing there or I would have been too nervous. She blushed as I looked her up and down. She was wearing a black sweater, a leopard-print miniskirt, black tights, and patent leather creepers. Damn, she looked good. "I didn't think you were coming tonight," I said.

"I made it back from Orange County early, so here I am. Wow, you have pretty eyes. I didn't notice them at Deluxe. They're so light green, almost yellow like a cat." She studied my face, and I didn't know what to do.

"Jason, c'mon!" Damien yelled at me to help him unload the gear from the van.

"We were nominated roadies for tonight." I turned away from Amy and grabbed a couple of drum stands. I handed one to Amy. "Here, follow me. I'll get you in for free." She was hesitant, but I pulled her along toward the club door. A bouncer with a clipboard saw us coming.

"She's going to need to pay," he said, holding up his clipboard.

"She's with the band," I said.

"She's not with the band. She needs to pay."

"No, really, she's in the band."

"Is she *with* the band, or is she *in* the band?" The bouncer was annoyed.

"Uh, both. C'mon on, man. She's with the band. She's helping me roadie." I held up a drum stand for emphasis.

"It's only five bucks to get in. I really don't mind paying," Amy said to me. I stood my ground.

"Listen, man. Is it really worth the hassle?" the bouncer asked, trying to reason with my drunkenness.

I looked at the bouncer and shrugged, pointing at him with my free hand. "You have a good point." I reached into my pocket and found a five-dollar bill and handed it to him.

"I'd like to pay," Amy insisted.

"No, no, I got it." I pushed her money away, and we went inside. The club was a dump. It looked more like a basement with a makeshift bar and stage. "I gotta get the rest of the stuff...See you soon?"

"Yeah, I'll go find my friends." She smiled.

I helped unload the rest of the equipment and arrange it on the stage. When I was done, I found Amy sitting at a table with two girls. I walked over. "Hey."

"I saved you a seat," Amy said.

"Thanks."

"J., this is Mary and Laura."

"Hey, ladies. Nice to meet you." I kissed both their hands, and they laughed. Amy and her roommates were all pretty. I was a bit intimidated.

"So, you're friends with Matt?" Laura asked.

"Nope!" I laughed.

"What? I thought you knew each other." Laura looked confused.

"That depends. Do you like Matt?" I asked.

"Well, sure. He's cool," Laura said.

"Okay, then, yes. I'm friends with him." I smiled.

"Uh, okay."

"Hey, you can't be too careful these days. Especially with friends like mine!" I said. They all laughed at that. "But seriously, Matt is one of my best friends. I would do almost anything for that guy."

"Everything, except admit that you're his friend?" Amy teased.

"Well, yeah. There is that."

"I got you a beer, but they only have PBR." Amy slid a giant mug of cold beer in front of me.

"I knew there was something I liked about you." I took a big gulp from the beer. "Next round is on me, ladies."

"Cheers to that." Mary lifted her mug. We all followed suit and clinked our oversized mugs together.

"So, you know the band?" Laura asked.

"Yeah. The singer is my friend from back home, and well, you know Damien over there." I pointed to Damien, who was in line to get a beer.

"Oh yeah. We know him. He's the creepy guy who delivers pizza to us," Mary said.

"Yep. That would be Damien. Just so you know, whatever he does or says, I totally do not have his back, so please don't hold it against me!" The girls agreed to my plea of disassociating myself from Damien's future rudeness. I felt great! I was in the city, about to see one of my best friend's band play, and I was sitting with three super-hot girls, especially Amy. I was completely void of sadness. I hadn't cut loose in a long time, and it felt good.

I noticed the girls were almost to the end of their drinks, so I jumped up. I acquired four more giant mugs of beer and returned. "Beer fairy!" I yelled as I passed them out around the table.

"I like this guy, Amers," Laura said.

"He's a keeper," Mary said.

"I'm beginning to think I'm a stray cat." I grinned. "I guess you should know I haven't been fixed, but I am potty-trained."

"It's good to know that you won't pee on my floor, but please don't spray or bring me a dead mouse!" Amy laughed.

"I promise not to bring in any strays, and I'll work on my socialization skills," I said.

"I see. Well, you seem to be doing good so far," Amy reassured.

I smiled at her, and for the first time, our eyes met. Instead of nervously turning away, I continued to gaze into her eyes. She looked back for what seemed like minutes. It was a substantial moment, and at that point, I was in trouble. *What is it with this girl?* I thought. I had no intention of getting serious with anyone, but whenever I thought about Amy, I would get lost in thoughts of possibilities.

"So, what do you do for work?" Laura asked, interrupting my thoughts.

"I dress mannequins at the Gap."

"What? Ha-ha, I never would have guessed that," Mary said.

"Why? Because I'm super good-looking?" I joked.

"Yeah, that's it exactly," Mary said sarcastically.

"I'm a graphic designer, but I had to take something to pay the rent until I can get some freelance work."

"That's odd," Amy said. "I have a degree in graphic design!"

"Really? That's cool. Where did you go to school?"

"I went to FIDM in LA."

"LA? So, you are from Los Angeles?" I asked.

"I was born in LA, but I grew up in Lake Forest."

"Lake Forest? That's only fifteen miles from where I grew up."

"Yeah, I know."

"You do?"

"Matt told me. He said you were roommates in Laguna and other stuff."

"Oh shit! So, I should just leave now."

"No, silly, you're fine." She laughed.

"So, you are a working artist in the city, huh? That's really cool."

"No," she said. "I'm a registrar at a local graduate college. It's the complete opposite of a working artist." She sighed.

"How'd that happen?"

"My graduating class was the last group to do traditional graphic design without computers. We did everything by hand. When I graduated, I couldn't get a job because my skills were obsolete. Companies had already switched to computers, and they wanted a designer with proven computer skills. Since I worked full-time to put myself through school, I ended up staying in the corporate world because I had experience and it paid well. I worked my way up from receptionist to registrar."

"That sucks."

"It does, but I was able to pay off most of my debt, and I like where I work. It's amazing, though, how quickly computers took over the art world."

"I know. I use Photoshop and Illustrator for everything. You really do need computer skills these days."

"I miss art and wish I made a living from it, but I lived on my own and I needed to get a real job to pay off my student loans, blah blah blah. Anyway, enough of that!" She smiled.

"It's cool that you are an artist. I'd like to see your stuff sometime. Cheers to art." We clinked our beers together.

"You guys are pretty." A drunk Damien walked up and hung his arms over the necks of Laura and Mary and slowly started rubbing their shoulders.

"Ew, get it off!" Mary squirmed out of Damien's grasp and swatted his hand away.

"What. You can't take a compliment?" Damien said.

"Yeah, I can…just not from you."

"Oh, I see. I'm just the pizza guy," Damien slurred.

"Well, you are the pizza guy," Laura said, and we all laughed.

"Fine. I'll just go over there and fuck off in the corner." Damien disappeared into the crowd. We all laughed.

"What a little shit." Mary rolled her eyes.

"In his defense, he's a boob-a-holic, and you two are like crack to the poor kid." I shrugged.

"What about you?" Amy asked.

"What about me?"

"Are you a boob man?" Amy wasn't flat chested, but compared to Laura and Mary, she might as well have been.

"I'm an equal opportunity lover. I do not discriminate."

"Oh God," Amy said.

"I do, however, want my woman in the kitchen," I declared.

"What?!" Laura said.

"Yep, like I always say, 'Woman! Get in the kitchen and let me make you a sandwich!'"

"You, sir, are funny," Mary said.

"Why, thank you, ma'am." I pretended to tip an invisible cowboy hat.

Amy excused herself. I assumed she went off to the ladies' room, but she quickly returned with another round of beers for us.

"Yay, Amy is the best!" Laura cheered the bringer of beers.

"You know the way to a man's heart, darlin'!" I accepted her liquid offering.

"Is that so?" Amy smiled.

"Well, at least one way," I said, holding up the beer.

"Amy, this boy keeps calling you darlin'," Laura interjected.

"I know. I like it," Amy said.

I was sitting next to Amy on a bench seat, and every so often, our knees would touch. At first, I would instinctively pull away because I didn't want her to think I was too forward. But now, I got the sense she liked me. The next time our knees touched, we let it linger. I even pushed against her knee a little bit, and to my delight, she pushed back. The band was about to start, and the crowd got loud. It was impossible to carry on a conversation, but it didn't matter. Amy and I were having a very intense discussion without saying anything at all.

The set started, and everyone in the room stood and rocked to the band's fast rhythm. It was as if Amy and I were moving in slow motion, oblivious to the rocking crowd. I rested my arm on her back. With my hand, I made gentle circles on her shoulder. Her left hand fell onto my knee, pulling it close to hers. *Oh my God, oh my God*, I thought. I was freaking out inside. I felt like I had left my drunk body and was floating in space with Amy. It was us alone in that moment, and I never wanted it to end.

The band's final song was met with cheers from the crowd, and soon the room's roar was replaced with conversations. Laura and Mary, out of breath from dancing, sat back down and quenched their thirst with cold beer. I snapped out of the trance I'd been in with Amy and excused myself from the table to use the restroom. I waited in line, and after what seemed like forever, I came out of the restroom to find the club mostly empty, including the table we'd been sitting at. Amy, Mary, and Laura were gone. *What the fuck?* I thought.

I rushed outside to see if they were still there, but I didn't see them. *You would think she would have at least said goodbye.* I went back inside to find Damien and saw that Amy was sitting at our table alone. I walked over. "Hey!" I said, smiling.

"Hey." She smiled back.

"What's up? Where's Laura and Mary?"

"They headed home."

"What about you?"

"Well, I was planning on going to a friend's party, but I don't really want to go alone," she said.

"Oh. Well, I can go with you."

"You sound really excited about it." Amy chuckled.

"No, I just didn't want to invite myself is all."

"That's why I waited. I want to hang out with you."

"You do?"

"I do."

"I think that's probably a really good idea." I grinned.

"Okay, good." Amy stood up and grabbed her purse.

"Let me just find Damien and say bye to the band."

"Okey-doke. I'd like to get some air, so I'll meet you outside."

I found Damien fallen over, drunk backstage. I stepped over him and said goodbye and good show to the band, then hurried outside to Amy. "Hey, darlin'!" I shouted, coming up behind her.

"Hey, you." We stood face-to-face, our eyes locked. I moved in for a kiss, but she grabbed my hand before I could and dragged me off into the night. She led me down the street and through back alleys until we popped out on Market Street. We walked and talked about the show and how annoying Damien was. It was a nervous conversation, at least for me. After a few blocks, Amy planted us at a bus stop.

"You sure know your way around this town," I said.

"Oh, I work right up the street, so I walk this way most days to catch the bus."

"So, where's this party at?"

"Um, I guess I should've told you this…it's my ex-boyfriend's party," she said guiltily.

"Oh really?" I laughed. "That really sucks!"

"It does." She joined in the laughter. "But really, it's cool. We're still friends."

"Oh, well, that still sucks!" I chuckled.

"No, *trust me*. He cheated on me last year with my friend who is now his fiancée, Margery. To be honest, I'm grateful it happened. She can have him!"

"Sounds like a great guy."

"He used to be, but things changed. He just became too controlling and emotionally abusive, and I got tired of all the games."

"I know that story all too well," I said.

"You have a bad ex too?"

"You could say that. She goes to college here."

"Oh really. Is that what brought you to SF?"

I proceeded to tell her about Ashley, all the drama she created, and how I ended up in the city, minus the adventures at the cabin.

"Wow! I guess that's what happens when you fall in love with a young girl." She patted my knee.

"I guess."

"Well, you and I have something in common. Someone that we loved and trusted tore our hearts out."

"Yeah, I guess you're right."

"Do you still see her?"

"I saw her when I first arrived in the city, but, well, it was…never mind."

"No, not never mind. You have to tell me now that you said that," Amy insisted.

"Okay, to be honest, it was kind of a revenge visit."

"Revenge?" Amy looked a little concerned.

"Well, it didn't start out as a revenge visit. It just ended that way," I chuckled.

"What did you do?"

I told her about how I had sex with Ashley and how I'd slapped her on the butt in front of the guy she'd been with.

"That's terrible," Amy said.

"Yeah, it was kind of mean, but it also felt great!" I smiled.

"Geez. I hope I never get on your bad side," she teased.

"Yeah, you don't want to be there." I laughed.

"I never sought revenge with Chad. He's his own revenge."

"It's never too late to at least put on a good show."

"Wait, what?"

I seized Amy by the waist, slid her close, and kissed her. Her lips felt wonderful, and my heart raced as our gentle kiss became passionate. Our mouths danced and teased. I squeezed her hard until she winced, breaking away. "I'm sorry," I said, releasing my hold on her.

"It's okay. I like how you hold me."

"Good," I said. "I plan on doing it a lot." I hadn't kissed anyone in a long time, and it felt incredible. She felt amazing to hold. She had an energy about her. It was difficult to explain, but when I touched her, it felt familiar. I was having a hard time keeping my brain from falling quickly for her. As soon as I leaned in for another kiss, the bus came and squashed my plan.

The bus was packed, and the only seats available were singles across the aisle. Amy sat down, and I took the seat across from her. I looked over at her, and she smiled. She shied away and then turned back, locking eyes with me. It wasn't uncomfortable at all. Looking at her made me feel good even though I was trying hard to play it cool. But each second I fell for her more, and each moment I became closer to the point of no return. The next few stops filled the bus until the standing riders blocked all connection between us. I looked out the window into the speeding city. My heart was full and my spirit alive for the first time in a long time.

I must have lost myself in the neon flashes because the next thing I knew, Amy grabbed my arm and pulled me from my daydream and off my seat. "This is our stop," she said. We rushed off the crowded bus and spilled out onto the equally crowded street.

"Oh, is this Haight Street." I recognized the Ben & Jerry's ice cream shop on the corner.

"It is. Chad's place is just down the street." Amy wrapped her arms around my arm, squeezing it. As we walked, she nuzzled her head into my shoulder. I flexed my arm, trying to give her some muscle to hold.

"Are you *flexing*?" Amy grabbed my arm with both her hands and laughed.

"No! Uh, no!" I couldn't help but laugh. "You see, my arm is so buff it sometimes just does that."

"Oh, I see. It must be difficult being so buff!" Amy teased.

"Don't worry, you'll get used to it." I did some impromptu muscle poses, making her laugh harder. She grabbed my arm again, and we continued down the road, my bicep unflexed. I could hear the music and see people laughing and dancing in an upper apartment. "This must be it," I said.

"Yep, this is the place," Amy said as she reached for the buzzer.

"Wait." I pulled her arm back.

"What's wrong?"

"Nothing, but if we are going to do this, let's do it right."

"Do what?"

"Put on a show," I replied.

"Um, okay. What did you have in mind?"

"Teach me a few dance moves so we can cut a rug to start. I have a plan for something else that will drive your ex crazy."

"We don't need to do this," Amy insisted.

"Oh, but we do. Trust me. A little revenge is the best closure ever."

"You're so bad."

"Thank you!" I chuckled.

Amy taught me a few swing dance moves, and being a quick study, I was able to set our plans in motion. Amy pressed the buzzer, and we waited to be let in.

"Amy!" a voice shouted from above. We looked up at a smiling guy in the window.

"Hey, Keith!"

"I'll buzz you in." He disappeared from the window, and soon the door buzzed. We headed up the long staircase and opened the door to a large apartment crowded with people drinking, laughing, and dancing.

"Hey, Amy!" the same guy from the window said.

"Keith!" Amy said, hugging him. "Keith, this is J."

"Hey, man." With a big smile, he shook my hand. "Nice to meet you."

"Yeah, you, too," I replied. Keith was a good-looking guy who appeared to be in his early thirties. His thick brown hair was slicked back, and he was wearing a T-shirt with Bettie Page on it. "I like your shirt," I said.

"Thanks, man. I made it. Well, I didn't draw it. I silk-screened it."

"Oh cool. Is that what you do?"

"It's one of the many hats I wear."

"Keith is really talented. He makes furniture and restores antiques," Amy piped up.

"Oh really? My friend Maddison is really into restoring antiques. I used to help her from time to time."

"You should show J. your shop one of these days," Amy said.

"Yeah, sure," Keith said.

"Cool." It was almost as if Amy was helping me make new friends. She was already great and quickly becoming one of the nicest people I'd ever met. I was in trouble for sure.

"Let me grab you guys a drink," Keith said.

"Nice, thanks!" I said.

"Sure thing." Keith walked away.

"He seems cool," I said to Amy.

"Keith's a sweetheart. He and his girlfriend, Annie, buy and sell vintage clothing and furniture. Annie grew up with my roommate Mary in Washington."

"What a great way to make a living. I would love to do that," I said.

"Me too. It seems like a lot of fun." Keith came back with two beers for us. A tall Aryan-looking guy followed behind him.

"Thanks, man," I said.

"Sure thing."

"You made it," the other guy said, hugging Amy as if he had a million times before.

"Yeah, I thought I'd stop by after the show," Amy said. "Chad, this is J. J, this is Chad."

"Hey, man," the tall blond guy said, reaching his hand out.

Assuming this was her ex, I quickly snatched up his hand and squeezed it hard, shaking it. "Nice to meet you, Chad." I grinned.

He tried to quickly match my grip. I could tell he was annoyed. I released my grasp and excused myself to the bathroom. As I was making my way back, I noticed that another girl had joined Amy, Keith, and Chad. She was also tall and blonde. *That must be Chad's girl*, I thought. *The girl that Chad cheated on Amy with.* I came in, sneaking up behind Amy. I slipped my arm around her waist and lifted her up, kissing her on the neck.

"You scared the shit out of me," Amy said.

"Sorry, darlin'. Just keeping you on your toes." I planted a kiss on her mouth. Amy blushed, and I could see by the look on Chad's face he was pissed. *This is working perfectly.* "Who are you?" I said to the blonde standing next to Chad.

"This is Margery," Chad said.

"I'm J. Nice to meet you, Margery." I kissed the top of her hand. Chad looked uneasy. "You look familiar," I said, still holding her hand. "Aren't you a singer?"

"I am," Margery said excitedly. I had no idea who this chick was, but Amy had told me she was a singer in a band. I knew feeding her ego would do the trick.

"I've seen you sing, you're great!" I released her hand.

"Thanks!" Margery beamed.

"Do you tour a lot? I'd love to see you play again."

"Not right now, we're on a break," she said ruefully.

"Oh, that's too bad. You should be onstage."

"See!" Margery jokingly slapped Chad's arm.

"Oh, did I say something wrong?" I asked.

"No, you didn't. Chad just hates my fans is all."

"I don't hate your fans," Chad said. "I don't like that the guys just want to fuck you!"

"Oh. Well, isn't that how you met me?" Margery scoffed. "J., it was really nice meeting you. Amy, glad you could make it." Margery walked away mad. Chad followed quickly behind.

"Whoa, drama town!" Keith said as he downed the last of his beer. "I'm out of here, kids. I need to work early."

Amy hugged Keith, and I shook his hand. We planned to meet up sometime.

"What the hell was that?" Amy said quietly, as if we'd just pulled a caper and didn't want anyone to know.

I put my arms around her waist and laughed. "That went way better than I thought it would."

"Oh my God," Amy said.

"C'mon, you have to admit that was pretty funny," I said, pleading my case.

"No, don't get me wrong. That was amazing. I just had no idea that was going to happen."

"The best plans are never planned."

"I actually feel sorry for Margery. It looks like Chad is starting to control her." Amy shuddered. "Her band used to play all the time, and if I know Chad, he wants all the attention. Battle of the egos." Amy chuckled, then her eyes lit up and opened wider. "This is my favorite song to dance to, 'Flip, Flop, and Fly.'" The music played a rhythmic tune. It was a fast-paced 1950s big band swing tune.

"Well, I guess we should put that lesson to use." I grabbed Amy's hand. "Can I have this dance, my lady?"

"My pleasure, sir." We hit the makeshift dance floor in the living room. Amy had quickly taught me four basic swing moves before we rang the bell to Chad's apartment. I got the feel for it and even added some freestyle moves. It wasn't long until I heard some people cheering us on. I had no idea what I was doing, but I did know that I was having the time of my life. "You're a natural," Amy shouted.

"Thanks," I shouted back. We flipped, flopped, and flew. By the time the song ended, we had a cheering section. "That was great," I said.

"I predict that you will be very good at swing dancing." Amy winked.

"Well, with you as my partner, how could I not?"

"Oh, partners, huh?" Her eyes sparkled as she grabbed my face and kissed me. *Is this happening?* I thought. It wasn't long ago that I was in a pit of despair, and now I was on top of the world dancing with the most beautiful girl. The universe was at work, and at least for now, it was working in my favor.

We grabbed two more beers at the bar they'd set up in the living room. Margery was bartending. "You guys were great!" she said.

"Thanks," Amy said.

"I just learned tonight," I said.

"Really?" Margery sounded surprised.

"Yeah, it's super fun. You should try it," I said.

"You think I can do it?" Margery asked.

"Well, let's see." I held out my hand. At the same time, I squeezed Amy's hand with my other, assuring her that this was all for her.

Margery jumped at the chance and snatched up my hand. We hit the floor. It was a total disaster. It was the blind leading the drunk and blind. I knew four moves that she didn't know. I spun her out and back in, and each time we would clumsily bump into each other and laugh. It was so much easier dancing with Amy, but I had a plan, and it was working. I looked across the room and saw Chad standing next to Amy at the bar. He watched us intently, and he was *not happy*. I could see the muscle of his jaw line jut out as he clenched his teeth. Amy smiled at us. I could tell she knew exactly what was happening right next to her. Chad was seething, and Amy just laughed, enjoying the spectacle. The song ended, and Margery hugged me and kissed my cheek, leaving a lipstick-stained mark. She laughed breathlessly, fanning herself as she walked back to the bar, toward Amy and Chad.

"You guys look good out there." Amy laughed as she wiped the lipstick off my cheek.

"Yeah, I think I need a few more lessons before I try to teach someone else."

"That was so much fun! Thanks, J.," Margery said.

"No, thank you."

"You guys should learn how to swing dance," Amy said to Margery and Chad.

"Oh no. Chad doesn't dance," Margery said.

"Oh, that's right. I forgot," Amy said, half smiling at Chad.

Chad was still stone-faced and trying to hold it together. I pulled Amy close, and still catching my breath, I kissed her again, in front of Chad and Margery.

"You guys are so cute," Margery said. "How did you meet?"

"Uh, through a mutual friend." Amy grinned.

"Let me take your picture." Margery produced a Polaroid camera from behind the bar. "Say cheese!" Cheek-to-cheek we smiled, and the moment was recorded. She handed the picture to Amy.

"Thanks, Margery," Amy said.

"Sure!"

"Well, darlin'. Let's say you and I take a walk," I said to Amy.

"Okay. Nice party. Have fun, you two," Amy said.

"It was really nice meeting you guys, and thanks for the beers." I looked at both Chad and Margery.

"Thanks for the dance lesson," Margery said. Chad nodded. His arms were folded across his chest, and I could tell he was still pissed.

Amy and I slinked out like a couple of mischievous school kids. We rounded the corner and stopped about a block away. We looked at each other and busted out laughing.

"Oh my, did you see the look on Chad's face?" Amy exhaled.

"Yep. I thought he was going to burn a hole in my head with that look." I sighed from laughing. "That couldn't have gone better."

"Too bad we had to leave. It was a good party, but if we stayed any longer, I have a feeling it would have ended badly, and I think it was good to leave on a high note." She chuckled.

"Always leave 'em wanting more." I grinned.

"Chad certainly doesn't want any more of you! On the other hand, Margery had me wondering if I was going to lose another guy. I mean, well, not that you're my guy…"

"Yeah, we wouldn't want to say that." I laughed.

"C'mon, let's go back to my place. I can teach you some more moves."

"Oh?"

"Dance moves, Mr. Man!" She punched my shoulder.

"Oh yeah, that's what I thought you said."

We walked, swinging our held hands down the street and through the park. I recognized the Panhandle and realized we were close to the tree. The Urban Giant's tree. I thought to tell Amy about that, but for some reason, I didn't. I was worried that she would think I was strange. I wasn't ready to tell her about my gate. I had zero desire to go to my secret place, as my reality was with Amy, and I wanted to stay right here.

"Here we are," Amy said. We climbed the stairs to her second-floor apartment. "Hello? Anyone home?" Amy shouted. "Looks like we have the place to ourselves. Laura and Mary must have gone out." Amy directed me down the hall into the living room. "There are beers in the fridge. I'll be right back."

I grabbed a beer and plopped myself on the couch. My mind raced with thoughts of what was to come. I was suddenly nervous. *Am I about to get laid? Is this happening?* I said to myself. *She really doesn't seem like the one-night-stand kind of girl. I'm here in her apartment, though.* I started to panic and downed my entire beer in a few gulps. "Braap!"

"Oh, nice," Amy said as she appeared in the living room.

"Sorry! I kind of drank that fast."

"You want another one?"

"Yeah, I better."

"Are you nervous?"

"No, why?"

"Just asking." She smiled, walked over, and sat down next to me.

I cupped her face and kissed her. She felt so good. I wanted to be with her. We kissed for a few moments, learning each other's techniques. She was a good kisser. I decided to go for second base, but she immediately shot me down.

"Uh, I was just trying to see something." I shrugged sheepishly.

Amy laughed. "You were just seeing something?"

"Yeah. I was just seeing something."

"What does that even mean?" She laughed again.

"If I got into trouble when I was a kid, I would simply tell my dad that I was just seeing something."

"Oh wow. Well, you're not in trouble nor will you be *seeing something* tonight. I don't perform on a first date," Amy said.

"Is this a date? I'm sorry. I would never have tried something like that on a first date!" I laughed.

"Oh, I'm sure you're a perfect gentleman." Amy grinned.

"If the shoe fits…anyway, sorry. I just got carried away, and those cute boobs of yours were talking to me."

"You are such a flirt."

"It's your fault for being so damn pretty," I said.

"Compliments will get you everywhere."

"Good, because I have tons of them for you."

"Aw, you are sweet!" She sat next to me and grasped my hand, playing with my fingers.

"I try to be…Well, I think I should be going. Do you know which bus I take to get back to Russian Hill?"

"Oh, Russian Hill is all the way across town. You can stay here if you want."

"Really?" I perked up like a puppy dog.

"To sleep, just sleep."

"Got it. Where shall I lay my pretty head?"

"Um, you don't want to sleep out here. You may get attacked by two drunk girls when they get home."

"Yeah, that would suck," I said.

"C'mon, silly. You can sleep with me, but no funny business."

"Scout's honor," I said, holding up two fingers then switching to three fingers. "Is it two fingers or three? I always forget."

"Were you even in the Boy Scouts?"

"I was, but I got kicked out."

"You got kicked out of the Boy Scouts?"

"Yep."

"That's funny. I got kicked out of the Blue Birds when I was five or six for fighting over a stuffed animal." She laughed. "What did you do?"

"Well, we had to carve boats out of bars of soap for a float race, and I kind of carved my boat to look like a wiener."

"Oh my God, you did not!"

"Oh, I did, and they immediately kicked me out."

"No second chance, huh?"

"You would think, right? Nope, that was it."

"So, your Scout's honor thing really holds no water, then."

"Uh, pretty much." I laughed.

"Okay, just so I know whom I'm dealing with."

"I'll be a good boy," I said, following Amy down the hallway and into her room.

"This is my cat, Blixa. Blixa, this is J.," Amy introduced us. Her cat opened one eye, stretched, and resumed its nap. Amy grabbed a T-shirt, pajama bottoms and excused herself. "I'll be right back…I need to take a quick shower."

I stood there scanning her room. Amy's room was filled with the smell of incense and furnished with antiques. She had shelves full of books on esoteric things like tarot, goddess religion, and other witchy, paranormal, and psychic stuff. She even had a book on astral projection. *Wow. Cool*, I thought. The other side of her room was lined with vinyl records and CDs. She had an impressive music collection.

I was a confident guy, but right now, I was a nervous wreck. *What do I do? Just get undressed and get in bed? Do I wait for her to come back? We're just going to sleep. I'll just get undressed and get in bed*, I decided. After struggling with my thoughts, I took off my shirt. When I unbuttoned my pants, I realized I'd made a really, *really* bad mistake. I was wearing my oldest, holey pair of tighty-whities. *Oh shit!* I thought. I generally wore boxer shorts, but I hadn't had a chance to do my laundry, so I had put these on. I was going out with the boys, and I hadn't planned on going home with a girl.

With only a moment to think of what to do, I decided I would just get undressed, get into her bed, and hope she wouldn't notice. It wasn't like we were going to get it on. I was good.

I pulled my pants down and off. At that moment, the door started to open. I jumped behind it and hid. I stood quietly behind the door in nothing but an old pair of tighty-whities. I was trapped like a scared animal.

"J...?" Amy said hesitantly.

"Uh, yeah?" I said from behind the door.

"What are you doing?"

"Um, nothing. Just seeing something." I reverted to my twelve-year-old self.

"Why are you behind the door?"

At that moment, I did what I do best. I turned an awkward moment into a more awkward one. I giggled nervously and jumped out and onto Amy's bed. I jumped up and down singing, "I'm in my tighty-whities, I'm in my tighty-whities." I saw Amy's jaw fall open. I stopped jumping and looked at her. She was searching for some explanation for my strange behavior. "What? Don't you do a dance before bed?" I asked.

She didn't answer and just continued to stare at me, openmouthed.

I forged on. "That was my tighty-whitey dance because, as you can see, I am wearing tighty-whities today. You're lucky I'm not doing my commando dance."

"You're insane," she said.

"No. You are crazy if you don't do a celebration dance before bed. C'mon, just a little dance." I beckoned her to the bed.

"I'm not doing a bedtime dance." Amy laughed.

"Fine, but you're missing out." I patted the bed, and we both got under the covers, facing each other. "You smell really good," I said.

"Thanks, it's Angel oil."

"I like it." I scooted closer to her. Our knees touched, and I put my hand behind her back, pulling her against me. Our stomachs touched as we started to kiss. She pulled away for a moment and started laughing hysterically. "What's so funny?"

"Really? The *tighty-whitey* dance?"

"Oh, that." I'd hoped we were forever over that moment. I came clean and told her that I was embarrassed about my underwear and, at the last second, I couldn't think of anything to do except jump on her bed and dance.

"That's really adorable," Amy said.

"Oh good. I thought you were going to kick me to the curb." I sighed.

"No worries. It's just funny because you were so cool all night and then the next thing I see is you dancing on my bed in tighty-whities. I mean, they're funny all on their own. Anyway, your dance made my day."

"I guess I should do it more often."

"No. You should never do it again." She laughed. "Once was enough!"

"Oh really?" I jumped up and stood above her. "You sure you don't want an encore?"

"No! I'm good."

"I'm in my tighty-whities…" I danced.

"Noooo, please stop!" She belly laughed and covered her eyes with her arms. I collapsed on top of her, panting out of breath. "You're crazy!"

"I will take that as a compliment," I said.

"Okay, get back in here. I'm cold and tired."

I kept my word that night. As frustrating as it was, we remained at first base all night.

Chapter Twenty-Eight

I awoke intertwined with Amy. She was facing me, her eyes closed. I kissed her on the forehead. "Morning, darlin'," I said.

She blinked a few times before fully opening her green eyes. "Hey, handsome."

"How'd you sleep?"

"Good, considering I think we only slept a few hours."

"Yeah, I'm pretty tired."

"I had a really good time last night." She stretched and yawned.

"Me too. It was definitely one for the books."

"I haven't had a night like that in a while."

"You've got to shake your tail feathers once in a while. So, it's Saturday," I said.

"Indeed, it is."

"You up for another adventure?"

"Sure. What do you have in mind?"

"Well, as you know, I am wearing my last awesome pair of underwear. I really need to do some laundry. Why don't we meet up later?"

"Okay. I really need to get some sleep…so later is good."

"I'll come by and get you around four. How does that sound?"

"That sounds perfect," Amy said.

I hopped out of bed and quickly pulled on my pants. "I'll see you later." I leaned over and kissed her before turning to leave.

"J?" Amy said, stopping me.

"Yeah?"

"Thanks for being a gentleman last night."

"No problem, but beware. I used up all my gentlemanly behavior last night."

"Oh really?" Amy laughed.

"Yes, so you better watch yourself…you just might be in trouble."

"Okay, we'll see." She smiled.

I didn't want to leave, but I turned and quietly opened her door, not wanting to wake up anyone else in the house. Once in the hallway, I stopped and listened for any sign of life. There was none. Holding my shoes in my hand, I tiptoed down the hallway and into the bathroom. After relieving myself, I snuck into the kitchen and stole a banana from their fruit bowl. I laughed to myself as I slid the banana into my back pocket and snuck out like a mouse. After a lengthy walk and a couple of buses, I was happy to find no one home. I chugged a glass of water, plopped myself on my bed, and fell asleep.

I was awakened by laughter. I looked over at my clock. It read 2:30 p.m. "Oh shit!" I had slept all day. I jumped up. I didn't have time to do all my laundry, so I dug through my dirty clothes piled in the corner. I just needed enough for my date. I found my favorite pair of vintage pants and a shirt, a pair of boxer shorts, and a white undershirt. I stuffed my outfit into a pillowcase and hurried out the door.

"What happened to you?" Maddison laughed when I entered the living room.

"Uh, hi," I said, still half-asleep.

"Nice hair!"

"Oh yeah. I just got up."

Maddison was lying on the couch. She had her staple blanket, a book, and a cup of tea.

I felt the top of my head and could tell my hair looked like a greasy mop. "Oh wow. Is it as good as it feels?"

"Oh, it's better!"

"I take it you had a good time last night?" I asked, trying to get the attention off me.

"I went to bed late, but you were still out. How was the show?"

"It was good...I got a little drunk."

"Did you stay at Damien's?" she asked.

"Not exactly."

"What! Did someone meet a friend and have a sleepover?" She grinned.

I couldn't contain my excitement, and my face turned bright red. I smiled.

"Oh wow. Spill the beans, mister."

"I'll tell you later. I need to do some laundry."

"Wait, tell me now!"

"I gotta go," I said as I turned and ran down the stairs before Maddison could stop me. I hurried to the laundromat down the street. One washed load later, I headed back home with my clean outfit. I was ready for my official first date with Amy. I tossed my clothes on my bed and grabbed a towel for a desperately needed shower.

"Hey, you!" Maddison called from her room. I walked over to her door. I knocked gently even though she had just called to me. "Come in, silly."

I turned the antique glass doorknob to her room and poked my head in like Jack Nicholson and said, "Here's Jason!"

Maddison laughed. "Don't you mean J? Okay, details! Who's the lucky lady?"

"Well, actually, I spent the night with Amy."

"What? No way."

"Way," I said. I told Maddison about my adventure and how I was taking Amy out again tonight.

"Ooh, an official first date, huh?"

"I'm pretty nervous."

"Why? You just spent the night with the girl."

"Yeah, but this is a date, and I have no idea what to do."

"Just be your charming self and you'll be fine."

"Thanks. Well, I better take a shower and get ready."

"Okay, lover boy. You have fun!"

"Will do." I showered, put on my clean clothes, and took off to pick up Amy.

The air was strangely warm, and the bus ride to Amy's seemed to take forever. I was fidgety and nervous. I felt like I did the first time I kissed a girl. What a disaster it was. I was thirteen, and she was my cute neighbor, Sky. My dad had dated her mom, and one day, he told me I was going over to her house. I was excited, thinking she liked me. I was a scrawny, greasy little kid. She was a beautiful angel, aged fifteen. I remembered being so nervous that I almost threw up. I was a puberty disaster, with sweaty palms and a pimply face. I went over, and Sky answered the door, rolling her eyes at me. "Come in, I guess," she said. I should have run home right then, but no, I went in. I was never good at taking a hint. Other kids were there whom I didn't know, and they were all dancing. I didn't know how to dance like them. An older guy who looked about sixteen stood out from the group. He danced like a spastic Michael Jackson, spinning and kicking everywhere. Sky started dancing with him, and she looked great doing some sort of full-body-wave-gyration thing. He got behind her, and together, they did the gyration dance move. I wished I were him. Their bodies were rhythmic and in sync. I sat alone, watching. Sky looked over at me, and I guess she pitied me because she motioned for me to join her. I reluctantly did. Her dance partner stepped aside for me to take his place.

She began moving her hips in a wavelike motion. I moved in behind her, doing my best to follow her rhythmic movements. *I think I got it*, I thought. I was having fun as I held onto Sky from behind. Then I heard it. *Laughing.* I looked over, and Sky's friends were rolling with laughter and pointing at us. I thought I was doing it right. *It feels right,* I thought until I saw it in the mirrored closet door. My rhythm was off, and I looked like a dog trying to hump Sky. I pulled off the conga line and looked at Sky. She was laughing hysterically. I didn't know what to do, so I just said, "I'll see you Monday at school."

"Whatever," she replied. They continued to laugh as I hurried out of the house. "What a dork," I heard the older guy say. A few minutes later, Sky was at my door.

"Uh, hey," I said.

"Sorry about my friends. They can be jerks."

"It's cool, whatever."

"Look, I just wanted to say I was sorry."

"Great, *thanks,*" I said.

"Why don't you come back?"

"Um, I'm good. I think I'll just stay here. You should go back and hang out with your cool friends."

"C'mon…"

"Why should I? You and all your friends laughed at me. I don't even know how to do that stupid hump dance anyway."

"I'm so sorry," she said, trying not to laugh.

"See! You're still laughing."

"I'm sorry, it's just…"

"It's just what?"

She started belly laughing. "You totally looked like a dog trying to hump me!"

I realized she was right. "I did, didn't I." I laughed.

"Yeah, you totally did."

"Well, okay. I accept your apology."

"So then, you'll come back over?"

"Not a chance."

"Well, if you won't come back over, I better give you this now."

"Give me what?"

"This." She walked up to me and planted her lip-gloss-coated lips right on mine. My arms were in shock and hung at my sides. She pecked at my lifeless lips. I woke up and finally realized a girl was kissing me. I put my hands around her waist and, with a head tilt, melted into Sky's magical mouth. She thrust her tongue into my mouth, and I followed suit. It was amazing.

She pulled away and smiled at me. "Okay, see ya on Monday." She turned and ran back to her party.

I stood in my doorway, stunned. *Did that just happen?* I thought. I went to my room. My whole body tingled. I thought about how she had rolled her eyes at me, laughed at me, and then kissed me. *Man, do I need to learn more about girls*, I thought. *Or at least how they think.* I sat in my room, my palms dry and my nerves in check. I could still taste her lip gloss, and I thought I'd never forget that bubblegum flavor.

I arrived at Amy's building and rang the buzzer. Moments later, I could hear someone descend the stairs. My heart raced with nervous anticipation. I took a deep breath and reassured myself, forcing a nervous smile. The door swung open, revealing Amy. Her eyes sparkled, even in the dim afternoon light. She was wearing a plaid vintage dress.

"Hey! Long time no see!" I smiled at her.

"Yeah, it's been a minute." Amy smiled.

"How was your sleep?"

"It was awesome. I slept all day."

"Me too. I fell asleep as soon as I got home," I said. She leaned out and met me with a kiss. "I remember those lips." I grinned.

"Well, you should. You hung out with them most of the night." She giggled.

"I think my mouth is sore," I said, and we both laughed. We hugged and lingered on the front stoop. I could feel her energy, and it felt amazing. Her svelte frame felt wonderful in my arms. I squeezed her hard. "You feel good in my arms."

"You, too." Our lock separated. She grabbed my arm and led me upstairs. As we climbed the stairs, I spied her long legs peek in and out from the side split of her dress. I felt lucky to be going out with such a beautiful woman. Halfway up the long flight of stairs, Amy turned and smiled, knowing I was taking inventory of her features. Like a kid caught with his hand in a candy jar, I fumbled a smile back. I heard people laughing upstairs, and as we topped the stairs of the century-old Victorian flat, the laughter grew louder. *It must be Mary and Laura*, I thought. *Just be yourself and relax.*

Amy led me toward the living room, where the laughter turned into smiling faces. "Hey, ladies, you remember J. from last night?"

"Hey, J.," Mary and Laura said in unison.

"Hi." I waved to them. They both looked at each other and giggled. Both Mary and Laura made me nervous, and their laughter didn't help until I realized they were stoned as they hovered over a shared bag of Doritos.

"So, Mr. Jason—I mean, *J.*—would you like a Dorito?" Laura said in a slight Southern drawl that I hadn't notice at the concert. Mary continued to giggle.

"No, I'm good, thanks."

"Miss Amy?" Laura held out the bag for her. Amy declined as well. I relaxed a little, knowing they were more interested in eating chips than interrogating the new guy. "No one can resist the Dorito," Laura said as she cracked up.

"The first one's free!" Mary chimed in.

"Well, ladies. It looks like you have your hands full," Amy said.

"Yeah, *full of Doritos*," Laura said. They both laughed as if it was the funniest thing they'd ever heard. "We'll stop when we find the perfect chip."

"Okay, ladies...have fun with that," Amy said.

"Nice to see you," I said to Mary and Laura as Amy grabbed my hand to lead me down the hall to her room. As we walked down the hall, I heard one of them whisper, *He's cute.* A smile came across my face. When a guy hears that from any breathing girl on Planet Earth, it's a good day. Not to mention, Amy must've heard it as well, which helped calm my nerves.

"I just need to change before we go," Amy said.

"Change? Why?"

"What do you mean?"

"You in that dress is the best thing I've seen all day," I said. A smile came to Amy's face. "Really. I think you look great, like *really great.*"

Amy walked over to me and came close. Her hands slid down my arms. She looked at me like no one had ever looked at me before. "I'll wear this then if you like it so much."

"Great," I said, still in her trance.

"By the way...where are we going?"

"I thought we'd go to the Wharf and just play it by ear." I hoped she would like my no plans plan.

"Great. Do you mind if we stop by Walgreens on the way? I need to pick up a prescription before they close."

"Yeah, sure. That's fine."

She grabbed her purse and a sweater. "Okay, ready to go."

As soon as we were about to leave, I heard the girls yell, "Carson!!!"

"Hey, ladies. Where's the little woman?" Carson asked in his deep voice.

Little woman, who was that? I thought. *Ugh, not this guy.* Amy turned to me, looking worried. "Oh shit! I forgot I was supposed to practice with Carson today."

"Oh well, then you better—"

Amy stopped me. "No. I'll just tell him that I can't. C'mon," she said, grabbing my arm and leading me back to the Dorito party, which had moved to the kitchen.

"Hey! There's the little woman," Carson said. There he stood, all six feet two and looking very Abercrombie & Fitch.

"Hi!" Amy said as he engulfed her in a hug. She literally disappeared into his arms and then reappeared. "Carson, you remember J.," Amy said as she came back over to my side.

"Hey, buddy!" He spoke to me as if I were a little boy.

Buddy? I'll show him buddy, I thought. "Hey, Carson." I met his outstretched hand for a man shake. His hand pretty much engulfed mine. I wasn't a small guy, pretty average in build, but Carson was a giant. Both in size and looks. My mind raced, and I felt foolish because it wasn't my place to care. After all, this was just a date, but seeing the girl I liked being hugged by Captain America made me feel outmatched.

"Do you mind if we practice later?" Amy asked.

"Yeah, no worries. Where are you guys off to?"

"To the Wharf," I answered like I'd already planned a great time.

"Okay, you kids have fun," Carson said with a smile.

"Okay, Dad," Laura said. Laughing, she licked her orange fingers. "You sound like a Dad, Carson." She cracked up more. Still grinning, Carson looked at Laura. He didn't get the joke. It went straight over his head…his handsome but dumb head. I felt less outmatched.

"So, I'll see you later, then?" Carson said to Amy.

"Yeah. I'll meet you upstairs when I get home."

"Nice to see you all again," I said with a general wave.

"Oh wait!" Carson said suddenly. We stood waiting to hear what last-minute thought Captain America had to say. "Uh, your fly's down," he said, gesturing to me.

"Oh!" I quickly reached for my crotch. I zipped it up, and with a bright red face I said, "Thanks, man."

"No problem, buddy. It happens," he said as he turned to leave.

"Bye, Carson!" the girls said in unison.

"Shall we go?" Amy asked.

I looked at her and replied with a chuckle. "Yes. Please!"

We left Amy's flat hand in hand and made our way down the street to the bus line. Thank goodness for the efficient and timely SF transportation system. Waiting around for a bus on a first date is a recipe for uncomfortable silences. Even though we had spent the entire night together, this was official. We were on a romantic date, and I didn't want to blow it, especially with a girl like Amy. The key was to keep this date interesting and moving forward. We sat at the bus stop. Amy watched the traffic, and I fell into thought. I thought about what just occurred at Amy's place. Mary, Laura, Doritos, and of course, Carson. As my mind wandered, Amy snapped me out of my thoughts.

"Just so you know, Carson's my dance partner, and we generally practice three times a week." She was trying to assure me that there wasn't a romantic connection between them. This was thoughtful of her because it was really bothering me.

I replied as nonchalantly as I could. "Oh yeah. It's cool." Guys like Carson got what they wanted, and why wouldn't he want Amy? She was beautiful, smart, and incredibly nice. She was the nicest person I'd met since moving to San Francisco. I still couldn't wrap my head around why Matt didn't pursue her. I thought for a moment how strange it was. Just six months earlier, Matt had returned from a trip to San Francisco. I remembered him telling me about these girls he had met. I thought about the box of trinkets from Chinatown and the postcard with Amy's lipstick kiss on it. I replayed the entire conversation we'd had about Amy, the girl I was now sitting next to. Thankfully, I didn't remember him telling me if they'd had sex, and I was glad he hadn't. That was the last image I needed in my head right now. I laughed thinking about how strange life could be and how small the world could be.

"What's so funny?" Amy asked.

"Uh, well. I was, well…"

"What?" she insisted.

"I was thinking about Matt."

"And what about Matt?" She raised an eyebrow.

"I was thinking how strange it was that Matt had shown me the box you sent him. I'd told him he should get you before someone else did. I'd told him not to let you get away because you seemed so cool."

"And what did he say?"

"Honestly?"

"Well, that would be better than a lie." Amy laughed. "I don't like lies. The truth may suck, but it's easier to work with. So, go on. Lay it on me."

"If you must know, when you sent that box of goodies to him, he was dating two other girls at the time."

"Oh really? Nice to know," Amy said.

"Not to mention that one of his girlfriends was a girl I had brought over to his place for a BBQ years ago. Let's just say by the end of the evening, she was his date."

"He stole your date? Doesn't sound like a great friend," Amy said.

"I was better off without her. My taste in women is a little different than Matt's."

"It kind of doesn't look that way!" Amy laughed and nudged me with her elbow. "I had an idea that Matt was possibly a player, but at the time I didn't really care. When I met Matt, it had only been five or six months since I'd ended my five-year relationship with Chad. He was so controlling, and after moving out and living on my own, I enjoyed making my own decisions and living my life. With Chad, I was living his life, not mine, and the last thing I wanted was to get involved in another relationship. I was free, and Matt was entertaining. He lived far away, and we had fun when he visited, but that's all. He was just a brief break. Does that make sense?"

"Yeah, I can see that."

"So, back to what you mentioned earlier…What is your taste?" Amy grinned.

"Well, if you must know…"

"I must."

"I like a woman that can cook and clean *really well*. I don't mean just light dusting, I mean on all fours, scrubbing hard." I stifled my laughter.

"Oh, I see. Well, that's totally me!" Amy said. We both laughed.

"But seriously. Let's just say I'm a romantic and we can leave it with that," I said.

"Fair enough." Amy smiled at me. "But now I feel a little foolish for sending that package. In hindsight, I wish I hadn't."

"I stole most of the stuff in the box anyway!" I laughed.

"Well, then. I guess you got even with him for stealing your girl."

"Some trade-off. I got a box of Chinese trinkets, and he got the girl."

"No, I wasn't referring to the trinkets." She leaned in, and our lips met. We hovered, suspended in some other dimension. A place where time stopped while our lips touched. When we finally separated, our eyes locked, and we smiled.

"I see. I guess you have a point. You are definitely better than a box of trinkets!"

"I should hope so." Amy reached into her purse and pulled out her red lipstick. I watched intently as she reapplied it to her lips and placed it back in her bag as the bus pulled up.

We got on the bus, and I paid our fare and asked for a transfer. I assumed the driver handed one to Amy. We sat down toward the back.

"Shoot! I forgot to get my transfer," Amy said.

"That's okay. I'll get it for you." I made my way back to the front of the moving bus. I swayed back and forth and grabbed onto one of the chrome bars next to the driver, holding myself steady. "Hi, bus lady. Um, we, I mean, she didn't get her transfer. Can I get another one, please?"

"Who is *she*?" the driver barked, obviously not having a good day.

"Uh, we just got on the bus. I paid for both of us, but you only gave me one transfer." I smiled big. "We just need the other transfer."

"Transfers need to be asked for when boarding the bus only, not after!"

"Right, but we just got on," I said, pointing to Amy, who was sitting pretty at the back of the bus. "You saw us, she's right there," I said, still pointing at Amy. "Can I please have another transfer, ma'am?"

"Transfers must be asked for when boarding the bus and not after. Now please sit down, sir!"

I looked back, and the bus was nearly empty. I understood the policy. People were always trying to get an extra free transfer, but it was obvious that we weren't doing that. There were only about six other people on the bus, and she hadn't stopped since we'd gotten on.

"Really?" I insisted. "You won't give me the transfer I just paid for two minutes ago. We were the only people to get on the bus at the last stop…Really?"

"Sir, you need to *sit down*. I am not going to ask you again. Or you can just get off my bus. It's up to you."

"This is bullshit." I turned and weaved my way back to Amy, who was unaware of the drama that had unfolded.

"Did you get the transfer?"

"No! She won't give it to me," I said, frustrated.

"Really? You're joking."

"'Transfers must be asked for when boarding the bus and not after,'" I quoted. "That's what she said. She told me she would kick us off the bus if I didn't sit down."

"What a bitch!" Amy glared at the front of the bus.

"Total bitch!" The situation with the bus driver played over and over in my mind like a movie clip on loop. Why was it so hard for her to just tear off another transfer? She obviously knew we'd just gotten on the bus. She was being stubborn, and in fact, I was entitled to that bus transfer. *She has no right to deny us!* I thought. With my manhood inflamed and my ego bruised, it was on. I grabbed Amy's hand, and without forethought, I stood and led her to the front of the bus. The driver saw us in her rearview mirror. She called out, insisting that we take our seats. We managed our way to her, and again, I grabbed onto the chrome bar to steady myself. I put my hand up and pleaded for any kind of reason. I pointed at Amy's face. "You don't remember us just getting on the bus. Why will you not give her the bus transfer I paid for? Is it really that hard to be a nice person?" I pleaded.

In an instant, she slammed the brakes and looked at me with disgust. "This is my bus and my rules! If you don't like it, then get *off*!"

"Fine! We'll be getting off your fucking bus, then. Open the door," I demanded.

"Exit the rear of the bus," she commanded.

"Why? Open this door right here and we will get off."

"The rear door," she insisted.

That was it. I snapped. I was not about to look like a pussy on my first official date with Amy beside me. I'd seen many drivers open the front door for people. I grabbed the big chrome-plated lever that just happened to be within arm's reach and pulled hard. The door flung open. I grabbed Amy's hand and quickly led her down the bus steps.

"Was that so fucking hard?" I said to the driver. The driver, in an attempt to foil my mutiny and stop our escape, grabbed the door lever and, with a stern pull, tried to close the door on me. I was so close to the outside, I could smell freedom from this disaster. I powered forward like a charge in battle. I met the closing door with my shoulder, and the struggle ensued. The driver, steadfast, held onto the lever. Her grip was strong. I struggled to keep the half-open door from closing in on us.

"Sit down, now!" the driver yelled at us.

"Open the damn door!" I said, leveraging my weight against the door. The traffic ahead started to move. The driver had to let go of the door handle to take the wheel. Simultaneously, she let go and I applied all my weight against the door. The next thing I knew, the door flew into the open position and the door's safety glass shattered everywhere. My eyes popped open in an *Oh shit!* stare as I looked at Amy. Her mouth was making an *Oh shit!* shape as well.

The driver yelled, "Oh no you didn't!" She grabbed her radio to call what I could only think would be some sort of bus police.

I squeezed Amy's hand a little tighter and yelled, "Run!" We darted off the bus and down the block. We ran as if we were Bonnie and Clyde who had just robbed a bank. We darted into a bookstore, startling the quiet customers.

"This way," I said, holding her hand tight. I led Amy to the back of the store. Without hesitating, we passed an "Employees Only" sign and ran through the back room and out the back door to the alley. I stopped and let go of Amy's hand. I leaned forward, placing my hands on my knees, and breathed hard for several seconds.

I looked up at Amy, who was also catching her breath. Thinking I'd blown this date for sure, I waited for her reaction to my brutish behavior. To my surprise, Amy gathered herself and then started laughing. Elated, I joined in. "Did that just happen?" I hugged her and pulled back. "Are you okay?" I examined her for wounds from the shattered glass.

"I'm fine, how about you?" she said.

"I'm good. I am so sorry! I had no idea the glass would shatter."

"It's all right…she was so mean!"

"We laughed about it for a moment then decided to move on in fear of the bus police or whomever she might have called.

We made our way hand in hand through the alley and down a couple of streets to the subway. We hurried down the steps, through the turnstiles, and onto the platform. As we waited for a train, I felt Amy squeeze my hand, getting my attention. She had that look that I knew meant *Come here*. She pulled me to her and, without hesitating, embraced and kissed me passionately. I reciprocated and was overjoyed that this debacle was ending in a kiss. I held her tightly, so tightly she winced. I didn't let go because I knew she liked being held.

"I feel safe in your arms," she said.

"Uh, you might want to rethink that." I chuckled. "I did almost get you arrested or injured." We kissed again. I could feel the wind from the approaching train. I pulled my lips from her mouth and looked into her eyes. "Wow," I said out loud.

"That was nice." She smiled.

"Yes, yes, it was." My lips tingled. The doors to the train opened. Hand in hand, we hurried onto the train, completing our escape. We sat down, and I suddenly remembered that we hadn't stopped at Walgreens for her prescription. "I'm sorry. I forgot about your prescription." I was concerned.

"It's okay. I can go tomorrow."

"If you don't mind me asking, what medication do you need?"

"Oh, it's just a new medication for chronic headaches and migraines."

"You must get them bad if you need a doctor for them."

"Yes, I do. I get them all the time, and unfortunately, I have one right now. I usually don't talk about them. Most people don't understand…"

I put my hands on her temples and gently rubbed them. I kissed her forehead. "All better," I said. She was right, I really didn't understand, but I wished I could take her pain away.

She smiled as if it worked and said, "Yes, all better."

The train slowed, and the digital banner read "Embarcadero." We got off and walked the short distance to the famous Fisherman's Wharf and Pier 39. You could smell and taste the sea. Amy and I held hands as we walked toward the festive marketplace. I really had no idea where I was going, and after a few blocks, I think Amy knew this too.

"You want to see something cool?" she asked.

"Yes, definitely."

"There's a tiny little museum around the block. I think you'll like it."

"Sounds great, I love a good museum."

"This museum is a little *different*." She led me down the street and around the corner. We came to a small store frontage. In large, aged letters, it read "The History of Torture Museum EST 1980."

"Oh wow. You're right, I didn't expect this." I laughed. "What the hell is this place doing here?"

"I know. I thought the same thing when I came here a few years ago."

"This is pretty awesome," I said. It was morbid, but I was excited to see what might lie inside the cryptic, dark building. "What could be more romantic than to browse ancient torture devices?" I laughed.

"Exactly," she said. "Plus, we get to learn about the demise of the unlucky victims." We both giggled.

The museum was what you might expect from its name. Each torture device displayed a history of the origin and how it was used, though some of the devices were self-explanatory just by looking at them. One device was called the triangle. It was a good seven feet tall, and the poor soul would have to sit on the top point. Slowly, weights would be added to their feet.

"Talk about a pain in the ass," I said, horrified.

"Yeah, I think I would rather endure the iron maiden," Amy said.

"Hmm, being slowly split in two or being forced into a suit of steel spikes. That's a tough one," I said. We laughed, trying to pretend the devices hadn't really been used on people, but deep down it was a tragic place filled with a history of misery.

"Well, that was interesting," I said once we were outside.

"Yeah, it's pretty dark," Amy said.

"Well, all that torture has given me quite an appetite. You hungry?"

"I am."

I knew they had fresh crab at Fisherman's Wharf. My mom used to bring me here when I was a kid, and I remembered the big pot of boiling water. A guy wearing the traditional Gorton's yellow slicker would drop screaming crabs into the boiling water then fish them back out. With a few cracks and a side of butter, he'd pass crab legs out to hungry tourists.

"How about crab?" I said.

"Uh, I'm sorry. I don't eat seafood," Amy said.

"It's fine, I thought everyone likes crab, but hey, I guess you're just different than everyone, aren't you?" I teased.

"I guess I am, and I'm absolutely okay with that!" She smiled.

"Honestly, I was just trying to impress you with a fancy, overpriced bug from the bottom of the ocean." I chuckled.

"You don't need to impress me. I like you the way you are."

I looked at Amy intently and scratched my chin. "Hmm, let's see. You look like a hamburger kind of gal. Am I right?" I waited for her response.

"I do like a good burger. I'm impressed. You can really read a girl's mind." She laughed.

"It's a gift." I proudly puffed out my chest. "So, considering that you live here and it's obvious that my planned date is not planned, do you have any recommendations?"

"Well, there's a Hard Rock Cafe down the street from here."

"I love their burgers!" I said.

"I know, right? They're delicious."

"Let's do it."

"Sounds good!" We walked down the street talking about the torture device museum and the mean bus lady. As we walked, I grabbed Amy's hand, and she instantly wove her fingers into mine. She looked over at me coyly. It was strange holding a new hand, as I was used to Ashley's. She would always fold her thumb a certain way to lock my finger to hers. Holding Amy's hand was different but better. Her energy radiated through me. In a strange way, it was like holding my own hand. Her skin felt familiar. I looked over at her as we slowly walked. I walked slower than usual, wanting this moment to last longer.

"I had fun last night," I said.

"It was pretty great. Fun times were had." She sighed.

"I kind of feel bad for causing so much drama at your ex's house."

"You shouldn't. That was the highlight of my night." She grinned.

"The highlight?"

"Well, aside from the tighty-whitey dance."

"Oh, please don't remind me! God, how could I forget about that? I will never live that down."

We rounded a corner and opened the door to the Hard Rock Cafe. The hostess smiled and walked us to a booth. Amy sat close, and our knees pressed against each other's.

"Can I get you something to drink?" our waitress asked. I motioned to Amy. My father brought me up as a gentleman. She smiled, noticing.

"I'll have a Tom Collins," Amy said.

I'd never heard of a Tom Collins. I was about to order a coke, but since Amy ordered a cocktail, I ordered the same.

"You like Tom Collins?" she asked me.

"Never had one."

"Oh, you'll love it."

"I hope it's not super fruity."

"No, well, it has a little sugar in it, but it tastes kind of like a tart lemonade."

"Cool, sounds good."

"So, what else do you have planned for our unplanned date?" She chuckled.

"I thought we would go to Alcatraz Island. I went there when I was a kid, and I thought it might be fun."

"Oh, um…unless you made reservations a month ago. I'm sure it's sold out this time of year."

"Oh shit. I didn't even think about that."

"It is one of the biggest tourist attractions here." She laughed.

"Well, we can check it out, and if not, I guess we can go skydiving."

"Really?" Amy was surprised by my suggestion.

"It's plan B." I smirked, obviously joking.

"I was going to say…I would love to skydive, but I'm not really dressed for it." She laughed.

"Thank God for that!" I smiled at her. She smiled back and gave me that *come here* look again.

Our drinks arrived, and we ordered burgers with fries. "This is good!" I sipped my first Tom Collins. I noticed that my drink had a cherry in it, and I remembered a trick my dad showed me when I was a kid. He taught me how to tie a cherry stem in a knot inside my mouth by wedging one end in between your teeth and carefully maneuvering the stem into a loop with your tongue. It took some practice, but it wasn't really that hard. I announced my performance to Amy and proceeded with the magic. She watched my mouth move as I went to work, trying to get it right. Sure enough, after a minute or two, I produced one cherry stem tied in a knot from my mouth.

"That's crazy. How did you do that?" Amy was clearly impressed with my trick. I tried to teach her, and it was fun watching her try to tie her cherry stem in her mouth for the next fifteen minutes.

Our waitress came with our burgers, and Amy finally gave up. "Ugh, I can't do it," she said.

"Don't feel bad. It takes practice," I said. We ate our burgers and finished our drinks.

"I know this really cool bar in North Beach that we can go to, unless you have something else planed like bungee jumping or scuba diving." She grinned.

"Actually, since you like seafood so much, I thought we could go crabbing."

"Screw that…I don't like going on the water." She laughed.

"What! You hate the sea?"

"No, that came out wrong. I love the sea. I love looking at it, and I love living near water. I just avoid going in it. I can't swim." She laughed more, knowing it sounded strange.

"You grew up in Southern California and you don't know how to swim?"

"I can doggy paddle and do the frog, but that's about it." She laughed at herself. "I got a horrible ear infection when I was little, and my eardrum burst. It was so bad that it didn't grow back, and my parents couldn't afford the surgery to have one grafted. Ever since I can't go underwater. I almost had the surgery done a few years back, but honestly, I've lived so long this way that I really don't mind anymore."

"That sucks. I practically grew up in the ocean."

"It sucked when I was young...I was horrible at Marco Polo. I was always *fish out of water*." She laughed.

"Okay, so no seafood and literally no sea. I am seeing a pattern." I laughed.

"Pretty much. Now that you know all my baggage, do you still like me?" Amy teased.

"Yeah, I guess I can live with that."

"Good. Ready to go?"

I paid the check, and we ventured onward to North Beach. We walked silently for a while.

"I like that you call me darlin', by the way," Amy said.

"Oh good. It reminds me of my grandma," I said. "She always called her grandkids darlings. She said *swell* all the time too."

"I love that word."

"It's funny how she still uses the same slang words from her childhood. I can see her smiling face. 'That's just swell,' she would say."

"That's cute," Amy said.

"Thanks."

"Not you, your grandma, but you're cute too, I guess."

"Why, thank ya, ma'am. I think you're purdy as well," I said in an exaggerated Southern drawl.

Amy laughed. "You should use my middle name...it's Mae."

I laughed. "Amy Mae, you git your butt in here and wash that doggy!"

"I'll be right in, Ma!"

We laughed, talked, and walked for what seemed like a long time. Amy held my arm with both of her hands, and I made a conscious effort to stay in perfect step with her as we walked to North Beach.

"I love North Beach," Amy said. We approached streets filled with Italian restaurants and bars. "It's just so romantic."

"Wait, is this where the Purple Onion is?" I asked.

"Yep. It's just down the street."

"So...I'm still wondering about you," I said.

"What do you mean?"

"Well, the first time you met me was at Club Deluxe. I had an embarrassingly greasy Afro do, thanks to Damien's Brylcreem. And then, the second time you saw me, I was falling out of a van and into the street at the Purple Onion. At least my hair looked normal, but I'm just wondering why you haven't run for the hills like a respectable girl would."

"Oh right. Okay, well, see ya, then." She let go of my arm and started walking the other way.

"Hey! Wait!" I walked after her.

"You know what? You're absolutely right. What kind of girl would possibly see herself with someone like you?" she replied seriously. She stopped and looked at me, crossing her arms, clearly annoyed. I didn't know what to do. I looked down then back at her. She cracked a smile and jokingly slapped my arm.

"Oh man, you had me going. That wasn't funny." I grabbed her and held on to her tiny waist tightly. "I think I'll keep you right here," I said.

We kissed for what seemed like minutes, right there on the street. I heard a couple of guys yell from a car, "Get a room." I heard another woman walk by and say, "How romantic." I opened my eyes and let go of my squeeze, just enough for her to breathe.

"Scary," Amy muttered.

"What do you mean?"

"Just scary," she said again. "It's a good thing."

"Oh okay, you as well." I sighed.

We walked to the bar, and I was surprised to see that it was the same dive bar that Maddison had taken me to when we first met up in the city. "I've been here," I said as we walked in.

"Really?"

"Yeah, Maddison brought me here. We live just up the hill from here."

"Maddison, huh?" Amy teased.

"We're just friends."

"I'm just joking. I'm not the jealous type, and besides, this is only our first date."

"I know, but it feels like we've been together longer. I don't know how to explain it. I feel comfortable around you."

"I feel the same way. Weird, huh?" She smiled.

We sat down and enjoyed a few Tom Collins cocktails and got a bit tipsy. We talked about each other and our lives growing up in Southern California. We both agreed that we weren't in any hurry to get seriously involved with anyone. Amy had ended her relationship with Chad a year ago, and I'd only been away from Ashley for a few months. It was only natural that we didn't want to offer our hearts so soon after being hurt, so we agreed that we would just have fun…no strings attached. Our intent was there, but I think we both could tell it was a losing battle. We were falling for each other, and a web of strings was already attaching us together. Our conversation was far different than the one we were having with our eyes. That conversation said much more. *Man, I think I'm in serious trouble*, I thought.

"Hey, since I live up the hill, why don't we go to my place?" I asked.

"Your place, huh?" Amy said, as if I was trying to get her into my bed.

"It's my turn."

"Your turn?"

"Yes. Last night we had a sleepover at your place. It's only fair that tonight we have a sleepover at my place."

"Oh, I see. Well, since you put it that way, it would be the fair thing to do," she said. We left the bar, and arm in arm we climbed the hill to my place.

We were both out of breath as we reached my front door. It was late, and the apartment was dark. "Shh," I said as we climbed the stairs.

"Bathroom?" Amy whispered. I directed her to the bathroom and waited for her so I could guide her to my room. I'd forgotten that I needed to lift the corner of my bed to open and shut the door.

"Wait," I whispered to Amy as I did the maneuver.

She tried her best to keep her laughter in. I, too, was beginning to giggle. It was hard to be cool at the same time I was lifting my bed to let a cute girl in my room. Things were not adding up as I tried to figure out how to get us both in. "Okay, I got it. Hop on."

With delicate grace, Amy climbed onto the bed. I lifted the corner of the bed with her on it and closed the door. With the added ninety-eight pounds, the bed slammed on the ground as I dropped the corner. I looked at Amy and placed my finger to my lips, reminding her to remain quiet, but it was no use. We both laughed with our hands covering our mouths. I flopped down on the bed, laughing. I silenced our laughter by kissing her.

It was like the night before, but we both knew this would end differently. I wasn't wearing tighty-whities, and Amy was in my bed. Kissing led to groping and then to sex. We made love with the full moon shining into my tiny room until we collapsed in exhaustion.

Chapter Twenty-Nine

I awoke to Amy sleeping next to me. She was beautiful. I had been with pretty girls before, but this was different. The light draped over her as if it was happy to do so. Every curve and shadow was perfection. Even the texture of her skin was perfect. I carefully slid my hand across her violin-shaped side, making sure I didn't wake her. I imagined I was one of the great Impressionist artists of the seventeenth century and Amy was my muse. Here in this moment, I was inspired. About what, I had no idea, just inspired. The light of the sun began to fill the room.

"Curses!" Amy said as the sun's rays hit her eyes. "Go away, sun," she hissed like a vampire. She attempted to bury her head in my chest to hide from the day.

"I don't think it's going to go away." I laughed.

"I know." She sighed. I folded my arms over her head, creating a little cave for her to hide. "Thanks."

"Welcome to the J. Cave."

"I like the J. Cave. Hey. Can I ask you a question?" she asked.

"Uh, sure, as long as it's a good question."

"Well, that depends on your answer, I guess."

"Okay, shoot."

"Was last night good for you?"

"What, you couldn't tell?" I was joking and playing it cool. The fact was it was incredible and strange all at the same time. I had never felt so connected to a human being in my life. I wanted to tell her, but I was scared. Scared I would scare her off.

"Yes, but it was different...never mind, it's stupid." She buried her head deeper in the J. Cave.

I sensed she was embarrassed by her question. "No, it's not stupid," I said. "I think I know what you mean. Are you talking about the energy?" I could tell she was feeling the same thing as me.

"Yes!" She popped her head back out, knowing what I meant. "There's definitely an energy between us."

"It was like we were two perfectly fitting puzzle pieces," I gushed.

"Yes! That's exactly what I mean. I have to say, I didn't expect to feel this way. It's powerful." She drew circles on my chest while looking up at me.

"Me too. I think we better stop this conversation right here." I chuckled.

"I agree."

At the bar, we had both agreed we weren't looking for anything serious, but last night was the best sex we had ever had, both physically and emotionally. We were a good fit, and there was nothing either of us could do about it.

I could hear Maddison talking on the phone somewhere in the apartment. Amy heard her too. "Ugh, the walk of shame," Amy said.

"Walk of *shame*?" I said.

"Oh no. I didn't mean I was ashamed of you."

"Oh, I get it. Not cool," I said sarcastically, letting go of my embrace. She wrestled with my arms, trying to get me to hold her.

"It's just other people see a girl still dressed up from the night before, and they assume she had a one-night stand. Mary, Laura, and I laugh every time we see it. Once, we were eating breakfast at a diner the day after New Year's Eve and we saw a girl dressed in a red sequin gown walking up Haight Street holding one shoe with a broken heel. Her hair was a tangled mess, and her eyes were ringed black from her smudged mascara. It was so sad, but we couldn't help but laugh. It was funny."

"Let's hear your walk of shame story," I teased.

"You first!" Amy pointed her finger back at me, laughing.

"Uh, never mind."

"Yeah, that's what I thought!" she said. "Are both your roommates here or just Maddison?"

"I don't know. I never see Audrey."

"I really need to use the bathroom." Amy dragged her fingers through her hair, attempting to tame her mane.

"You look great." I grabbed Amy's hand, pulling her up. "Hold on. I need to lift the bed corner to open the door. It's never not funny."

"You will never forget living here."

"Well, I don't think I'll remember it for the door, but more about you and our wonderful night we shared."

"You know how to make a girl feel special," she said as she wrapped her arms around me.

"It's all those *How to Seduce a Woman* books I've read."

"Very funny."

"What? It's good information."

"Please open the door now." She started doing the "I need to pee" dance. I laughed and lifted the bed to let her out.

Maddison was still on the phone and smiled at us as we walked by. Amy waved quickly and hurried into the bathroom. I sat on the couch and thumbed through an *SF Weekly*. I could tell Maddison was on the phone with Brad. Her tone was always the same when she talked with him.

She hung up the phone forcefully. "Ugh, that boy is driving me crazy!"

"Drama with Brad?" I asked.

"You could say that. He just won't give me my space."

"Well, I don't think I'm the best person to talk to about that."

"Yeah, you're probably right." Maddison looked toward the bathroom then back at me. "So last night went well, I presume?" she whispered.

"Yep. You could say that." I winked.

"Good for you! She's really cute."

"Yeah, I know." I smiled to myself.

"You want me to disappear?"

"No, no, you're good. Thanks, though."

Amy came out of the bathroom with newly applied makeup and combed hair. She smiled and sat down next to me as if we were kids in trouble.

"Hi, Amy." Maddison smiled at her.

"Nice, to see you again. You're so cute," Amy said to Maddison.

"Aw, this old face?" Maddison laughed. "You are the pretty one and look at all that hair!"

Amy touched her long dark hair. "Oh, sorry. I used your brush, or at least someone's brush."

"That's fine, as long as you don't have lice," Maddison joked.

"Not that I know of, but I did sleep in J.'s bed," Amy said. They both laughed at my expense.

"Wow, you're so funny," I said to Amy. "Hey, Mad, we ended up at that bar you took me to in North Beach."

"That's cool. I love that place."

"We had a great time." I couldn't help but smile.

"So, what are you kids up to today?" Maddison asked.

"Uh, I don't know." I looked at Amy. "I think Amy has plans of hiding from the sun," I said, laughing.

She rolled her eyes at me. "I'm a little hungover."

"Sounds like a good plan…Well, kids, I am off to lunch." Maddison got up.

"Ooh, lunch date?" I asked.

"Maybe." Maddison winked.

"What? Who's the lucky guy?" I asked.

"The new guy from work."

"Nice!"

"A girl's gotta eat!" She laughed. "Amy, it was super nice seeing you, and I'm sure I'll see you again soon."

"You, too. Enjoy your lunch date." Amy smiled.

"Ciao, you two." Maddison grabbed her purse and sweater and walked toward the stairs.

"Later," I said. After she left, I turned to Amy. "Well, that wasn't so bad."

"No, it went well. She's pretty. I'm shocked you haven't tried to date her."

"I didn't know you swung that way, but I can see what I can do," I said.

"Oh, shut up!" Amy punched me jokingly.

"Man, you are a hitter. I'm not sure about you. I think I'm being abused."

Amy leaned in and kissed my chest where she'd punched me. "All better," she said.

"It hurts a little lower." I laughed and instantly blocked another punch. "Ouch!"

"You deserved that one," she said.

"Okay, okay. You win," I surrendered.

"I think I'm gonna go home and take a shower."

"I totally understand. After being with me all night, I would want to shower too."

"Very funny, but it's not like that. A girl just likes to be fresh. Besides, I was thinking you could come over later. I'll make you dinner."

"I think I would like that. Dinner sounds good."

"Can you lift the bed for me? I need to get my stuff." Amy laughed. "You're right, it's never not funny."

"I'll get your things. Be right back," I said. I grabbed her stuff from my room and headed back to the couch. Amy put on her shoes and stood up, swinging her purse over her shoulder.

"I'll see you later, then." She looked up at me. I kissed her, and she lightly bit my lip before breaking away.

"Uh, you better leave now, or you won't be leaving at all." I grabbed her tightly with intent.

"Oh no, don't start. I need to go," she said.

I slowed my advance. I held her and picked her up off the ground and kissed her passionately.

"Come over at six," she said, breathlessly.

"I'll be there." I set her down. After one last kiss, she tiptoed down the stairs like a mouse. I went to my room and looked at my bed where we had lain last night and smiled. Something different had happened, and I was worried. Worried I was falling for her too soon. It was bad timing. I wasn't sure how ready I was to fall in love again. I thought about everything that had happened to me in such a short period of time. It wasn't that long ago that I'd arrived at my mom's cabin. I was in such a fragile state then, and I had felt so alone, but I was thankful for what I had learned during my time there. I was by no means enlightened, but I'd had a taste of something. Something that I couldn't explain. All I could do was move forward and let fate land me where I was supposed to be. I knew that I was on my path and that it included meeting Amy.

Chapter Thirty

It was only five fifteen when I arrived at Amy's building. I was still getting the hang of the bus routes and the timing from one part of town to the other. I always assumed it was going to take a lot longer than it did. Not wanting to be too early, I decided to walk through the Panhandle where I'd found the giant oak tree. Amy lived only a few blocks away, and I had the time, so I decided to walk to the tree. It was a nice day, and as I expected, there were dozens of people in the park. I was happy to see that no one was occupying my spot by the tree. I sat beneath it and looked around at the people busy having picnics and playing with dogs. I looked up and rested my head against the huge oak tree. I thought about the spot where I'd placed the pebble in the forest at my mom's and imagined the tree being there. I tried to close my eyes and concentrate, but all I heard was a chorus of people. I opened my eyes and relaxed against the tree and just tried to feel its energy. I wished the people away, but I knew they wouldn't go. I'd been caught up in the energy of the city, and I knew the longer I waited, the harder it would be to find the way to my gate. I promised myself I would return to my special place soon. I sat at the base of the tree, and all I could do was think about Amy until it was time to head over to her place. As I got up, I placed my hand on the giant oak and thanked it.

I walked up the hill toward Amy's flat, but for some reason, I stopped and turned to take a final look at the tree. To my surprise, there was a child hugging it. It startled me. I watched until the child ran back over to his family. I knew it didn't mean anything, but it was still odd to me. I thought about the Urban Giant and his tales of people feeding his tree. I wondered if that little kid was feeding the tree. I laughed, but still, I wondered. I thought of my dad's friend, the lady who told me to look out for coincidences in life. I could feel the universe directing me, and as much as I wanted to fight it, I could feel the universe's energy in Amy. I knew I was supposed to meet her, but I didn't know why, yet.

I was perfectly late when I finally arrived. I rang the bell, and the door instantly buzzed. I opened the door, and Amy was at the top of the stairs. "Hi," she said with a big smile. "C'mon up."

I walked up the stairs and followed her into the kitchen. "Smells good." I inhaled deeply, and my stomach grumbled in response. I was suddenly starving.

"Hope you like lasagna."

"Oh really? I hate lasagna."

Amy snapped her head around only to find a big smile on my face. "You suck!" she laughed and threw a kitchen towel at me.

"Gotcha!"

"Gosh, you better like it because I made enough for an army."

"Sounds good to me," I said. Amy poured us some wine, and we sat at the table.

"It should be done in about an hour."

"Oh, that's enough time," I said.

"For what?"

I looked at her with a mischievous grin.

"Oh...*that*."

"Well, I was just thinking..."

"I can see that. We do have the place to ourselves." She sipped her wine and gave me that look I loved so much.

We hurried down the hallway and into her room. We frantically tore into each other, kissing and taking off our clothes as quickly as possible. We made love until the oven timer went off.

"Oh my, a girl could get used to this."

"You're not kidding."

"Where did you come from?" She traced my lips with her finger.

"Uh, the bus," I said, and we both laughed.

"I'm starving! Let's eat." Amy jumped up from the bed and quickly got dressed and ran to the kitchen to turn off the timer. I followed suit. We sat enjoying the lasagna, drinking wine, and talking about trivial stuff.

"Where is everyone, by the way?" I asked.

"They went to a music festival. Laura works for a promoter."

"That sounds like a fun job."

"She's a star fucker."

"Star fucker?"

"Yes. She embraces it happily...she even has a T-shirt! She's so funny."

"How'd she get the name?"

"She fucked Nick Cave, allegedly."

"Wow. Well, I like Nick Cave, but I'm not sure that's bragworthy." I laughed.

"Yeah, he's not the prettiest guy." Amy laughed back.

"Anyway, how about a dance lesson?" I asked her.

"Sure, I'll be right back."

Amy returned with a handful of old vinyl records of big band music. We spent the better part of the night dancing in the kitchen. I learned a few more swing moves.

"I can't believe how fast you are learning this," she said.

"Probably a past life."

"Do you think?" Amy sounded excited.

"I was joking, but you never know."

"Do you believe in past lives?" she asked.

"I do."

"Me too," she said. "I think I may have been alive during the Holocaust."

"Really?"

"Yeah. When I was a kid, I had recurring dreams of hiding from German soldiers. I've always been interested in the Holocaust. Well, not necessarily interested, more like drawn to it."

"That's weird. I've always thought I was in World War II, specifically D-day. I can watch any movie from any war, and I don't feel emotional about it. I mean, I feel bad that it's about war, but if I watch a World War II documentary or movie, I cry every time. Also, I've always loved clothes, cars, and furniture from the forties."

"That's really interesting. Wouldn't it be strange if we knew each other back then?"

"You never know."

"Hey, do you want a tarot reading?" Amy asked.

"I noticed some books on tarot in your room. I would love one just as long as your reading puts *you* in my future."

"Well, if it doesn't, I'll fake it." Amy laughed.

"Deal, let's go."

"Okay, but all jokes aside, you need to take it seriously."

"Yeah, of course."

We went into her room, and she made her bed, smoothing out her comforter. We sat cross-legged on the bed. She reached up and grabbed a red silk bag off her shelf and pulled out a deck of tarot cards.

"Do you do this a lot?" I asked.

"No, I mostly read for myself, but I'm curious what the cards say about you."

"Well, I can save you time. They will say I am awesome!"

"Uh, yeah, I don't think they'll say that, but nice try." Amy chuckled. She mixed up the cards and laid them out in three separate stacks. She asked me to place the right stack on top of the middle one, then the double stack onto the left one. She shuffled one more time and carefully laid three cards out side by side. "Hmm…interesting."

"Does it say that I'm awesome?" I laughed.

She looked up at me. "Remember your promise to take it seriously?"

"Oh yeah, sorry."

"The cards say that you will be going through some big changes and that you should watch out for coincidences or patterns around you."

"Really?"

She ignored me, concentrating on the cards. "I also see a business opportunity coming your way."

"I won't be dressing mannequins and folding T-shirts forever?"

Amy looked at me pointedly and motioned for me to be quiet. "You've been wandering, are wandering, but soon you will find what you are looking for when you least expect it."

"The cards say all that?"

"It pretty much says you will go through a major change, you'll most likely start a new business, and a substantial love is in your future."

"Love? Yuck!"

"Sorry, I'm just the messenger." She smiled. I reached over and kissed her. "I'm not done," she said.

"Yeah, but I've always wanted to kiss a witch." I grinned.

Amy cleared the cards, and we found ourselves naked again. We talked most of the night, listening to music and making love. It was amazing, and neither of us could get enough. I couldn't remember ever feeling this way about anyone, including Ashley, not even close.

"I know I keep saying this, but you really scare me," Amy said.

"I'm right there with you. I feel an intense connection, and I really like sex with you," I said bluntly.

"Me too. I'm not usually this sexual," she said.

"Wow! You could have fooled me."

"No, really. It's you. I'm serious," she said. "You are doing this to me."

"Oh, so it's my fault?" I laughed.

"Exactly." Amy poked my chest.

"Well, let's sleep on it."

"Good idea, I'm a little sleepy."

"Oh shit! I forgot my Gap shirt. I work tomorrow, and I need a Gap shirt."

Amy giggled. "Wait. I think I have a Gap shirt. It's large on me, and I think it might just fit you." Naked, she jumped up and tiptoed over to her closet.

"I love how you do that," I said.

"Do what?"

"Walk on your tippy toes, especially when you're naked!"

"Don't look at me," Amy said, trying to cover her bottom with her arm. She looked for the shirt in her closet. "Here! Yep, it's a Gap shirt." She threw it at me.

"This is a Hawaiian shirt," I said, laughing.

"Well, it has a Gap label on it." She giggled.

"They did say I could wear anything as long as it's made by the Gap. This should be fun."

The next morning, we woke up early. Both of us had to work. We were exhausted, and for the second day in a row, we were going on about three hours of sleep.

"Oh man. I am sore." I stretched my arms.

"Yeah, me as well."

"That was quite the workout," I said.

"I'll say." We showered together and barely made it out. Amy was in a business suit and looked adorable. I, on the other hand, was in her Hawaiian shirt.

"Oh boy, this shirt is loud," I said.

"Yes, yes, it is. I'm going to enjoy the image of you working in that shirt all day!" She belly laughed. "It's too funny."

"Why do you even have this? It's hideous!"

"I bought it for a Hawaiian-themed party. It's pretty obnoxious." She snorted.

"Did you just snort?"

"Sorry." She giggled. "We should get going."

It was way too far for me to stop by my place to grab a new shirt and get to work on time. I was stuck with this ugly Hawaiian shirt. We held hands as we walked through the park to catch a bus to downtown. As we walked along the path, I noticed a chubby guy standing on a small hill practicing with a samurai sword. He was deeply focused, concentrating on his movements. We slowed to watch him. He silently drew his sword from his side and took a few steps forward and quickly slashed at his imaginary opponent. He repeated the same move over and over, trying to perfect it each time. It was cool, and Amy and I stopped to watch him, completely enthralled. Just as he was about to do another run of movements, the large park sprinklers all around him turned on.

By mid-slash, the samurai was completely drenched. Amy and I couldn't help but laugh. It was funny, but our laughter died as he, undeterred, continued his movements with the same intense concentration. He kept in perfect motion and continued his practice, sprinklers and all. We were both impressed with his unyielding devotion to his craft. We silently passed by and walked down the other side of the hill. Once we were out of earshot, we busted out laughing.

"Did that just happen?" Amy asked.

"Uh, yeah. I think it did. That guy was amazing!"

"He was. This is a moment I will never forget."

"Me too." I kissed Amy. "Hey, that's my tree." We approached the huge oak.

"What?"

"This one, right here."

"It's huge. Wait, did you say *your* tree?"

"Well, it's actually not mine. It belongs to the Urban Giant."

"What are you talking about?" Amy looked confused.

"Never mind." I chuckled. I didn't tell her anything more about the tree, nor did I tell her about my special place and the gate. I wanted to share those things with her, but I still had my guard up, and I was trying my hardest not to fall in love with her. I took comfort in knowing she was doing the same thing.

"This is you." Amy pointed at a bus heading toward us a few blocks away.

"You don't take the same bus as me?"

"Nope, I take a different one."

"Well, then I guess this is bye." I held her hands in mine.

"I had fun." She smiled. "I guess I'll see you later."

"Yeah, okay." I could see in her eyes she didn't want me to go, and I didn't want to go either. It was a "We can survive on love" moment. I kissed her as the bus pulled up.

"Good luck with the shirt!" she said.

"Oh shit, thanks for the reminder…I almost forgot!" I boarded the bus and sat so I could see her out the window. She looked so beautiful standing there in her little business suit. She waved to me and smiled. Our eyes locked, and I waved back as the bus pulled away taking me to another world. I think I smiled the entire bus ride.

Chapter Thirty-One

All eyes were on me as I walked into work and clocked in. I knew this shirt would be an issue even though I was technically following the rules. By the time I reached the visuals room, my boss, Ron, was waiting for me, and by the look on his face, I knew someone at the managers' station had already warned him about my attire.

"Wow, Jason. That is some shirt," Ron said.

"Thanks." I played along as if I was unaware.

"Do you think that shirt is appropriate?"

"I do, it is a Gap shirt." I grinned. I hoped my good cheer would win him over. I was wrong.

"That's a Gap shirt?" He challenged me with a look.

"Yeah, look!" I pulled the back of my collar, revealing the tag.

His face softened. "Wow, it is a Gap shirt. When did they make that gem?" The Gap was about solid colors, basics, and a preppy style, not loud and Hawaiian. "Well, I know it's the rule, but I just can't have one of my visuals team members wearing a Hawaiian shirt."

"I'm sorry. I didn't think I was breaking the rules."

"You're not, but we like to wear the clothes that are available for purchase here."

"Of course, I totally understand. Honestly, I don't get paid until the end of the week, and I don't have the money to buy a new shirt today." I did have the money. I just didn't want to buy another Gap shirt.

"Well, I'll give you credit for a shirt, and you can pay for it on your next payday."

I was in a fantastic mood, and I really didn't want to rock the boat, especially since it was a new job. And no matter how stupid the job was to me, I needed it to wine and dine Amy.

"That sounds great," I said. "Thanks, Ron, for understanding."

He responded with a smile and patted me on the shoulder like I was a good boy. I knew my days were numbered here. I could feel it in the air. The universe was telling me I wouldn't be working here for very long, and I couldn't wait for that day to come. *Cheers to Amy's tarot reading*, I thought. Her reading affirmed that I didn't belong in a corporate environment, and I decided I would listen to the universe and begin a new business venture as soon as I could.

Chris was out sick, and I dressed mannequins in the window all day. It was fun watching the people walk by. I felt like I was an animal at the zoo. I fantasized I was a performance artist and dared myself to do something radical like remove my clothing. *That would be one way to get fired*, I chuckled to myself.

Ron stopped by, interrupting my daydream. "Jason, there is a girl downstairs waiting for you." He looked at his watch.

"For me?"

"Yes, she asked for you. Your shift is up. Why don't you clock out and call it a day? I told her you would be down soon."

"Okay, thanks. And thanks for the shirt!" I raised my voice as he sped away.

"My pleasure. Oh! And good job today."

As I took the escalator down, my heart skipped a beat to find Amy waiting for me. She was sitting on "the Dad's Chair." They were utilized for husbands or grandpas waiting while their spouse or family members shopped. Amy was looking in a pocket mirror, checking her makeup, and didn't see me. I snuck up on her. "Ma'am, you can't do that here."

She looked up quickly, startled, and then grinned. "Hey, handsome!"

"Hey, darlin'. What are you doing here?"

"I was on the bus going home and I decided to stop by. Is that okay?"

"No!" I joked. She disregarded it and flung her arms around my neck and gave me a quick kiss on the cheek.

"Oh good. I need to talk to you about something."

"Okay, is it bad?"

"No, nothing bad. Are you hungry? There's a super yummy Mexican restaurant not far from here."

"Well, I don't think I can turn down super yummy. Let's do it."

It was chilly outside, and we cuddled as we walked. Her body felt so good. I wished we were going to my place so I could get her out of those business clothes and into my bed. I could tell she felt the same way. She would periodically look up at me and kiss my neck. That look she gave me was deadly. I thought about what she wanted to tell me. We had just started dating. *What can it possibly be?* I thought. *An STD or another guy?* I thought the worst. *If it's something bad, at least she's telling me now before I get too attached.* My anxiety level was beginning to rise.

"This is it," she said. It was your typical Mexican restaurant with a neon sign that flashed "Ricardo's Cantina." The inside was dark and lit by candlelight. There was a giant fountain in the center and a stone wall with plants and a small, trickling waterfall. The ambiance was cool. I felt like I was outside in a courtyard.

"Isn't this place great?" she asked as we sat down at a table near the flowing water.

"I like it." I smiled, trying not to show my nervousness.

"Hello, my friends! Can I get you some chips and guacamole or a drink perhaps?" the server asked.

"I'd like a Cadillac Margarita with Hornitos, please," Amy said.

"Yes, ma'am. And you, sir?"

"I'll take a Pacífico."

"Great! I will leave you to decide…" The waiter walked off.

Amy was quiet and seemed a little nervous. She kept fiddling with her napkin. All I could think about was what she wanted to talk to me about.

"What's a Cadillac Margarita?" I said, breaking the silence.

"It's an after-work glass of deliciousness." She smiled. "It's a regular margarita that comes with a shot of Grand Marnier on the side."

"So, it's a Margarita with two shots, just one is on the side? Why don't they just pour the other shot in?"

"The Grand Marnier is supposed to float on top. I guess people get weird and want to make sure an entire shot is floated on top, not just splashed in by the bartender. It's silly, but I kinda like the ritual."

Sure enough, the waiter came back with a margarita on the rocks and a side shot. Amy happily poured the shot, carefully, over the top. I couldn't help but laugh.

"Don't ruin my drink," she said playfully.

"Sorry, it's just funny. You just stirred it in!" I laughed again.

"I know. You're not supposed to, but it's a habit." She laughed at herself.

"Cheers!" I lifted my beer.

"Cheers." Amy clinked my glass and took a sip from hers.

I couldn't take it any longer. "So, what's the story? You need to talk to me about something?"

"Yes." She took another sip of her drink. "Remember my friend Sean? You met him and Angie at Deluxe."

"How could I forget the night of the great white Afro!" I smiled. I waited for her to tell me something awful.

"Exactly. Well, when I was down visiting my parents, I also visited Sean. He offered me a position at his clothing company. He wants me to manage it."

"Wow. That sounds like a good opportunity." I smiled, relieved. "Is it better than what you do now at the graduate school?"

"The money isn't as good, but there's potential for growth. I'm pretty much at the top of my ladder where I am now, and fashion design is far more interesting than record keeping."

"Seems like a no-brainer. I assume you get to work from home?"

"I wish, but the job is in Orange County, and I would have to work on-site…that's the catch."

"Oh, I don't know why I didn't think of that." *Fuck, fuck, fuck*, I thought. I knew Sean didn't live here. I just didn't compute that detail when she was talking about the job. "Oh, well, that's something to think about." I didn't know how to respond.

"Yes, it is." She fell silent and looked at me, waiting for a reaction. I wanted to say, *there is no way in hell you are leaving now.* But the fact was, I'd just met her, and I didn't have the right to say that. I struggled to find my words. The silence was deafening as we sipped our drinks. Thankfully, I noticed our waiter walking toward us.

"Have we decided?" he asked.

"Yes, thank you. I'll have fajitas with chicken," Amy said.

"For you, sir?"

"I'll just have a bean and cheese burrito."

"You sure you don't want something else? My treat." Amy smiled at me.

"No, I'm good. I'd like a bean and cheese burrito," I confirmed to the waiter.

"You got it, amigo."

I took another couple of sips of my beer and shook my head. "Fuck!"

"Are you all right?" Amy placed her hand over mine.

"Yes, no. I just didn't see this coming. I mean, I'm having fun. I didn't want to get serious, but I also don't want the fun to end either."

"I feel the same way. It just feels stupid to pass up a great opportunity because I just met a guy that I like." Her words stung deep, but I agreed with her.

"I know," I said. "That would be stupid, but I just have this weird feeling."

"What kind of feeling?"

"It's hard to explain. I just feel this powerful energy toward you. I don't want to say it, but it's a serendipitous feeling. I'm supposed to know you," I said.

"I understand."

"Honestly, I would hate it if you left." *There, I said it.* "You just met me, and yes, I would hate it if you left. Don't go. Just don't go." I looked down.

A few seconds passed silently. "I don't want to go either. I wanted to see what you would say, and I'm happy you want me to stay here."

"Really?" I looked up at her smiling face.

"Yes, really."

"That's great! I really like hanging out with you. If you left now, it would just suck."

"Well, we can't have that."

"So, you're not going to take the job?" I asked.

"Nope. I'll call him tomorrow."

"Cheers to that!"

"You better be worth it!" She laughed.

"Oh, I'm not, but too late. You already committed." I grinned. "You just passed up a great opportunity for a guy who is broke, dresses mannequins for a living, and lives in a room so small he has to lift the corner of the bed just to open the door." I took a swig of my beer.

"Hey, don't go changing my mind. I haven't called him yet."

"You're right. I should probably just shut up," I said. "Well, cheers to the unknown and hopefully not to bad decisions!"

Chapter Thirty-Two

Amy's decision to stay was clearly the right choice. We were inseparable and very much in love even though neither one of us admitted it. We both still seemed to be sticking to our guns that we didn't want a serious relationship. We spent every moment that we could together. After work, I would meet up with Amy, and she would teach me how to swing dance. We spent our nights drinking gin and tonics and dancing in her kitchen. On the weekends, we would go to the very club where we'd met and dance to live music. I was having the time of my life.

A month passed, and I hadn't been home except to grab more clothes. One evening we were lying in bed, watching a movie, and eating popcorn. The phone rang, and I heard Maddison's voice leaving a message on the answering machine. I picked up the receiver and said, "Help, Mad. I'm being held hostage from a sex-crazed witch. She put a love spell on me. Help!" Amy kicked me. "She's beating me, I don't think I have much longer."

"Uh, you sure don't sound like you want rescuing. Torture him, Amy!" Maddison yelled so Amy could hear. "Do you still live here?"

"I know. I haven't been home much. Amy and I are getting to know each other."

"Oh, is that what you're calling it? Well, I am so happy for you. I had a feeling about that one," Maddison replied.

"It's weird. I just can't get enough of her, and I don't mean just sex." I saw Amy give me a look.

"I'm happy someone is getting laid," Maddison said. "Before I forget, Koji called wondering if the city ate you up."

"Oh shit. I haven't spoken to him since I moved out. I'll give him a call. Are you doing okay?"

"Oh, you know me," Maddison answered. "I'm good, just dealing with jealous boys."

"Is Brad still harassing you?" I asked.

"Let's just say he happened to call the gallery when I wasn't there and spoke to my boss. He was trying to find out if I was dating anyone."

"That sucks. My grandma always said that people are never given anything they cannot handle."

"Yeah, she never dated Brad."

"This is true. At least he's five hundred miles away," I said.

"There is that. Well, hey, don't be a stranger."

"Let's get drinks this weekend. I think we are going to Club Deluxe. Carson will be there," I teased.

"Oh God. He is cute, though," Maddison replied.

"He's a pretty boy all right. Just make sure you bring some antibiotics."

"Oh gross. Well, I guess I'll see you soon. Have fun being in love."

"Thanks, Maddy."

Just as I hung up, the phone rang again. It was Keith, Amy's friend whom I had met at Chad and Margery's party. He was surprised when a guy answered Amy's phone and was doubly surprised that it was me because I was the one he was looking for.

"How's it going?" I asked.

"Hey, man. I called Amy hoping she would give me your number. I need to talk to you."

"Uh, I didn't do it," I said.

"Yeah, me either." Keith laughed. "When I met you at the party, you mentioned that you were looking for a job. Is that still the case?"

"God yes! Why?"

"I'm assuming you don't like your current job."

"Dressing windows at the Gap?"

"Oh right. Enough said. So, listen. I need a guy to help me pick up and deliver antiques."

"Awesome, I'm your guy."

Amy looked at me oddly. She was probably wondering who I was talking to. Keith gave me his address, and I told him I would be there in the morning. Luckily, it was my day off.

I ended up quitting my job at the Gap and working full-time with Keith for an antiques dealer. The pay was the same as the Gap, but the job was a lot more fun. I was happy to be out of the corporate world. Keith and I got to drive all around the city, and we became really good friends.

I got back in touch with Koji and told him all about Amy. He invited us to a party at his house for his birthday. He also said he wanted me to be there for something special but didn't elaborate. He said Star would be there along with a few other people he worked with. I was surprised that he didn't give me a bunch of shit about falling for Amy so quickly. I think he could tell I was happy and didn't want to rain on my parade. I was excited for Amy to meet Koji. He was an important person in my life, and his opinion meant a lot to me. Regardless of what he thought, I didn't think anything could break the spell that seemed to envelop us both.

Amy had finally given me a key so I wouldn't have to wait on her front step for her to get home from work. It was six p.m. when I heard the front door open and the sound of Amy's heels walking up the stairs.

"Hello, sweet man," Amy said as she walked into the bedroom.

"Hey, darlin'!" I grabbed her around the waist and pulled her onto the bed. I didn't give her a chance to put down her purse, which flopped onto the bed with us. I held her and kissed her, then nuzzled my nose in her hair and inhaled her scent. "I love the way you smell."

"Ew, I'm all gross from work and walking home from the bus stop."

"Well, if you're gross, then I love gross." I kissed her again, and we laid holding each other tight before she got up to brush her hair at her vanity.

"What?" she said, looking at me as I watched her in the mirror.

"Just watching you. So, I have some news."

"Oh yeah, what is it?"

"Koji's having a party on Saturday, and he invited us."

"Really. I finally get to meet the famous Koji? What if he doesn't like me?"

"He will love you."

"Not so sure. Especially after, well, your ex." She looked a little concerned.

"There is that, but you're different."

She turned from the mirror and faced me. "How so?"

It was a good question that I didn't have a good answer for. It was more of a feeling. My soul knew Amy was different.

"Trust me, he will love you," I said.

Amy didn't seem entirely convinced. She turned back to the mirror.

"There's another thing I wanted to talk to you about," I said.

"Oh, this sounds serious." Amy stopped brushing her hair.

I got up and stood behind her with my hands on her shoulders and looked at her in the mirror. She looked up at me, and I sensed that my unusual serious demeanor had caught her off guard.

"I just want to say…well…I want you to know—"

"I love you," Amy blurted out.

My heart burst open. Every fear that was holding me back melted in that very instant. I slid my arms around her until my cheek met hers.

"I love you so much," I said.

Amy pushed her face against mine like a cat wanting to be pet. I spun her chair around and, in one motion, picked her up in my arms and kissed her deeply.

"God, that was terrifying," I said.

"Yeah, for me as well. You better not break my heart." She poked my chest.

"Could never happen," I assured her.

Chapter Thirty-Three

I could hear Koji's laugh before we even knocked on the door, and it made me smile.

"That's Koji," I said to Amy. She squeezed my hand hard as the door opened.

I was surprised to see Star open the door, even though Koji had told me she would be at the party.

"Hey! How are you?" Star said. Her happy expression changed a bit when she saw Amy holding my hand. I squeezed Amy's hand back with reassurance.

"Hey, Star!" I said. "It's good to see you. It's been a while."

"Yes, it has. Koji tells me you're adapting to the city and, uh, making friends." Star's eyes flashed to Amy.

"I have. Star, this is Amy. Amy, this is Star. Star is the first person I met in the city."

"Nice to meet you," Star said to Amy.

"Likewise." Amy smiled.

"Aren't you two the cutest," Star said, rather flatly.

Amy raised her eyebrows in confusion. I was a little shocked with Star's rudeness. I didn't understand why she was being cold toward Amy. I mean, we'd never dated. *Did she like me more than I thought?* I let go of Amy's hand and put my arm around her, holding her tight. "Where's the birthday boy?" I asked.

"Oh, he's in back hitting his piñata like a samurai warrior."

"What! A piñata?"

"Yeah, you realize Koji is never growing up."

"Yeah, I guess not. I gotta see this." I grabbed Amy's hand again and led her through Koji's flat to the backyard. I glanced over at the couch I had used as a bed and momentarily thought about how far I had come in such a short period of time. We stopped at the steps to the yard below. Koji was blindfolded, and in true traditional samurai-warrior style, he crouched with his broomstick, waiting to strike. His friend Kyle pulled a rope, tossing the Sombrero-shaped piñata up and down, and in his other hand held a beer.

I laughed when I saw Koji swing and miss. "Strike one," I yelled.

Koji frowned in frustration and moved in for another strike. Kyle took a swig of beer and pulled the rope up just in time for Koji to miss the piñata, but the broomstick landed a direct hit to Kyle's beer bottle. The bottle flew to the ground and shattered. The dozen people surrounding the action simultaneously jumped back, shouting, "Ohhhh!" Koji quickly took off his blindfold to see his beer-soaked and surprised friend.

"Dude, what the fuck?" Kyle said.

Realizing Kyle wasn't hurt, Koji's lion face grew into a big crocodile smile. He swiftly thrust the stick in the air and demolished his prey. The piñata soared and split like a pumpkin on Halloween. Candy and shredded colorful paper flew everywhere, intermixing with the glass. The onlookers turned into children and madly went after the candy, not caring about the glass.

I hurried down the stairs and patted Koji on the back. "Happy birthday, man." I bear-hugged him.

"Dude, thanks for coming."

"Wouldn't miss it. So, what's this special thing you wanted me to do? I hope it wasn't the piñata."

"Nope. You'll see." Koji grabbed two beers from a cooler and handed them to me. He looked up the stairs where Amy was standing. "She's pretty, good luck!" He clinked my beer with his.

"Something tells me I don't need it."

"Whoa, Mr. Confident," Koji said.

"No, it's just…well, I can't explain it, it's just a feeling. Anyway, come on up and say hi." I gestured toward the deck above. Koji and I climbed the stairs, snaking around the people who patted him on the back and congratulated him on a good kill.

"Amy, this is Koji," I said.

"Happy birthday, Koji. You have some serious sword skills! It's great to finally meet you." Amy smiled and hugged Koji.

"Okay, dude. She's too good for you." Koji laughed.

"We are just right for each other," Amy said, grabbing my hand.

"I think you got yourself a keeper," Koji said.

"Thanks." Amy blushed.

"Did you see Star? She's here somewhere," Koji said.

"Yeah, she answered the door," I said.

"Did she tell you about your big fat face?" Koji laughed.

"What are you talking about?" I asked.

Koji patted me on the shoulder. "Oh, dude. Wait here, I'll go find her." He continued to laugh as he walked away.

"What is he talking about?" Amy looked confused.

"Crap. I have a feeling—oh no." I downed my beer in one gulp and grabbed another from the cooler on the deck. I was about to be embarrassed. I made Amy a cocktail at the makeshift bar, and we mingled for a while until Koji returned with Star. He looked like a kid who had just gotten a new bike for Christmas.

"Okay, tell him, tell him."

"Koji, I don't know why my art is so funny to you," Star said. "Jason, remember when I took the photo of your face for my art show?"

"How could I forget. How'd the show go?"

"We had an amazing turnout."

"Oh good. So, what is Koji all giggles about? Did my face look funny or something?"

"No, not at all. It sold!" Star said.

"What? My face sold. Like, someone bought it to hang on a wall?" I was shocked.

Koji doubled over with laughter, holding his stomach. I looked at Amy, and I could tell she was confused by this inside joke.

"Tell him the best part," Koji gasped.

"Koji, it doesn't matter." Star looked annoyed.

"Oh, it totally matters."

"What? Just tell me and get it over with." I felt my face flush.

"Fine, fine. So, the guys who bought it own a bondage shop here in the Castro."

I watched Koji sit on the ground, unable to no longer stand. He was laughing so hard that he began to cry.

"What is this all about? I need details!" Amy looked really happy to know what was truly embarrassing for me.

I told her about the quick photoshoot with Star and how it was just a blown-up picture of my face. Star told us the photos were three feet by four feet in size.

"So, you're telling me that there is an enormous photo of just your face possibly hanging on a wall in a gay, sex dungeon? Oh my god, that is awesome!" Amy covered her mouth, trying not to laugh at my expense.

"Yes! Yes! That's it exactly, Amy," Koji managed to get out.

"Yeah, great. Me and my big face. That's really funny." I looked at Amy, and she lost it, joining in Koji's laughter. "You too? I give up," I said.

"I'm sorry, but it's really fucking funny. Wait, are you smiling in it or serious?" Amy looked like she was dying to know.

"If you must know, I am serious in the photo," I said.

Amy and Koji couldn't stop laughing, and Star didn't appear to be amused that Amy thought it was just as funny as Koji did.

"It was a really great show, you guys," Star defended.

"Yeah, fuck you guys. Star, I take it as a compliment to your work and to my face." I tried not to laugh.

"Dude, you're famous." Koji stood up and wiped the tears from his eyes.

"Aw, I love your face." Amy squeezed my cheek like a grandma. "Star, can I buy a copy?" Amy asked.

"No! No, you cannot get a copy," I said.

"Actually, I did make two," Star said.

"Oh God, please tell me there isn't another one floating around."

"Well, the first one was too dark, so I printed another one."

"Oh crap. Can you tear it up?" I pleaded.

"It's my art! Thanks, guys." Star walked away.

"Star, Star, c'mon," Koji called after her. "I think she's pissed."

"Can you blame her?" I said.

"I feel kind of bad. I wasn't making fun of her art, just your situation," Amy said.

Koji was still amused. "J., you have no idea how hard it was not to tell you."

"I was wondering why you went so far out of your way to track me down."

"Dude, I really wanted you to come to my party, but seriously, it wouldn't be the same without your face here." Koji resumed his laughter, right along with Amy. "Okay, okay. I'll stop. You know I love you, bro."

"I love you, too," Amy said to me. "How could you not love this face." She squeezed my cheeks together and kissed me on my smooshed lips.

"Seriously, seriously?" I said.

"I couldn't resist. It wrote itself." She smiled.

"I like this one, J.," Koji said.

"She's all right." I winked at Amy.

"Okay. I'm glad you are here, but now I need you for that favor I mentioned on the phone." Koji became serious.

"What is it?" I asked.

"I want you to cut my hair."

"What, why?" I asked.

"No! Your hair is amazing," Amy said.

"It's time." Koji nodded at me.

I looked at Koji's long, long hair, and without hesitation, I said, "Absolutely!"

"You cut hair?" Amy asked me.

"No, well, yes, well, not exactly. I have cut my own hair since I was a teenager, and sometimes, I cut my friends' hair. It's not rocket science."

"Wow, okay," Amy replied.

"So, when is this going down?" I asked.

"Now or never," Koji said, holding up his ponytail. He pointed to a plastic chair in the courtyard. Next to it was a box containing a pair of scissors and hair clippers. "It's time! Time to cut the hair!" Koji shouted to his friends.

We walked down the stairs, and people gathered around the plastic chair. Koji sat down and tightly gripped the armrests. I held his ponytail with my left hand and the scissors with my right.

"You ready?" I asked.

"Ready as I'll ever be." Koji closed his eyes. "Do it!"

I held the scissors above my head as the partygoers started loudly cheering, "Cut that hair! Cut that hair!" I gave the people what they wanted and cut into Koji's thick mane, sawing away until the last section released from his head. I held the three-foot-long ponytail in the air and waved it. Everyone hollered and cheered. Koji got up and took a bow. He and I walked up the stairs to finish his haircut in the bathroom. I gave him the best haircut possible with my novice hands. It turned out better than I expected, and a few people asked for my card. Koji was transformed. He ran around laughing with friends, drinking, and enjoying his party. A few people took turns rubber-banding his ponytail to their hair and impersonating him. Amy and I stayed for another hour or so before sneaking out.

The early afternoon sun was slowly disappearing into the incoming fog, and Amy's arms filled with goose bumps. I took my flannel off and wrapped it around her.

"You're going to be cold," she said.

"I'm fine." I was freezing, but I wasn't about to let her know.

"So, I heard that Indigo Swing is playing at SF State today at five o clock."

"Indigo Swing?" I asked.

"Yeah, we saw them last week at Deluxe. They play that cover song I love, 'Flip, Flop, and Fly.'"

"Oh right. They were good. You want to go?"

"Sure."

We headed up to Market Street from Koji's and descended into the Muni station. We caught a train to the college, and in about forty minutes, we were walking among students from all over.

"They said it was supposed to be in the cafeteria," Amy said.

"That's a weird place to have a swing band."

"That's what I was thinking."

The cafeteria was more like a student mall. There were a couple of shops selling clothes with "SF State" printed all over them. They even had a Taco Bell. As we looked around, I noticed Carson and a few other people I'd seen at Club Deluxe.

"Look over there." I pointed to the group.

"There's the little woman!" Carson yelled out to Amy as we approached them. He wrapped her in his massive Captain America arms.

"Hey, buddy." Carson smiled big and shook my hand.

"Still J.," I said. *Not Buddy.* I wasn't jealous, but he just bugged me.

Amy introduced me to the gang, and a couple of people remembered me from Deluxe. They were all nice and seemed genuine. It felt good to think that I might have a group of friends here in the city. One of the guys mentioned to me that the band had asked them to come and dance for the crowd. *Crap*, I thought. I had only just learned how to swing dance, and these people really knew what they were doing. One of the couples were swing dance instructors. I was worried. I had no business dancing with these people. I thought we were seeing a band, not dancing in front of college kids. I started to panic.

As the band tuned their instruments, all the partners paired up to dance. I looked around, noticing that the cafeteria had filled up with college kids waiting for the spectacle. In my head, I quickly went over the very few steps I knew, and I could feel myself starting to sweat even though I wasn't moving. Amy looked at me with a huge smile, and I mustered a nervous *I'm going to puke* grin in return. Just then, Carson came to my rescue.

"Hey, buddy. You don't mind if I take the little lady for a spin, do ya?" Carson asked. All the other pairs were walking to the center of the cafeteria for the show. I looked at Amy, and even though she would've proudly danced with me, I could tell she also understood I wasn't quite good enough for this moment.

"Sure, just bring her back in one piece!" I slapped him on the back

"Will do, buddy. Uh, I mean, J.," Carson said as he outstretched his hand to Amy.

She gave me a quick kiss and then headed to the dance floor with Carson.

The band started playing, and the dancers were great. After a couple of songs, I really needed to pee. As I made a beeline to the bathroom, I heard a familiar voice.

"Jason? Jason!"

I stopped in my tracks and turned around, finding myself face-to-face with Ashley. She was standing alone by a door, holding a mountain of books and looking very collegiate, and surprised.

"Hey! What are you doing here?" I asked. I gave her an awkward half hug.

"I go to school here, remember? The question is, what are you doing here?"

"Oh right. The swing band in the cafeteria. I'm with the band. Wait, no, well, not with the band—my girlfriend is swing dancing, and well..." I realized what I had just said by the look on Ashley's face. I'd just told her that I had a girlfriend. She had seemed happy to see me until those two words, *my girlfriend*, came out of my mouth.

"Girlfriend, huh? That didn't take long."

"Yeah, I was surprised too. We just seemed to hit it off right away," I said.

"Well, I'm happy for you."

"No, you're not," I replied.

She looked at the ground, and I could tell she was about to cry. Her forehead always crinkled up when she was about to cry.

"Hey, hey, don't cry."

She walked past me, and I followed her to a bench. She sat and continued to hide her face from me. I didn't know what to say, and I didn't know why she was crying. She was the one who broke my heart.

"What's wrong?" I said, standing in front of her.

Ashley wiped away her tears and finally looked up at me. "I fucked up."

"You fucked up. What do you mean?"

"I fucked up. With us."

I knew I was about to hear what I had wanted to for months. She was going to apologize for breaking my heart. The words I had longed to hear, I no longer cared to. My heart was one hundred percent with Amy, who was dancing away with Carson, a.k.a. Captain America, as we spoke. "Why are you telling me this now?"

"I don't know. When you told me you had a girlfriend, something triggered inside me and I realized I wanted you back."

"So, you're saying that if I didn't have a girlfriend, you wouldn't want me back?"

"No, I don't know. I just know how I feel. I love you."

I was numb, surprised, and in shock. But most of all, the only thing I could think about was Amy and how every part of my soul was screaming for me to go to her.

"Look, Ashley, I am sorry you are sad right now. I loved you. I loved you with all my heart. But now, after everything, hearing you say you want me back, I don't know what to say to you." I shook my head as she looked up at me with hope. It didn't feel good at all. I didn't want revenge. I didn't want her to feel sad. "I'm sorry, Ash. I gotta go." I turned and ran back to the cafeteria, down the stairs, and toward the increasing sounds of Indigo Swing. I saw Amy looking for me. She whispered something in Carson's ear, and he nodded and walked away. She gestured for me to join her. Seeing her smiling face, I was no longer nervous, and as far as I was concerned, we were the only two people in the room. I grabbed her by the waist, and the band began playing Amy's favorite song, "Flip, Flop, and Fly."

"I was hoping to dance this song with you," Amy said, looking up at me with her magic eyes. "Flip, Flop, and Fly" was a fast song, but we managed to keep up, and with my three moves, we danced. I messed up several times, but we didn't care. In that moment, it felt as if we were the only ones out there.

On the bus ride home, I thought about telling Amy about running into Ashley, but I kept quiet. This had been a perfect day, and I didn't want to ruin it. Amy leaned in, and I put my arm around her. She caressed my hand as we silently watched the people and buildings pass us by. I thought about the giant and his mighty oak. I thought about my special place and the forest, my gate and the beach beyond. I wondered if I should share my astral projection with Amy. I was worried she might think it too strange or think I was some New Age weirdo. *Am I?*

"You okay?" Amy asked, pulling away.

"Yeah, just resting my eyes."

"But your eyes are open, silly," she pointed out.

"You're the silly one." I smiled.

Amy rested her head back on my chest, and I cradled her like she was the most precious thing in the world.

"I love you," she whispered.

"Thanks," I said.

Amy popped up, giving the evil eye. "That was mean."

"Sorry, I couldn't resist," I joked. "I love you, too." I kissed the top of her head.

We cuddled the rest of the way home. I was excited for our future, and I believed she was too.

I was so happy where my life had led me. I was following my path and trusting in the universe. I thought about Old Man Dave and Jenny. I hoped Amy and I would have a love like theirs. I could feel it in my soul that Amy was truly my Jenny.

Chapter Thirty-Four

One Saturday, we went window-shopping to all our favorite vintage stores. A new shop had opened, and we excitedly went in looking for new treasures. We came across a nice mid-century living room set. Before we knew it, we put a down payment on it. The store owner agreed to hold it in his warehouse for a month.

"Did we just buy a living room set together?" I asked once we were outside the store.

"Yeah, I think we did."

"Where are we going to put it?" It seemed like we were on autopilot and some kind of force was making decisions on our behalf. It didn't make sense for us to buy furniture when we shared Amy's bedroom in an already furnished apartment, but it didn't matter.

"I don't know, but I just couldn't pass it up," Amy said.

"Same here. We have about thirty days to figure out what to do with it."

"Hmm, what do you have in mind?"

I looked at her, holding both of her hands. "Maybe it's time we got our own place." I squeezed her hands.

"You think?"

"Unless you don't want to."

"No. It's the right thing to do, considering our furniture needs a place a live," she said.

"So, we're doing it?"

"Yeah, it looks that way." She smiled at me. "I love you."

"I love you, too." I kissed her and looked into her eyes. "I'm really happy I met you that night, and that you saw past my Afro."

"Ditto."

"You know, it's not too late for you to take that job." I winked.

"Shut up," she said. "Let's go home and celebrate. I'm starving, and I want a big salad."

"A salad, huh? When I'm starving and want to celebrate, that's the first thing I think of, salad," I teased.

"I want some crispy lettuce." She punched my arm.

It was late afternoon by the time we reached her apartment. I plopped down on her bed with a tired sigh. "I'm pooped," I said.

"I think I'll go over to the store and grab some wine for our celebratory dinner. You want anything?" Amy asked.

"Yes, a Coke, please."

Amy kissed me on the forehead before leaving. I laid my head down for a quick nap, but the phone rang. I usually ignored her incoming calls, but something told me to answer this one.

"Amy's phone," I answered. A girl's voice asked for Amy. "Sorry, you just missed her. Can I take a message?"

"Uh, will she back soon?" the voice asked.

"Yeah. She just went across the street to the store. Maybe ten to fifteen minutes? Everything all right?"

"Oh yeah. Just tell her Eliza Cohen called."

I jumped from the bed, and the hair on my neck stood at attention. "Did you say Eliza Cohen?"

"Yeah, why? Who is this?"

"Eliza! This is Jason Romero," I said excitedly.

"What? You're fucking kidding me. Why are you in SF? How do you know Amy?"

I had met Eliza Cohen in a local alternative clothing store I worked at when I was fifteen. She came in one day, and we became fast friends. We had dated for a bit, and for about a year, we'd been inseparable. She was beautiful and stole the hearts of most guys she came across, and I was young and infatuated with her. She had tugged at my heart, and I had chased her around like a lost puppy dog. She wasn't the best of people, but I didn't care back then. We ended up going our separate ways when she became involved with another guy.

"Hello?" she asked.

"Sorry, I'm freaking out a bit," I stammered.

"What are you doing at Amy's house?" Eliza asked.

"Amy is my girlfriend."

"No way. I can't believe it."

"Wait! Why are you calling Amy? How do you know her?"

"This is fucking crazy," Eliza said. "You met Amy when you were fifteen."

"What? No, I didn't. I would have remembered her."

"You didn't meet her face-to-face. You talked to her on the phone that day we went to the Grateful Dead show to watch the hippies."

"I did?"

"Yes. You were waiting for me in my room while I was getting ready for the show," she said.

"Well, that was most days." I laughed.

"Funny. Amy had called, and I ended up handing the phone over to you so I could finish getting ready. Remember?"

"Oh shit! I totally remember that! That was *my Amy*?"

"Yes! Amy was one of my best friends. We went to high school together, and she lived at my house for a few months."

"Are you serious?"

"Weird. You met her way back then, and now you guys are together."

"This is really freaking me out. I can't believe your name was never brought up."

"I haven't seen or spoken to her in over six years."

"So, you randomly called today?"

"Pretty much. I found a photo of her and knew she moved to San Francisco with Chad. I wanted to talk to her, so I tried her old number from high school, hoping her parents still lived in Lake Forest. Her mom answered and gave me her new number."

"This is weird. I mean *weird*! If you knew how I met Amy, it would seem even weirder." I heard the front door open and Amy running up the stairs. "Amy!" I called out. "Amy!"

"I'll be right there. I need to pee!" she yelled as she ran down the hallway.

"Uh, she's peeing," I said.

"Yeah, I heard." Eliza laughed.

"Wow. How are you, by the way?"

"I'm good."

"Eliza Cohen. Man, I can't believe I'm talking to you on the phone. I can't believe I talked to Amy way back then."

"I know, this phone call is freaking me out too. Hey, can you hold on a sec?"

"Sure." My mind raced as I waited on hold. *I talked with Amy when I was fifteen!* I thought. I remembered Eliza handing the phone to me. I remembered talking to a girl, but I didn't remember what we had talked about. It was probably just a stupid teen conversation.

As I sat waiting, my mind jumped to Matt. I thought again about the package Amy had sent to him and how I'd told him he should go out with her. I remembered him telling me that Amy was my type. At the time, I was in love with Ashley. I couldn't imagine being with anyone else. My mind raced to the night at Club Deluxe with Damien when I walked up to two random girls, knowing one of them was Amy. *How did I know that Amy was there? Why did I feel compelled to ask?* I thought. I noticed the Polaroid picture taken of us at Chad's party. It was pinned next to Amy's vanity. I touched her dark hair in the photo, and my mind reeled faster and faster until Amy's cat, Blixa, jumped up on the bed and startled me. I looked over at Blixa. *Black-and-white furry animal*, I said to myself. Blixa was a super-fluffy black-and-white cat. "No fucking way," I said out loud. The phone was still dead, in true Eliza Cohen fashion. She'd put me on hold for a long time just like when we were young. I would have continued holding, but what was happening was too overwhelming. I hung up, knowing she would call back. "I'll be back," I shouted to Amy as I hurried out the bedroom door, down the stairs, and out of the house.

A cab approached, and I hailed it down, jumped in, and gave my address to the driver. My fingers drummed my knees, and my mind twisted and turned until we stopped outside my place.

"Can you wait here?" I asked the driver. "I just need to grab something. I'll be right back."

"It's your dime," he replied.

I fished for my keys and shakily unlocked my front door. I sprinted up the steep stairs, lifted the corner of my bed, and started madly rummaging through my boxes of trinkets. I was looking for something specific, a piece of paper. The same paper that my mom had written her psychic reading on the day I left for the city.

More coincidences popped into my head. I worked with antiques, and Amy's hair… *Oh my God*, I thought. When I met Amy, she had long, straight hair, but after seeing her with wet hair, I found out that she straightened it. Her natural hair was curly, *super curly ringlets*. It was all adding up. *Could my mom's predictions have all come true?* It didn't seem possible, but they seemed to be. *Found it!* I removed the note card that was tucked inside the astral projection book my mom had given me. Touching the book instantly brought me back to my time spent at the cabin. I'd been so busy lately and so in love that I hadn't ventured to my gate. My special place was *Amy*. I grabbed the book, along with the paper, and ran back down the stairs to the waiting cab.

The door to Amy's room was open. She was sitting at her vanity, brushing her long, curly hair. Blixa was on her lap. She looked up at me and smiled. "Where did you go?"

"Did she call back?" I asked.

"What are you talking about?"

I couldn't speak, so I just handed her the paper.

"What's this?" she asked, looking at it.

"Just read it."

"You're scaring me."

"No, it's a good thing."

Amy carefully unfolded the paper and read it. Her face looked confused. "What is this? Why is this all written down? Is this me?"

"I think so."

"I don't understand. What is this about?" She looked at me with concerned eyes. I could see she was shocked by the predictions. Almost every prediction on the list represented something that was in our lives, together.

I was so caught up in my life with Amy that I'd totally forgotten about my mom's prophecy. When Eliza called and told me that I had met Amy years ago, I was reminded of my mom's reading and how she'd said I already knew the woman I would be with. When Blixa, Amy's black-and-white fluffy cat, jumped on the bed, it all came together. It all made sense, and my mom was right. I did already know Amy.

"My mom gave me a psychic reading before I came to the city, and that's what she wrote. I totally forgot about it until Eliza called."

"Eliza? Who is Eliza?"

"Eliza Cohen." I was still breathing heavy from running up the stairs.

"Eliza Cohen? When did she call?"

"While you were at the store. I answered the phone."

"Gosh, I haven't spoken to her in years. What did she want?"

"Well, funny thing. She called out of the blue. What's strange is that I know Eliza. I met her when I was fifteen, and well, this is going to sound crazy, but I talked to you when I was at her house one night."

"What?"

"Yeah. We were getting ready to go out, and she handed me the phone—"

"Wait," Amy stopped me. "I talked to you! I totally remember that." She looked at me intensely. "The Dead show night, right? I remember that night because Eliza and I were supposed to hang out, but she flaked as usual. I called her because she hadn't shown up at my place. She told me she decided to go to the Dead show instead and just handed the phone over to some guy and said, 'Talk to Jason.' I remember that night clearly because I was so pissed that she blew me off again. That's why I stopped hanging out with her. Wow, I can't believe this." She shook her head and seemed upset.

"Are you okay?"

"Yeah, I'm just a little freaked out. I spoke to your fifteen-year-old self. Bizarre."

"I know."

I showed her the book on astral projection and told her how I had traveled to the city during my time in the mountains. I told her how I'd been asking the universe to guide me to my true love. Amy's eyes filled with tears. I held her, wiping away the tears.

"I found her," I said. "I found you."

She regained her emotions and wiped her eyes clear. "I want to show you something." She went over to her bookcase and grabbed a purple binder. She opened it and fumbled through the pages. She found what she was looking for. "Here, look at this." She held the open binder for me. There was a handwritten page. I started reading and I was stunned. It was about astral projection.

"What is this?" I said, looking at Amy intently.

"Well, when Chad and I broke up, I was doing the same thing as you. I asked the universe to guide me as well."

"No way! That's impossible you were doing the same thing as me at the same time?"

"The real crazy part is that I projected to a forest in the mountains. I didn't want to be in the city, and I imagined flying over the same forest every night."

"Could this all be true? We talked on the phone almost ten years ago. You met Matt, and I happened to be with him the day he received your package. I was jealous of him even though I was dating Ashley. Ashley ended up breaking my heart. You and Chad moved to San Francisco, and he broke your heart. We both learned about astral projection, and at the time I was sending my light to the city, you were sending yours to the mountains. I moved here and met up with Damien, who delivered pizza to you. He invited me to Club Deluxe, and I randomly chose your table to walk up to. And there you were! You introduced me to Keith, we began working in antiques, and then we all started a business together. What are the odds? Aside from this, Eliza Cohen just happens to look you up, and I answer the phone. Blixa jumped on the bed right at that moment, and everything clicked. And your hair…your beautiful curly hair. How is this even possible?" I reached out and touched one of her ringlets.

"I have no idea, but I do know that we asked for each other." Her tears started falling again. The phone rang, and I turned to answer it, knowing it was Eliza, but Amy stopped me.

"It's probably Eliza. Don't you want to talk to her?" I said.

"I'll call her back." She looked at me intensely.

"What? What's wrong?" I asked, concerned.

"The list," she said.

"What about it?"

"It's full."

"What do you mean?" I asked.

She gently handed the list of predictions back to me. I read down the list and mentally checked off each thing that had impossibly, wonderfully come true. I looked at the last prediction. It read *This person will be the mother of your child.* I looked up quickly. Amy was smiling and crying as she pulled something out of the pocket of her robe. In her hand, she held a pregnancy test. She looked at me, and with the phone still ringing loudly in the background, she said, "I'm pregnant."

The End

For more titles from J.C. ROMERO please visit our website.

www.upandoverpublishing.com

www.ingramcontent.com/pod-product-compliance
Lightning Source LLC
LaVergne TN
LVHW051358080426
835508LV00022B/2877